Anna Neima is a historian with ~~~~ Cambridge. She lives in north Lon~~~~ This is her first book.

'Fascinating and richly documented . . . This is Neima's first book, and should not be her last. She writes with a novelist's eye for detail and clearly revels in the eccentrics she has to chronicle.'
John Carey, *The Sunday Times*

'Neima's diligent account focuses on six interwar endeavours, in Japan, India, America, Germany, England and France, each established by a charismatic leader, each with a goal of creating a more democratic, just and peaceful society.'   Olivia Laing, *TLS*

'Neima's brisk storytelling and eye for the illustrative quote and telling anecdote conveys the thrilling and sometimes scandalous strangeness of these experiments . . . highly readable.'
Mary Harrington, *The Critic*

'Anna Neima has picked a valuable and illuminating focus for her first book . . . Engagingly written with colour, warmth and unobtrusive erudition, *The Utopians* looks back to find some sturdy roots of hope.'   Boyd Tonkin, The Arts Desk

'A book that carefully recuperates the wild desires of a diverse group of dreamers who founded new societies between the 1920s and the 1940s . . . One of the great joys of the book is the kookiness of the projects [Neima] highlights.'   Joe P. L. Davidson, *Tribune*

'In the midst of crisis it's inspiring to read about men and women who dedicated themselves to creating new worlds. Neima's book, impeccably researched and beautifully written, will be an inspiration for anyone looking to an alternative future today.'
Stella Tillyard, author of *Aristocrats* and *The Great Level*

ANNA NEIMA

THE UTOPIANS

SIX ATTEMPTS TO BUILD
THE PERFECT SOCIETY

PICADOR

First published 2021 by Picador

This paperback edition first published 2022 by Picador
an imprint of Pan Macmillan
The Smithson, 6 Briset Street, London EC1M 5NR
EU representative: Macmillan Publishers Ireland Ltd, 1st Floor,
The Liffey Trust Centre, 117–126 Sheriff Street Upper,
Dublin 1, DO1 YC43
Associated companies throughout the world
www.panmacmillan.com

ISBN 978-1-5290-2310-7

Map artwork by ML Design Ltd

Typeset by Palimpsest Book Production Limited, Falkirk, Stirlingshire
Printed and bound by CPI Group (UK) Ltd, Croydon, CR0 4YY

Visit **www.picador.com** to read more about all our books
and to buy them. You will also find features, author interviews and
news of any author events, and you can sign up for e-newsletters
so that you're always first to hear about our new releases.

CONTENTS

LIST OF ILLUSTRATIONS

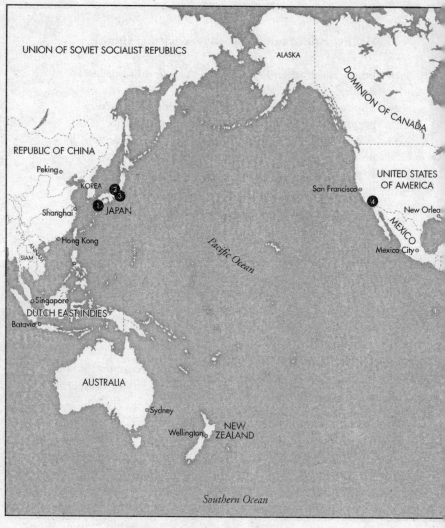

1. Kijō, Miyazaki – *Atarashiki Mura (first site)*
2. Moroyama, Saitama – *Atarashiki Mura (second site)*
3. Tokyo – *Mushanokōji Saneatsu's birthplace*
4. Trabuco Canyon, California – *Trabuco College*
5. Washington DC – *Dorothy Elmhirst's birthplace*
6. Estancia Primavera – *Bruderhof (fifth site)*
7. Houndhill, Barnsley, Yorkshire – *Leonard Elmhirst's birthplace*
8. Ashton Fields Farm, Wiltshire – *Bruderhof (fourth site)*
9. London – *Gerald Heard's birthplace*
10. Totnes, Devon – *Dartington Hall*

Utopian Communities Founded in the Wake of the First World War

(11) Fontainebleau-en-Avon – *Institute for the Harmonious Development of Man*

(12) Sannerz – *Bruderhof (first site)*

(13) Neuhof, Rhön – *Bruderhof (second site)*

(14) Silum, Triesenberg – *Bruderhof (third site)*

(15) Königsberg (now Kaliningrad) – *Eberhard Arnold's birthplace*

(16) Riga – *Emmy Arnold's birthplace*

(17) Alexandropol (now Gyumri) – *G. I. Gurdjieff's birthplace*

(18) Bolpur, West Bengal – *Santiniketan-Sriniketan*

(19) Calcutta – *Rabindranath Tagore's birthplace*

INTRODUCTION

'THE ART OF LIVING TOGETHER IN HARMONY'

On a damp autumn afternoon not long after the end of the First World War, a Japanese writer, Mushanokōji Saneatsu, crouched beside a wide, slow-flowing river, sawing up planks of wood. With him was a motley gathering of artists, intellectuals and idealists, working clumsily, none of them used to manual labour. They were racing to build a hut before winter gripped the island of Kyūshū. When his companions flagged, Mushanokōji urged them on again with his vision of how this hut would be the first step towards their new style of living. His voice rose as he enumerated the ways in which their community would revolutionize society: through its art, its writing, its music. It would, he said, be an antidote to the militarism that had triggered the global war.

On the other side of the world, outside one of the villages that speckle the pine forests of central Germany, another group of idealists were testing out their version of an improved society. Men, women and children inched across a field, bent double, their fingers frozen, gathering potatoes into their skirts and a few battered baskets. At the end of the slow-moving row of workers, a tall, bespectacled preacher, Eberhard Arnold, assured them that they were learning what the Bible meant by the phrase 'The kingdom of God is among you'.[1] Only a cooperative, pacifist mode of living like the one they were pioneering could avert the danger of another war. Their community would be an inspiration for Germany – and for humankind as a whole.

In England at about the same time, a young Yorkshireman, Leonard Elmhirst, rounded the bend of a West Country road to discover a ruined medieval hall. Its roof had caved in, pigeons roosted in the rafters, and the grounds were a mass of nettles and brambles – yet he was thrilled. He wrote to his wife in America, telling her that he had arrived at 'a veritable fairy land', the perfect setting for the revolutionary community they had been planning.[2] The couple aspired to create a modern version of the medieval village, a place that would prove that there was a harmonious alternative to materialism, competition and war.

Other groups of men and women were beginning similarly ambitious experiments from India to France, Russia to America. Across the world, idealists were reacting to the First World War with a horror and revulsion that drove them to try to reinvent society from first principles: rethinking everything from the amount of time spent working each day to the fundamental values by which people lived. They were building practical utopias – turning their ideal social visions into real places, model communities that could be visited and joined, places that they hoped would inspire imitation, and which might generate international change.

*

The First World War is one of the most commemorated events in history. It is hard, after more than a century of Armistice Day celebrations, to conceive of how unprecedented it was when it happened, or to imagine the depth of the shock that it caused. An estimated 61 million troops were mobilized. Of these, some 10 million were killed and 21 million wounded.[3] In the Napoleonic Wars, the most recent comparable international conflict, a century earlier, around 2.5 million soldiers died.[4] The First World War brought fighting on a terrible new scale. On a single day – 22 August 1914 – the French army lost 27,000 men: half as many Frenchmen dead as the United States lost in the entire Vietnam War.[5] And these mortality figures take no account of the wider damage: the millions blinded, maimed or otherwise permanently scarred by the war; the broken families; the dizzying sense of an entire social order destroyed.

Life on the Western Front was so savage, so like a nightmare, that it warped many soldiers' very sense of reality. One veteran remem-

bered a night spent trapped in a shell hole between opposing battle
lines: 'It stank. So did I when I fell into it. Arms and legs, dead rats,
dead everything. Rotten flesh. Human guts.'[6] As bad as the putrid
smell of the trenches was the noise – the constant shellfire that
reduced thousands of men to nervous collapse. Machine guns, high-
explosive artillery shells, poison gas and trench warfare inflicted
horrifying injuries; men were buried alive under the mud, or were
showered with the body parts of comrades during a bombardment.
One soldier, drafted from the Punjab and struggling to make sense
of the 'bodies upon bodies, and blood flowing' in France, wrote to
his brother that 'the Day of Judgement has begun'.[7] Conditions were
just as brutal along the Eastern Front, and in the theatres of war
that stretched across Africa, Asia and the Middle East. The soldiers
living through all this began to question the beliefs and structures
that many of them had previously accepted without challenge: their
nationalistic sentiments, their religious faith, the hierarchies of class
and the systematic oppression of empire.

Those on the home front experienced their own kind of suffering.
The First World War was one of the first conflicts to be reported
almost in real time to non-combatants: photography, film, the telephone and the telegraph gave the fighting a new immediacy. There
was a trauma to looking on helplessly. War was no longer a thing
convincingly elevated and distanced through poetry and patriotic
newspaper bulletins – its horror was all too present and tangible.
This was also the first war of mass mobilization and attrition.
Populations were forced to function for years at maximum output
in order to feed and equip huge armies, while their living standards
were undercut by strangled supply lines. The blockade by Britain's
navy meant that in the winter of 1916 – the 'turnip winter' – many
Germans were forced to survive on less than a thousand calories a
day. Chronic malnutrition led to scurvy and dysentery. The initial
enthusiasm for the war gave way on every side to pockets of disillusionment, and then to widespread anger at sacrifices that seemed
to serve no clear purpose. Growing numbers of people lost faith in
their leaders and in the principles by which they governed.

In 1918, the final year of the war, the world's weakened population was devastated by an influenza pandemic. 'It encircled the world,
visited the remotest corners,' remembered an American doctor,

'taking toll of the most robust, sparing neither soldier nor civilian, and flaunting its red flag in the face of science.'[8] Estimates of the death toll range from 50 to 100 million, with those between the ages of twenty and forty disproportionately affected.[9] Flu victims lay in bed: at home, in overcrowded hospitals or in makeshift field hospitals, locked for days in the struggle to breathe. Often, they began to bleed from the nose, ears and eyes. Their lungs filled with fluid. Their skin, starved of oxygen, turned blue, then black – a sign of impending death. The bodies of those who had succumbed to the virus overflowed the mortuaries. Exhausted doctors and nurses experimented with vaccines and almost every known medical compound to cure or prevent the disease, but to no avail.[10] People panic-bought masks and avoided one another in the streets. Public authorities closed schools, churches and pubs, and delayed celebrations to mark the end of the war. Nations sealed their borders, blaming each other for the disease's outbreak. The effects of war and pandemic compounded one another, and communities disintegrated under the strain – robbed of their young, afraid of contagion, uncertain what the future held.

The greatest public health catastrophe in modern history following so closely on the heels of the deadliest war caused something like collective trauma. Few could make sense of such monstrous suffering. Knowledge about infectious pathogens was still in its early stages, and no lessons, it seemed, could be taken from the pandemic – there was only a sense of immense, incoherent loss.[11] As a result, the memory of the influenza outbreak became shrouded in silence; its awfulness sublimated into the mass reaction to the war. Unlike the pandemic, the war had human perpetrators. It was read as an indictment of human brutality, one that had to be commemorated in order to prevent further violence on the same scale. Its horror was preserved in poems, novels, symphonies and paintings, and in the monuments that were erected on village greens. Expressions such as 'Never again' and 'The war to end all wars' were on the lips of men and women around the globe. The causes of the war, and how to stop anything like it from happening again, became topics of exhaustive discussion in homes, churches, lecture halls and political meetings.

To many, the combined destruction of the war and pandemic seemed so terrible as to destroy any hope for the future. 'So much beauty and pathos of old things passing away and no new things coming,' lamented D. H. Lawrence. 'For the winter stretches ahead, where all vision is lost and all memory dies out.'[12] A wounded Indian sepoy echoed Lawrence: 'Do not think that this is war,' he wrote to his brother. 'This is not war. It is the ending of the world.'[13] In Britain, those whose confidence in the future was destroyed in this period were lamented as the 'lost generation', while in France they were known as the *génération du feu* (the 'gunfire generation'). The American experience translated into the hedonism and cynicism of the hard-drinking expatriates crowding Europe's bars in the books of Ernest Hemingway and F. Scott Fitzgerald. But to the optimistic and the determined, the end of the war offered the possibility of a new beginning: the motivation for establishing an enduring peace, snatching paradise out of the jaws of hell. For such people, it seemed that there had never been a more apposite moment for radically rethinking how to live.

These idealists brushed past the debates over who to blame for the war, and instead condemned the Western political model itself. The pervading theory of the nineteenth century – at least after the Napoleonic Wars – had been that individuals pursuing their own ends would achieve the best results for society as a whole. According to the doctrine of laissez-faire capitalism then in ascendance, the state should intervene in the lives of its citizens as little as possible. Its sole duty was to promote and protect unregulated economic competition, freeing people to make or buy things cheaply and maximize profits, and thereby to bring about the wealth and well-being of the world. For most of the nineteenth century this formula had seemed to work, at least for those who made the rules and set the narrative – the upper and middle classes in Europe and America, who became ever more prosperous and powerful. The colonized, on the other hand, along with millions of peasants and industrial labourers, were made precipitously dependent on global trade cycles. Colonial expansion was a major feature of this era: European states competing to increase their economic power by taking control of vast tracts of Africa, Asia and the Middle East. 'I would annex the planets if I could,' wrote British imperialist Cecil Rhodes, the founder of Rhodesia. 'I often think of that. It makes me sad to see them so clear and yet so far.'[14] Along with empire-building came the rampant, competitive development of armaments. Nation was pitted against nation, making war all but inevitable. Across the world, people came independently to the same verdict: that this model had led inevitably to the First World War. The destructive pattern could not be allowed to repeat itself. An alternative social model had to be found.

Rarely had one ambition been pursued so determinedly in so many different regions. In London, Calcutta and St Petersburg idealists spoke longingly of communality, cooperation, self-determination and pacifism – the values that free-market capitalism had for so long pushed aside. Instead of concentrating on the old standards of material well-being and economic growth, discussions bloomed around the possibility of improving the inner life through psychological theories or spiritualism. European capitals thronged with Freudians and Jungians, with occultists, theosophists and spiritual gurus offering a fantastical array of panaceas for the world's woes. Others dreamed of reforming society by instigating new international organizations; the League of Nations was just one of hundreds founded in the hope of creating a system of global cooperation. This was an era of unprecedented international connectedness, with the telegraph, the telephone and railways snaking their way across continents and drawing millions of people together. Ideas travelled faster than ever before, movements flourished, and the ferment of people's social imaginings quickly triggered dramatic, real-world changes. In Russia, a communist revolution broke out in 1917, ending the country's participation in the war. In 1918, a socialist revolution swept Germany, forcing the Kaiser to flee. Campaigns for independence in Ireland, India, Egypt and other colonized countries galvanized populations who had fought on behalf of the imperial powers and now wanted the freedom to pursue their own political and social aspirations.

But for a small number of idealists the only solution was to start over, to reinvent the social model completely. Disparate groups around the world began setting up experimental communities outside the mainstream, where they hoped to discover and perfect new ways of life. German students and intellectuals took to the country to live collectively and farm cooperatively. In Russia, a group of young men and women espousing anarchic freedom and a return to a primitive lifestyle holed themselves up in a remote forest with a supply of black bread and ammunition, ready to defend their ideals with their lives. At the other end of the spectrum was Fordlandia, designed by the pioneer of mass production in the auto-mobile industry, Henry Ford. He created this vast, quintessentially capitalist rubber-producing town in the Amazon to demonstrate the harmonious society that paternalistic industry could produce if given free rein.[15] Attempted utopias appeared in hundreds of guises around the world. The ideologies that underpinned them varied wildly, but all of them tried in their own way to create a new social order.

*

Utopias are a kind of social dreaming. To invent a 'perfect' world – in a novel, a manifesto or a living community – is to lay bare what is wrong with the real one. Utopians refuse to settle for social improvement via the usual methods: civil disobedience, electoral politics, violent revolution. Throughout history, they have taken a different tack, articulating a vision of society transformed. Hungry peasants in medieval Europe dreamed of the Land of Cockaigne, where the roads were made of pastry, rivers flowed with honey and wine, and grilled geese flew straight into your mouth.[16] Sir Thomas More, faced with the fierce religious bigotry of sixteenth-century England, envisaged an island nation where men and women could choose their own religion without fear – coining the word 'utopia' in the process.[17] These two ostensibly different visions were both ways of imagining a world in which the wrongs of the day were righted: where famine was no more, or religious bigotry impossible. Both visions, examined today, offer a snapshot of the anxieties and hopes of the people who came up with them.

More took the term 'utopia' from the Greek ou-topos, 'no place': a play on the almost identical eu-topos, which means 'good place'. For this precise Renaissance lawyer and statesman, utopias were by definition impossible to build; it was this conviction that led him to write his book, a scathing satire on the shortcomings of contempor-ary society. But the word outlived More. Later idealists took the concept of utopia not as an indication of impossibility, but as a challenge. They questioned whether utopias did have to be 'no places'. Could there not be another option? Why shouldn't the 'good place' actually be created? Social reformers began to call their settlements, places where groups of idealists worked to embody their social dream in a real community, 'utopias'.

Practical experiments in utopianism tend to occur in waves, usually arising in periods marked by cultural and social dislocation. The urge to detach from society and start again is a way of finding new footing, of testing out unorthodox ideas by putting them into action. One wave – though by no means the first – arose in the sixteenth century, as part of the Protestant Reformation. Protestant thinkers throughout Europe had rejected Catholic dogma, but still needed to find new social modes that suited their beliefs. Gone were the pomp of the cathedrals, the silk vestments and the incense, and the gilded statues of saints. These people wanted to live in a way that mimicked the letter of the Bible, where worship was personal and not performative. As well as provoking the rise of the major Protestant sects like Lutheranism, Calvinism and Anglicanism, this quest sparked a series of smaller, more radical religious movements – among them the utopian communes of the Hutterites and the Mennonites, who lived in isolated 'colonies', rejected social norms and devoted themselves to self-sufficiency and Christian worship.

The nineteenth century brought another wave, with the founding of hundreds of secular and religious utopias across the United States. These were inspired by the optimism and social freedom that had followed the country's independence from Britain. Among these many experiments were the transcendentalist community Brook Farm, which aimed for the perfect balance of leisure, manual labour and intellectual activity, and the 'phalanxes' set up by the followers of the French visionary Charles Fourier, who hoped to inaugurate a new millennium of pleasure and fraternity in America. More recently, in the 1960s and 70s, a fresh wave of utopias emerged during the economic boom that followed the Second World War. From Kommune 1 in Berlin to the Kaliflower cooperative in San Francisco, large numbers of young people lived in communities, liberating themselves from the social conservatism of their parents by embracing free love, leftist politics, mescaline and mysticism.

But there are few periods in history when the world has been more widely seeded with practical utopias than in the two decades that followed the First World War. Most narratives of this era are dominated by the national-scale social experiments of fascism and communism, which dramatically changed the landscape of the modern world. These experiments relied on coercion: on military surveillance, purges, collectivization and oppression. Yet even as images of Mussolini and Hitler, Lenin and Stalin, surrounded by seas of raised forearms or clenched fists, were broadcast on newsreels around the world, and factories from Japan to Germany began churning out shells and steel helmets, dozens of small-scale, cooperative communities devoted to utopian living were also springing up.

The tools of these communities were shared property, democratic decision-making and progressive education. Their attempts at social reform were experimental, idiosyncratic and often bizarre: three hours a day of meditation in a darkened prayer hall; evenings of 'psychologically regenerative' dance; groups of soft-handed intellectuals labouring with spades while former farmhands were taught to play the violin. Yet these places were far more than just refuges for eccentric escapists fleeing an unsatisfactory social order that they couldn't change. The idealists who gravitated to them were devoted to devising new social structures, to identifying what the 'good place' would look like in reality, and to living in a way that would inspire change in others. They had a global vision: they wanted to better the condition of all of humankind, not just the immediate members of their community. They published books and journals, gave public lectures, and crossed oceans to sow the seeds of change. 'Fire from a single match / is capable of kindling everything flammable in the world,' Mushanokōji Saneatsu wrote from his settlement in Japan.[18]

The generation of idealists who founded utopian communities in the years after the war shared many characteristics, despite their different places of origin. A striking number of them had suffered serious personal losses during the war and pandemic. The Englishman Leonard Elmhirst lost two of his brothers in the First World War, at Gallipoli and the Somme. Eberhard Arnold, a German, lost his brother on the Eastern Front. The American Dorothy Straight lost her husband in the influenza pandemic, leaving her with three young children to care for on her own. Grief fuelled their determination to build a better world in memory of the departed. While they had different views on what the 'good place' looked like, these utopians were mostly united in what they rejected: the prevailing treatment of people as atomized individuals competing in the economic market. Many of them read and admired the same radical nineteenth-century thinkers, notably William Morris and Leo Tolstoy. They dreamed of social equality, self-government and back-to-the-land self-sufficiency, and withdrew to remote rural regions to build communities based on those dreams.

The post-war utopias reflected the power structures of the time: they were mostly run by people from middle- or upper-class backgrounds, and they tended to replicate patriarchal norms. Creating a utopia required capital, which was usually inherited, or given to the founders by rich well-wishers who supported their ideals. It was far easier to build a community that rejected the capitalist system if someone else had engaged with that system already, furnishing the necessary funds. Most utopian leaders were men, and few were notably visionary about the roles of women. Female idealists in the early twentieth century were often battling to expand their suffrage and social rights on a national level – they were more likely to be found organizing, marching, and enduring nights in jail cells than seceding from society to build utopias. For men, already secure in their social standing, detaching from the mainstream to create a community offered a welcome chance to experiment with how to live. While there were women with positions of influence within male-led utopias, few had the privilege necessary to found a settlement of their own. There were of course exceptions – like the Panacea Society, a community housed in a clutch of Victorian villas in the English market town of Bedford led by Mabel Barltrop, who believed herself to be sent by God to correct the gender imbalance of the cosmos and to lead people to immortal life on earth.[19] Other women expressed their ideas about good – or bad – alternative worlds through fiction: Charlotte Perkins Gilman's pacifistic female-only society *Herland*, for instance, or the eugenicist dystopia evoked by Rose Macaulay in *What Not*.[20]

The practical utopias of the 1920s and 30s tended to fit into two broad categories. The first tried to encourage complete self-actualization, uniting head, heart and hand. Three communities in this book represent this strand: Santiniketan-Sriniketan, a bustling, cosmopolitan centre that used education to promote a life of all-round fulfilment among the thatched huts of East Bengal; Dartington Hall, a lavishly endowed English country estate financed by the American heiress Dorothy Straight, where participants mixed chicken farming, open-air theatre, spiritual exploration and communal self-government; and Atarashiki Mura, a small collective of impecunious Japanese intellectuals who cultivated rice and strove for self-realization through artistic pursuits. While these were very different places, all sought to offer a more complete existence – one that fulfilled people creatively, intellectually, socially and spiritually, as well as economically. Their founders were not just interested in changing one particular area of human behaviour. They wanted to embrace and improve the whole person. For them, the way people lived required a total overhaul.

The second type of community was driven by spirituality. Many idealists feared that this vital dimension of life was in danger of being lost amid the material ambitions of industrial capitalism, empirical science, and the assault on religion and faith of all kinds brought about by the horror of the war and pandemic. Their version of the good life turned on strict adherence to spiritual systems – whether that meant orthodox Christianity or one of the new, syncretic faiths that were a feature of the era. Three communities in this book illustrate this stream of utopianism: the Institute for the Harmonious Development of Man, a bohemian commune run on a system of psychological shocks in the forests outside Paris; an austere, quasi-monastic Christian settlement in central Germany, the Bruderhof; and Trabuco College, a group of men and women following the 'third morality', a regime of celibacy, vegetarianism and silent meditation, amid the cactuses and scrub plants of California.

The stories of these utopias aren't stories of the cornucopian plenty, free-flowing intellectual debate and chamber pots made of gold to be found in More or the Land of Cockaigne. Their stories feature empty bank accounts and unsuccessful fundraising drives; freeloading followers and hostile neighbours; malaria, hunger and sleepless nights in mosquito-ridden huts; failed rice harvests, damp clogs and bitter squabbles over whose turn it was to feed the pigs. They are not stories of 'success' or 'failure'. In the end, utopias always 'fail' – at least in the sense that the 'perfect place' has not yet been created on earth, is unlikely to appear any time soon, and is, anyway, a concept that is inherently subjective. The wonder in revisiting practical utopias does not come from their demonstrating perfect solutions to the question of how to live, but from the imaginative ways in which they respond to the problems of their specific historical moment. As societies evolve, their problems evolve with them, and the corresponding vision of what the 'good place' is changes too. The old vision falls by the wayside.

Though the communities in this book were often small in scale, unrepentantly eccentric and dismissed even in their time, that doesn't mean they should be forgotten. They encouraged people to question the status quo, and to believe that private individuals could generate change through the examples of their own lives. These practical utopias pioneered a series of ideas that would be adopted by – or would at least influence – mainstream society: from child-centred education and universal access to the arts, to low-technology farming, composting toilets and making time for daily sessions of meditation or mindfulness. They would go on to shape government policies, to inspire and educate a new generation of politicians, scholars and artists, and to provide a model for the counterculture of the 1960s and 70s. They offered, and continue to offer, a rich store of lessons for those who aspire to improve society.

The communities set up after the war are examples of what Aldous Huxley called 'that most difficult and most important of all the arts – the art of living together in harmony and with benefit for all concerned'.[1] Theirs is a story of humankind's unrealized potential, of paths we might have taken and might yet take. It is a story of how the world can be shaped, even if only in a limited way, by a handful of odd and under-washed strangers trying to make a life together in the countryside – a story of absurdity, possibility and hope.

ONE

'LIFE IN ITS COMPLETENESS' ON
THE PLAINS OF BENGAL

Rabindranath Tagore's Santiniketan-Sriniketan

It was the late summer of 1901. A group of twelve-year-old boys dressed in yellow robes sat in the shade of a sakhua tree on a remote plot of land in the Indian province of Bengal. They were listening to the poet and social reformer Rabindranath Tagore – forty years old, his language marked by an unusual combination of passion and precision – talking about the kind of education he wanted them to have. He told them that they must be trained 'not to be soldiers, not to be clerks in a bank, not to be merchants', but to be the makers of their own world and their own destiny.' At his school, they would learn from their own observations, rather than from books written by others. Tagore gestured at a myna bird perched in the branches above their heads. Even from something as commonplace as birdsong, he said, they could piece together a personal understanding of 'a world which is their very own', rather than one shaped by conventional schoolmasters and British imperialists. By doing so, they would grow up conscious of the presence of the divine, 'full in all directions', and in charge of their own destinies.

Tagore's school was a shout against colonialism, and a precursor to the practical utopia he would establish at Santiniketan-Sriniketan in 1921. Although Tagore was already an ambitious social thinker and reformer when the twentieth century began, it took the First World

War to convince him that something more drastic was needed to change the way people lived: the building of a community that would demonstrate how cooperation and creative fulfilment could replace nationalism and material greed. He was perfectly placed to found such a place – a man with a comfortable income derived from his family's large estates, with access to land, with well-established philosophical principles, and a reputation for independent thinking.

By the mid-1920s, Tagore had transformed a few dusty acres of rural Bengal into a meeting place for idealists from across five continents. Santiniketan-Sriniketan was a whimsical confusion of Eastern and Western architecture. In one corner of the community, leading academics drank cups of the Darjeeling tea that grew nearby and discussed how the linguistic connections between ancient India and the West related to the underlying unity of humankind. In another, agriculturalists poked hopefully at a bed freshly spread with manure, where they were experimenting with how well Japanese vegetables could stand up to the dry conditions of Bengal. In a third, a clamorous group of children clustered around an American nurse who was teaching them how to distribute quinine, part of a project that combined education with combating the malaria that was plaguing the local villages.

When people think of Tagore, they do not often think of this experiment in rural Bengal. Usually, he is known as the first non-Western winner of the Nobel Prize in Literature. This single achievement dominates most accounts of his life. Biographers venerate him for it. In India, a country whose anthem he wrote, he is a national treasure. While the radiance of his literary career tends to obscure his work in social reform, Santiniketan-Sriniketan was vital to Tagore himself. Through it, he tried to turn the harmonious and vibrant world of his imagination into a real place shared with others. As a utopian leader he was flawed – indulgent, chaotic, contradictory, impatient, and inclined to take his privilege as a well-to-do Brahmin for granted. Nonetheless, his utopian community, one of the first in the wave that spread across the world after the First World War, was influential in India and beyond. It inspired new social experiments in England, Japan and Ceylon. Tagore himself became a figurehead for a generation of idealists: men and women who admired his blending of Eastern

spirituality and Western science, his melding of action with creativity, and his unwavering faith that a better future was possible
for humankind.

*

It is no easy thing to abandon the ruling doctrines and social norms
of the day, as Tagore did, in order to build a new kind of community.
The drive to pursue such a radical change depends on total disillusionment with the way things are, and complete confidence in an
alternative vision. Add to this the charisma needed to persuade others
to take part, and it is unsurprising that a certain amount of life
experience seems to be prerequisite for founding a utopia. All of the
idealists in this book were over thirty when they founded their
communities. But Tagore, who was sixty when he founded Santiniketan-
Sriniketan, had more life experience than most. The people he had
met and the ways of living he had observed in his first five decades
– growing up in late-colonial Calcutta, studying in London, managing
estates in the Bengal countryside and lecturing around the globe – all
went into shaping his vision for a better way of living.

Tagore was born in Calcutta in 1861, into the kind of family that
expected him to make a mark on the world. His grandfather
Dwarkanath – 'the Oriental Croesus', Charles Dickens called him
– was a middleman for the East India Company, and became one
of the richest merchants in Bengal by dealing in sugar, gold, newspapers and stocks and shares.[2] Tagore's father Debendranath reacted
against Dwarkanath's hedonistic lifestyle, materialistic ambitions and
collaboration with the British by helping to found a new religious
society called Brahmo Samaj.[3] This hugely popular Hindu reform
movement promoted sobriety, the worship of one God, the uplift
of the lower castes, and Indian cultural nationalism. The family's
achievements continued into Rabindranath's generation: among his
thirteen elder siblings were Swarnakumari, Bengal's first woman
novelist; Dwijendranath, a renowned philosopher-mathematician;
and Jyotirindranath, an accomplished composer who also staged
some of the most popular Bengali plays of the time. This distinguished
background provided Tagore with the confidence, connections and
funds that would facilitate his unconventional life.

Jorasanko – the sprawling mansion where Tagore and his extended family lived in north Calcutta – was a gathering place for the artists and writers of the late-nineteenth-century Bengali cultural renaissance. Its wide verandahs and airy front rooms echoed with music, plays and conversations about art, social reform and how to mitigate the effects of British rule. A more stimulating environment is difficult to imagine, but Tagore, an adventurous, romantic child, craved something further: to know the world outside. His puritanical father prohibited him from leaving the house on his own, worried that his son would be corrupted by the prostitutes who plied their trade in the backstreets behind the house, or by the British imperialists living in the neighbouring mansions.[4] All Tagore could do was lean wistfully out of the upper windows of his family house and listen. He craned to catch the sounds floating up from the nearby Chitpur Road – the squeaking cartwheels, the tinkling bells of Calcutta's first horse-drawn trams, the cries of kites fighting over household refuse – and dreamed of what the 'real' India was like.

At the age of seven, Tagore was sent to day school. Even sixty years later he remembered how it felt like a 'parrot's cage'.[5] Modelled on the British system, the school seemed designed only to prepare boys for government offices, the military and British businesses. Tagore rebelled against this regime of mechanical rote learning with such ferocity that, after trying him at four different schools in as many years, his family decided that it would be less trouble if he studied at home. As soon as his schooling was taken over by his lively minded, liberal elder siblings, he began to flourish. Aged thirteen, he published his first book of verse, and by sixteen he was contributing his poems and essays to the Calcutta journals. These were the first instalments in a stream of stories, dramas, verse and essays that would stretch to 18,000 pages across his lifetime. The lessons Tagore took from his education – that a set curriculum shouldn't be forced on children, and that people should be free to seek out the knowledge that genuinely interests them – were the seeds of his vision for Santiniketan-Sriniketan.

Calcutta, as well as being an important centre for the arts, education and social reform, had been the capital of the British Raj since 1772. Local opinion on the British presence was sharply divided. The colonial influence produced Anglophiles who saw the British as a vital force for developing their 'backward' country – a belief that the British naturally encouraged. It also bred nationalists whose chief hope was to sweep the British out of India as soon as possible and to proclaim Indian independence. Tagore's family was unusual in falling between these two camps. They resented the idea of their country being dominated by a foreign power. (Tagore mocked the local Anglophiles for collapsing 'into a mass of *jelly*, trembling and wobbling from top to toe' when they received some mark of British favour.[6]) At the same time, they admired Western liberalism and Western culture. The refusal to favour one side of the argument put the family beyond the pale of the Anglophiles and the nationalists alike. Through observing and then adopting his family's position, Tagore learned to take pride in rejecting mainstream thinking. 'That I do not belong to any group makes them all angry,' he would later write. 'No one will be able to put a chain on my feet.'[7]

At seventeen, Tagore was sent to England by his father, who wanted him to have the education that would allow him to become a barrister or a civil servant. He expected to find an island 'so devoted to higher culture that from one end to the other it would resound to the strains of Tennyson's lyre'.[8] But he was horrified by the reality of smog, soot-stained houses, commercial bustle and frostiness towards dark-skinned foreigners. Tagore briefly attended a public school in Brighton, then studied for a few months at University College London. He hated the constraints of formal education just as much as he had as a child, and he quickly returned to Calcutta. Once home, he wrote furiously, giving readings and lectures, and winning a reputation as 'Bengal's Shelley'. Yet he felt isolated by his fame, and he remained restless, drawn as he had been as a child to the world beyond elite Calcutta.

It's difficult not to be shocked at the fact that, aged twenty-two, Tagore accepted as his wife a near-illiterate ten-year-old, Mrinalini Devi, chosen for him by his father.[9] When he had daughters of his own, he married them off in the same way – aged fourteen and eleven, to men they had never met – despite the fact that he had by then written numerous articles campaigning against child brides. Tagore would always struggle to translate his professed ideals into action, a difficulty increased in the case of women's rights by the politics of late-imperial India. The British claimed the cause of female liberation as their own, while some nationalists defended women's lesser position – along with caste hierarchy – as an integral part of 'traditional', pre-colonial India.[10] Tagore wanted to combine his enthusiasm for progressivism and women's rights with his idealization of his country's past traditions, and to be associated with neither the British nor the nationalists. In choosing his marriage and that of his daughters, though, Tagore failed to live out his ideals completely.

Creating his own community would be, in part, an attempt to escape the pervading colonial–nationalist tensions by radically rethinking how society functioned. But it would take three more decades of mounting frustration with the values and systems that reigned in India before Tagore was driven to this drastic step. Through his thirties, forties and fifties, he continued to believe it was possible to improve society from within, whether through institutional change or education – until the shock of the First World War made it clear to him that a new beginning was necessary.

*

In 1891, at the age of twenty-nine, Tagore was seated at his desk by the open window of his wide, flat-bottomed boat, the *Padma*, which was drifting through the shallow waters of the Ganges delta. He was surrounded by the stacks of books without which he never went anywhere: classics in Sanskrit and English, treatises on anthropology and ethnology (everything, in fact, except what he called 'light' novels).[11] But for once he wasn't reading. He was in thrall to the pageant of daily life unfolding outside the window on the riverbank: old men gravely washing themselves; young girls in saris playing in the water before filling their vessels and carrying them up the bank; swarms of boats, fishing and carrying paddy and jute to Calcutta.[12]

This riverine existence, Tagore thought, was 'the lap of rural loveliness': the fierce power of the muddy water, the wild ducks haunting the white sandbanks, the waving clusters of bamboo shoots so tall that they hid entire villages in their midst.[13] He lifted his pen and wove the life around him into the short story he was writing – one of the forty-nine he would craft in the span of a decade. While Tagore was writing, he was also developing the idea that it was in the countryside that the true spirit of India resided: in small village communities rooted deep in the soil and water, where people were connected to the divine not by narrow religious traditions but by the beauty of the natural world around them. The life of the wealthy neighbourhoods of Calcutta, where educated, wealthy urbanites 'wander about in the high heaven of ideas like aimless clouds', seemed to him by contrast fundamentally profane and corrupt.[14]

A couple of years later, the *Padma* was moored by one of the family's estates in East Bengal, which Tagore was now managing. Tagore himself sat in a much-repaired thatched hut, whose roof would clearly leak all through the monsoon rains. He had gone through the tenant's accounts and was now listening to the man explain why he could pay only half his rent.[15] Tagore was learning that amid the beauty of the Bengal countryside, poverty was rampant. In former times, zamindars – landlords like Tagore – collected a flexible amount of revenue from farmers on behalf of the Mughal emperor. But in 1793, the British imposed a Permanent Settlement. This gave zamindars full ownership of land, rather than just the right to collect taxes. It also fixed the taxes zamindars had to pay to the government. The fixed tariff, which was designed to ensure a reliable stream of income for Britain, took no account of the vagaries of rural life. The same amount was to be paid regardless of drought, flood or famine.

To collect their revenue for the British, and to maximize their own profit, the zamindars forced their tenants to cultivate cash crops for the international market. This undermined the farmers' traditional survival strategies: growing diverse crops to guard against pest and disease, and building stores of grain for lean years. Poor farmers became poorer still, and ever more vulnerable. Under the pressure of the unremitting demand for money, the institutions of rural community life had atrophied. Social welfare, education and village festivities had fallen by the wayside as people struggled to keep on the treadmill of payments.

The paradise Tagore thought he had glimpsed on the riverbank only shortly before had turned out to be illusory. He shifted uncomfortably as his tenant begged not to be thrown off the land his family had farmed for generations. Tagore knew that summarily ejecting tenants was the kind of crude tactic that families like his had long relied on. He asked the man what he thought could be done to improve the situation in the countryside. The tenant was surprised and confused. He was too downtrodden and uneducated, Tagore thought, to even dream of an alternative to his situation. Back on his boat, the poet wrote that he found it 'a very shameful thing' that he should be spending his days 'engrossed with my own profit and loss'.[16] There must, he thought, be a better way for rural people to live. He had begun to dream of an alternative to the society in which he lived – and he was rich enough, and secure enough in his position, to try to make that dream a reality.

By the late 1890s, Tagore, his wife Mrinalini and their five children were staying at Shelidah, the family's main estate in East Bengal.[17] The poet was at his desk. Before him were the results of a clutch of experiments he had hatched to resolve rural India's problems. He had already established a judicial system on his estates, an impressive innovation that bypassed Bengal's complex law courts and gave farmers a voice. Now he wanted to set up self-governing bodies for each of the districts he ran, which he hoped would improve village life by supporting schools, dispensaries and grain banks.[18] His ultimate aim was to make the villages strong, self-reliant and rich in traditional culture. This, he believed, was how they used to be, before their vitality was sapped by colonialism and the forces of global commerce. But the measures he had thought up so far felt too light, too simple to produce fundamental change.

It dawned on Tagore that he already possessed the answer to the question of how to improve India; he had possessed it ever since his struggles at school at the age of seven. He pulled a fresh sheet of paper towards him. 'I know,' he wrote, 'all the evils, almost without exception, from which my land suffers are solely owing to the utter lack of education.'[19]

In 1901, Tagore opened his own school, Patha Bhavana, in a remote part of West Bengal.[20] It was located on a plot of family land called Santiniketan ('Abode of Grace'), which would later become the home of Tagore's utopian community. As Tagore navigated the practicalities of setting up his school, he was sidetracked from his hope of helping peasants and farmers by nationalist friends who suggested he devote his institution to promoting traditional Hindu values among the elite – thereby countering colonial influence. He followed this model: his pupils lived in mud huts, cooked their own dal and rice, and rose to meditate, pray and chant hymns from the Vedas before the sun had even risen.[21] Within a few years, the school grew from five to fifty students. Yet Tagore soon began worrying that, like his village-improvement measures, this elite, orthodox institution was too narrow an instrument to reform society in the way he wished. His discontent was aggravated by family tragedy. In 1903, his wife died. Less than a year later, he lost his daughter Renuka. His father died in 1905 and his youngest son Samindranath in 1907. This series of personal losses made Tagore all the more determined to devote himself to serious social change, but he did not yet know what his next step would be.

*

In the 1910s, while Tagore was still casting around for a better approach to social reform, the shape of his world was dramatically altered. He won the Nobel Prize in Literature in 1913. On the back of this award, he became one of the earliest international literary celebrities.[22] His work was soon available in the bookshops of Tokyo, New York and the European capitals, translated by well-known figures including André Gide, Boris Pasternak and Juan Ramón Jiménez – all of whom would subsequently become Nobel laureates in their own right. Tagore had barely begun to adjust to his new status when the First World War broke out – a war in which 1.5 million Indians participated and more than 74,000 died.[23] The colony endured Allied requisitions of grain and livestock, heavy taxes, and an influenza death toll of over 18 million. It was against the backdrop of this suffering that, in 1916, Tagore set off on a literary lecture tour of Japan and the United States.

Until this point in Tagore's life, his vision of a better world had been fuelled by the hardships he had witnessed as a zamindar, and by the debates about nationalist traditionalism versus Western liberalism that raged in Calcutta. His wartime travels reframed his world view. The people he met – from the elite students he lectured at Tokyo Imperial University to the wealthy New Yorkers he dined with in Manhattan – convinced him that India wasn't alone in her social problems. Humanity as a whole seemed in need of a change in philosophy to prevent such a cataclysm as the First World War from happening again. The book that Tagore was best known for outside India was *Gitanjali* ('Song Offerings'), a poetry collection celebrating spirituality, devotion and love.[24] Partly because of this, he found himself being treated on his travels as an enlightened Eastern guru who might have an explanation for where the West had gone wrong. He embraced the role, seeing in it a powerful way to convince others of his ideas, and he quickly conceived of an ambitious plan for averting future world conflict.

The plan was simple: the individualistic, materialistic West needed to learn from the communality and higher, more tran-scendent wisdom of the East. 'For is not the East the mother of spiritual Humanity,' Tagore asked in one of his addresses, 'and does not the West, do not the children of the West amidst their games and plays when they get hurt, when they get famished and hungry, turn their face to that serene mother, the East?'[25] The West's greedy, expansionist nationalism – its insatiable appetite for 'competition, conflict and conquest' – should, he argued, be replaced with a new era of cooperation and spiritualized international harmony.[26] No one nation was greater than the universal ideal of humanity. Tagore's words were received with relish in most places he visited – he easily filled the 3,000-seat auditorium of Carnegie Hall in New York.[27]

The enthusiasm for these ideas, along with the mounting toll of the war, convinced Tagore that it was time for action. Instead of continuing to try to reform society from within, he would separate himself from it and start again from scratch, working with others who felt the same way. During his stay in southern California, he wrote to his son announcing that he had come up with a radical plan. He wanted to set up a 'world centre' offering an idealistic education that would be 'the first step towards universal union'.[28] He imagined a place that would make people realize 'that artists of all parts of the world have created forms of beauty, scientists discovered secrets of the universe, philosophers solved the problems of existence, saints made the truth of the spiritual world organic in their own lives, not merely for some particular race to which they belonged, but for all mankind'.[29] Tagore's new community would promote international harmony, and it would offer to all who came what he called 'life in its completeness' – a social mode that met people's needs on every level: creative, intellectual, spiritual, social and economic.[30]

*

To begin with, all Tagore had was his vision and a piece of land. Santiniketan, which was already the home of his school, consisted of a few desolate acres amid miles of flat semi-desert studded with stunted shrubs, anthills and dilapidated villages. Santiniketan had once been dedicated as a public ashram by his father, who constructed a grand glass-and-iron prayer hall there, the structure ordered from the same firm that built Crystal Palace in London.[31] Since then the plot had been neglected. Apart from the prayer hall, it was marked out only by a few trees and the handful of mosquito-haunted mud huts that made up Tagore's school. This was not a promising setting for the 'universal union' Tagore envisioned – but when Tagore examined it, he began to envisage the 'good place' that he wanted it to become: a community that would generate a harmonious global culture, while also fostering strong local roots. He wanted it to be universal in its outlook, but particular in the richness of its day-to-day life. Internationalism would replace nationalism, cooperation would replace individualism. In the outside world, people were treated merely as economic 'machines', but here the focus would be on all-round fulfilment and the 'personal relationship between man and man'.[32] Visiting this community would, Tagore thought, 'be a pilgrimage. Let those coming to it say, oh what a relief it is to be away from narrow domestic walls and to behold the universe.'[33]

He threw himself into finding the funds for the buildings and staff that would make this vision a reality. It was a daunting task, but he had many factors in his favour, the most important being the very thing which had driven him so zealously into this project: the aftershock of the war. Enthusiasm for internationalism was flourishing across the world. Organizations sprang up to promote global cooperation in health, education, women's rights and in many other areas; in America, Salmon Oliver Levinson, a Chicago attorney, spearheaded an international 'Outlawry of War' campaign; in locations as distant as rural Japan and the European capitals, hundreds of clubs were started to encourage people to learn the international language Esperanto.[34] Tagore's idea was perfectly pitched to capture the imaginations of the internationally minded in Europe, America and Asia, promising to forge a peaceable world culture – the joint product of East and West – and to instil this culture in participants from across the world, creating a generation that would be incapable of succumbing to war.

By now Tagore had a wide web of acquaintances to draw on: businessmen in Bombay, millionaires in New York, esteemed academics in the universities of Europe, social reformers tucked away in obscure corners of the globe. He knew who would be won over by letters and telegrams, who was likely to contribute to or to help publicize his cause. With the assistance of various secretaries, he arranged a quick-fire journey around India, Europe and America to raise donations in person. In an earlier age, before steamships and railways, before the telegraph and telephone, it simply wouldn't have been possible for Tagore to raise funds so readily for a project in rural Bengal. As it was, he managed it with remarkable speed and ease – although he remained uncomfortably conscious of the irony of appealing for money to create an anti-materialist utopia.

As a zamindar, Tagore's strength had been coming up with ideas to improve villagers' lives, which he then left to be executed by the villagers themselves. Now that he had raised his funds and was attempting to enact his own ideas, his inability to engage in sustained, orderly practical activity became quickly apparent. Neither at this early point nor at any later time did he draw up a clear design for the community he intended to create. The well-regarded Scottish city planner Patrick Geddes – one of the many idealists attracted to Tagore's unique undertaking – tried to persuade him to organize his thinking before launching into the building stage of the project.[35] He sent Tagore a possible schema for his 'world centre', including a diagram adorned with such obscure labels as 'ethopolity' and 'psychorganics'.[36] But such theory-driven planning was anathema to Tagore. 'If I had in the commencement a definite outline which I was merely to fill in,' he wrote back, 'it would certainly bore me.'[37] He told Geddes that he preferred plunging right into the thick of the action, working out what should happen organically as he went along, just as he did when he was writing stories.

By the mid-1920s, the result of Tagore's haphazard approach was a community impressive in its scope, but far more disparate and disorganized than the vision he had described in his letters. The community crystallized into four projects based across two locations, all of them revolving around what, for Tagore, was the ultimate tool for creating a better world: education. There were hundreds of people involved, local villagers working alongside teachers, pupils and visitors from across Asia, Europe and America. At Santiniketan was Patha Bhavana, the school Tagore first established in 1901, which he had begun reforming along more progressive lines. Sharing the campus was the 'world university', Visva-Bharati, opened in 1921 to promote cross-cultural understanding between East and West through its cosmopolitan participants and wide-ranging courses. That same year, Tagore opened an institute of rural regeneration, intended to transform the countryside by modelling good agricultural practices. This was based at Sriniketan, a plot of land two miles away. Finally, in 1924, Tagore began a second school, Siksha-Satra, devoted to the education of village children. Throughout the rest of his life, Tagore would flit restlessly between these institutions, never able to articulate how they should relate administratively or ideologically, but convinced that together they pointed the way to a better mode of living.

*

Tagore first threw his energies into the university, which required more infrastructural outlay than his other projects. For a motto, he gave Visva-Bharati an ancient Sanskrit verse, *yatra visvam bhavati ekanidam* – 'where the world finds a nest'. Its nucleus consisted of a department of the arts, a department of music and a department of Indology (dedicated to the study of Buddhism and Asian languages and literature). All of these departments were intended, as Tagore told his professors, 'to help the realisation of the unity, but not of uniformity' – to emphasize and celebrate the diversity of cultures in the world, 'without losing the hold on the basic or spiritual unity'.[38] Students could pick and choose their courses at will, simultaneously studying subjects as diverse as modern Italian literature and the Vedic, Buddhist, Jain, Zoroastrian and Sikh traditions, the writings of medieval saints, and the cultures of contemporary China,

Japan and Tibet. If a student wanted to pursue a course of study that was not yet available, Tagore went out of his way to recruit a new teacher for them.

Even with Tagore's energetic fundraising, there wasn't enough money to spare for a professional architect, so a painter who joined the university's staff, Surendranath Kar, designed many of the buildings. He borrowed styles from Japan to Java, and took inspiration from Mughal palaces and Hindu temples, transforming Santiniketan into an appropriately cosmopolitan campus. Over the years, Tagore would add further structures as the whim took him: a single-storey hostel for students, traditional mud-built guesthouses, a clocktower paid for by the prominent Indian statesman Satyendra Prasanna Sinha of Raipur, and a fresco-adorned library specializing in books on Zoroastrian and Tibetan studies. Alongside these buildings stood the simpler structures of Patha Bhavana school, and the magnificent prayer hall, which was used as a gathering place for a weekly non-denominational service. Standing amid the thatched villages of the plains, thronging with students from across India and with an international teaching staff, Tagore's community looked like it had been built of fragments gathered from across the world.

Life at Santiniketan was not a comfortable one. The lodgings for students and staff were scorching hot for half the year, plagued by mosquitoes and water shortages, far below the standard of most universities. An American nurse, visiting a professor ill on campus, was horrified to find him lying on a string cot in a stifling, one-room thatched cottage with birds living in the roof.[39] Tagore was determined that his community's participants wouldn't be caught in 'luxury's noose', the preoccupation with material gain that he associated with the West's descent into war.[40]

It might be imagined that such conditions, added to a remote location, low salaries, and the lack of job security, would have put off all but those few fanatical idealists drawn to a life of hardship. But Tagore's invitation to join Visva-Bharati was taken up by scholars around the world, people who appreciated that this wasn't just a conventional academic institute – it was part of an effort to forge a new international culture. Soon Nandalal Bose, a pioneer of Indian modernism, was running the arts department. A noted singer, Dinendranath Tagore – the grandson of Tagore's eldest brother – was in charge of the music school, assisted by the classical musicologist Bhimrao Shastri. The contingent of foreign professors included two Czech Sanskritists, a Viennese art historian and a Russian Persianist. Chinese scholar Tan Yun-Shan joined the university to found Cheena Bhavana, the oldest centre of Chinese studies in South Asia. French Orientalist Sylvain Lévi, who had been invited to join Visva-Bharati and Harvard University at the same time, chose Visva-Bharati, and organized a department of Tibetan studies that was the first to be founded in the country. The enthusiasm with which established academics and experts gave up their old lives to join Tagore's experiment was testament to how ardently they believed in replacing the ideologies the war had shown to be so dangerous. As the Norwegian Indologist Sten Konow put it, 'The outlook in the West was hopeless when the poet came from the East, and asked us to seek salvation through faith in new ideals [. . .] The aim of the Visva-Bharati is life-giving, it is to achieve unity in diversity.'[41]

Once the university was under way, Patha Bhavana school was repurposed to fit Tagore's utopian vision. In 1901, he had set it up on the model of the *tapovan*, the Hindu forest ashrams of ancient India. As with the *tapovan*, its guiding principle had been *brahmacharya* ('continence') – which meant, as Tagore told his students, keeping away from 'the luxuries of European life and any blind infatuation with Europe', and learning 'the ways of the sacred and unsullied Indian tradition of poverty'.[42] But by the 1920s, Tagore had no time for such nationalistic Hindu sentiments. He wanted his school to promote international unity and religious inclusivity. His own faith, by this point, was what he termed a 'poet's religion', turning on the belief that an impersonal deity infused all of nature and humanity regardless of sect or theological persuasion.[43]

The remodelled Patha Bhavana was co-educational, with the boys and girls living together – an arrangement that was rare in India.[44] It followed no prescribed curriculum. Instead, pupils' education was to be driven by their own curiosity, their hunger for knowledge fed by giving them as much freedom as possible. Their teachers encouraged them to a full emotional and spiritual appreciation of the divinely created universe – of the natural world, the globe's varied civilizations, and their own powers of creative self-expression. Drawing inspiration from the fashionable progressive educators

Tagore had met in Europe, he cut down on the formal apparatus of the school, eschewing classrooms in favour of open-air lessons under the trees or on the verandahs of the dormitory. After class, students were encouraged to join in with any of the activities of the other parts of Santiniketan-Sriniketan – learning pottery or sculpture in the Visva-Bharati art department, for example, or joining the workshops on carpentry, tanning or midwifery that were being conducted a short walk away at Sriniketan. 'The highest education,' Tagore liked to say, 'is that which does not merely give us information but makes our life in harmony with all existence.'⁴⁵ In these early days, students felt they were pioneering a new and vital way of living, building a utopia that offered an alternative to mainstream values.

While many of the staff at Visva-Bharati and Patha Bhavana came from abroad, the students of both university and school were mainly Indian. Pupils arrived from as far afield as Gujarat, Madras, Kerala and Andhra Pradesh.⁴⁶ Several of them would go on to shape India's cultural landscape after it gained independence in 1947. They included the Bengali writer Syed Mujtaba Ali, the Oscar-winning filmmaker Satyajit Ray, the Nobel Prize-winning economist Amartya Sen, and Indira Gandhi, the first (and so far only) female prime minister of India. Satyajit Ray looked back on his years studying at Santiniketan as the 'most fruitful' of his life, a period that transformed him into 'the combined product of East and West'.⁴⁷ His appreciation of the unique, cosmopolitan atmosphere of Tagore's community was echoed by the visiting Italian Orientalist Giuseppe Tucci, who remembered Santiniketan as 'an island where those who had not lost faith in mankind and its destinies, or did not despair that the divine in us could sparkle again in full splendour, could find a congenial atmosphere to cherish and nourish their hopes'.⁴⁸ These appreciative participants became missionaries for the community's ideals, carrying them into the wider world.

There was a free, creative, cosmopolitan allure to daily life on the red clay campus of Santiniketan in the early 1920s. The bell rang at dawn, calling students and teachers from their huts, houses and dormitories as the sun rose. They walked out into what Satyajit Ray remembered as 'a world of vast open spaces, vaulted over with a dustless sky'.⁴⁹ Many sat cross-legged beneath the sakhua trees for half an hour of meditation before breakfast. Following the community's ideal of equality, everyone took turns serving and clearing at mealtimes. There were lessons in languages, literature, philosophy, history, economics, music and art until 4.30, on a schedule largely determined by the students themselves. These lessons had a fluidity and range that was a unique part of the peda-gogical style of Santiniketan: Amartya Sen remembered 'something totally remarkable about the ease with which discussions in the school could move from Indian traditional literature to contemporary as well as classical western thought and to China, Japan and elsewhere'.[50]

After lessons, scholars of all ages and nationalities met over tea to discuss the ideas that they'd encountered in the course of the day, parting ways for a cricket match or a conversational stroll through the shady mango grove. Days usually ended with a per-formance by students on the pillared verandah of Tagore's house – of drama, music, or dance in a unique internationalist style devised by Tagore, combining Indian folk tradition, Hindu classicism and the modernism of Europe and America.[51] There was no formal religious teaching at Santiniketan-Sriniketan, only the weekly meeting in the prayer hall led by Tagore, who recited from a Sanskrit text or gave a speech about his ideals, before a choir of students sang.[52] But to many visitors and residents it felt as if the community's day-to-day routine was imbued with 'a deep spiritual atmosphere' unlike anywhere else in the world, so focused were the people Tagore had brought together on pursuing higher values and modes of behaviour.[53] It 'induced contemplation, and a sense of wonder,' Ray recalled, even in 'the most prosaic and earthbound of minds'.[54]

News of the unusual community at Santiniketan-Sriniketan spread quickly across India, arousing considerable suspicion and hostility. The nationalistic elite complained that its participants were 'dissoci-ated from reality' in their internationalism and refusal to engage in the campaign for Indian independence.[55] The British and their Indian supporters were equally disapproving. Tagore had renounced his British knighthood, awarded in 1915 for services to literature, after the massacre of unarmed civilians by troops under British command at Amritsar in 1919. Suspecting him of dangerous nationalist sympa-thies, the British government in India had already tried to undermine Tagore's post-war fundraising tour by warning potential American

donors against him.[56] Now that his school and university were
established, the British declared them 'altogether unsuitable for the
education of the sons of Government servants' and gave the police
the power to open all letters addressed to Santiniketan.[57] In spite
of opposition from two of the most powerful factions in India, there
were still enough parents and willing young men and women to
keep the school and university dormitories full. In a country reeling
under British rule, sectarian tension and the memory of the war,
Santiniketan-Sriniketan was a beacon of liberal and outward-looking
ideals, and one that rejected religious and cultural divides.

The community drew a great deal of foreign interest. The aged
idealistic poet and reformer Edward Carpenter, whose home in the
north of England had served since the 1880s as a place of pilgrimage
for socialists, pacifists, environmentalists and advocates of sexual
freedom, wrote approving letters from afar. Visitors ranged from
Ramsay MacDonald, who would be the first Labour Party politician
to become prime minister of Britain, to wealthy Dutch musician
Mary van Eeghen, who stayed for a couple of months, and Andrée
Karpelès, a French painter and translator who would go on to spend
time at the English utopian community of Dartington Hall. Oswald
Mosley, later the founder of the British Union of Fascists, also visited.
Clearly he did not adopt the community's ideal of pacifist internationalism, but, like the other guests, he revelled in passing evenings
in philosophic discussion with graduates from Oxford, the Sorbonne
and Heidelberg, with the great plains of Bengal stretching out on
all sides 'like the inverted bowl of Persian poetry'.[58]

For the visiting German pioneer in quantum physics Arnold
Sommerfeld, the most impressive feature of Santiniketan-Sriniketan
was its founder. 'He is to India perhaps the same as old Goethe was
to the Germany of his time,' Sommerfeld wrote. 'Like Goethe he is
infinitely diligent: he works from early in the morning till night.'[59]
Tagore did work hard, devoting his energies to keeping the four projects
evolving in accordance with his philosophy of a complete life. To an
extent he retained the trappings of his elite upbringing, living with his
family in an elaborate complex of buildings, which were far more
comfortable than the accommodation for other members of the
community. But he was always busy, preoccupied with the work of the
community, despite being well into his sixties. When he wasn't striding

about campus, enthusiastically showing round a guest or conversing with a student, he would be found at his desk.[60] Doors and windows flung open regardless of heat or rain, he juggled the writing of poetry and stories with the more mundane demands of keeping his community running, paying bills, drafting courses, writing a letter to solicit yet another donation or an article to drum up wider support.

The task of fundraising in particular was a constant source of frustration for Tagore, who had intended his community to be a rejection of the materialism and inequity that he felt had taken hold by the end of the nineteenth century. Like many of the other utopians of the period, Tagore had inherited money. But his various projects were still prohibitively expensive to run and he found it impossible to keep them going without frequent new injections of capital. 'This is not my work,' Tagore wrote in frustration in 1923, as he was forced to go on yet another tour to beg for donations, 'and I feel that I insult myself when I let my ideals go out for the purpose of courting money.'[61] Yet in a very real sense, fundraising was a utopian's work; without it, their ideals would never have had the chance to become reality.

In this period, Tagore also found himself trapped in what he called a 'civil war' between his personality as a thinker and artist, 'who necessarily must be solitary', and that of 'an idealist who must realize himself through works of a complex character needing a large field of collaboration with a large body of men'.[62] This struggle between the private and the public was one that most practical utopians had to grapple with in one form or another, since they tended to combine a theoretical belief in cooperative activity with the intense independent-mindedness necessary to convince them of the merits of seceding from society. In Tagore's case, one of the results of this tension was that in spite of his energy and passion, he ran his community with a notable lack of efficiency.

His schooldays had instilled in him a horror of institutions and their administrative instruments. He still believed that 'great men' could improve the world far more effectively than formal organizations. While this was a persuasive idea in theory, in practice the demands of the four institutions at Santiniketan-Sriniketan far surpassed the abilities of any individual. But Tagore chose not to establish a formal management team to help him meet the multitudinous needs of his projects – raising funds, finding staff, getting rid of staff, recruiting pupils, soothing quarrels, solving minor and major hiccups. He addressed all of these duties himself, and only when they could no longer be ignored, giving each of them as short shrift as possible. To an extent, he justified this as being part of his philosophy of organic, independent community growth. When new teachers arrived, for example, he told them that he didn't like to set out their jobs for them like 'a cage for the bird', but that they would have to 'win themselves the seat which is their own'.[63] In the 1920s, this personal style of rule served Tagore's utopia adequately. Although it was exhausting and time-consuming, his energy, confidence of vision and practicality were sufficient to keep all the balls in the air and most participants happy. But it posed questions for the future. What would happen when the community's founder was no longer able, or willing, to man its helm?

*

Though two of the institutions in Tagore's community, Patha Bhavana and Visva-Bharati, focused on educating a mostly elite student body, he did not forget the plight of India's villagers. He intended his utopia to combine the evolution of a harmonious world culture with local roots, and to show how the nurturing of the mind and the soil could go hand in hand. Along with inviting idealists and intellectuals from around the world to exchange ideas and knowledge with each other and to teach well-to-do students, Tagore wanted his community to offer poorer, local villagers, farmers and children an education that was just as innovative and uplifting. While founding Visva-Bharati and reforming Patha Bhavana, he also initiated the development of an institute for rural regeneration. Located on a plot of land two miles away from Santiniketan, a property Tagore named Sriniketan – 'the Abode of Plenty'– this was devoted to enriching locals' lives economically and culturally.[64] Here, in 1924, Tagore would also found a second school, Siksha-Satra, which was designed specifically for the children from the nearby villages.

Tagore set up the institute for rural regeneration with the help of a young Englishman, Leonard Elmhirst – a rare example of his successfully delegating responsibility. It was while Tagore was in New York, raising funds for Visva-Bharati in 1920, that he met the twenty-eight-year-old Elmhirst, who was studying agricultural economics at Cornell University.[65] The pair quickly recognized in one another that rare brand of idealism that unites abstract, soaring hopes and a fascination with the concrete practicalities of social reform. Tagore sketched out his plans for reviving the Indian countryside. 'If I can free only one or two villages from the bonds of ignorance and weakness,' he told Elmhirst, 'there will be built, on a tiny scale, an ideal for the whole of India.'[66] Impressed by the Englishman's know-ledgeable and enthusiastic responses, Tagore asked if he might be willing to bring the agricultural theory he had been learning at Cornell out to India. Elmhirst leaped at the chance. The First World War, Elmhirst told Tagore, had forced on his generation 'beastliness we would never have chosen for ourselves' – but Sriniketan offered the kind of work Elmhirst had 'always longed to take a shot at'.[67]

In general, Tagore was a poor judge of character. Many of those he relied on to help him at Santiniketan turned out to be unreliable, incompetent or untrustworthy – what one commentator called 'absolutely feeble-minded enthusiasts' who were 'obsessed with some unpractical idea'.[68] Elmhirst, however, was organized and efficient, and had the youthful vigour and agricultural training that Tagore lacked. Perhaps most significantly, he also had a financial backer who agreed to underwrite the work at Sriniketan, and who helped connect the endeavour with a worldwide network of social reformers. This was the American heiress Dorothy Straight, a distin-guished figure in the world of New York philanthropy. Later in the 1920s, she would marry Elmhirst, and the two of them would set up their own utopian community, Dartington Hall.

By the end of 1921, Elmhirst had joined Tagore on campus at Santiniketan, where he began to hear of the challenges that awaited him a little further down the road. Like so much of India, the poet said, the area had been sucked dry by the rental demands of the zamindars. To meet their obligations, tenant farmers had deforested and overgrazed the land. Thousands of acres had been eroded down to infertile desert, the red soil raised in clouds of dust in the dry seasons, then carved out into treacherous gullies by the rains. Tagore concluded this depressing picture by warning Elmhirst that the countryside's problems weren't confined to agriculture. The trad-itional, culturally rich rural way of life had crumbled entirely. Villages such as Ballapur, a mile from Sriniketan, had once supported five hundred families. Now it could only sustain twenty-four. The surviving population was debt-ridden and weakened by malaria, the children swollen-bellied with malnutrition, the ill-maintained mud huts disintegrating annually in the monsoon rains.[69]

Dauntless, Elmhirst drew up plans for Sriniketan and talked them through with Tagore, who shaped the younger man's ambitions according to the first-hand experience that came of reforming his family's estates in East Bengal. Both men shared a passion for the ideas of the founder of the Irish rural cooperative movement, Sir Horace Plunkett, and they discussed strengthening community in the countryside by encouraging cooperation among farmers.[70] But Elmhirst was chiefly inspired by the pioneering approach of Cornell's College of Agriculture. As well as the usual academic facilities, Cornell had a farm for demonstrating techniques and an extension scheme that sent experts out into the surrounding countryside to teach farmers more efficient and profitable methods.[71] Tagore agreed with Elmhirst that Sriniketan should work in a similar fashion – running a model farm alongside an outreach programme that would help the surrounding Hindu, Muslim and Santali villages. He also urged Elmhirst not to limit his work to promoting Western-style scientific farming. He should, he said, take an 'integrated approach', encouraging villagers to live a 'complete' life: one that was socially, spiritually and creatively fulfilling, as well as economically profitable. Elmhirst should promote 'Eastern' self-sufficiency and self-government alongside Western expertise. Their ultimate aim, Tagore told him, wasn't to perpetuate a structure of elite control, but to 'rouse the will of the people to remove their own wants'.[72]

Elmhirst recruited ten students in their late teens and early twenties from the Santiniketan campus, students who had found themselves unsuited to academic life. Their task, he told them, was to defeat 'malaria, monkeys, and mutual mistrust'.[73] Together, they piled a Ford lorry high with pots, pans and tools and moved two miles down the dirt road to Sriniketan.[74] Elmhirst found the sight of his new home dispiriting. Set at a little remove from the run-down village of Surul, the plot was marked out by an overgrown thicket of teak and thorn trees, at whose heart stood the ruins of a house. Complete with carved balustrades and crumbling elephant stables, this building had once been a stronghold of the East India Company, when West Bengal was still fertile and flourishing, not yet sucked dry by British taxes. Elmhirst couldn't help contrasting Sriniketan's neglected acres with the cutting-edge farms he'd grown used to in America. But he was an optimist – as one would expect from someone willing to cross the world to dedicate himself to utopia-building. Putting aside his notebooks, which were full of notes on soil testing in university laboratories and the latest advances in tractor technology, he rolled up his sleeves and set to work.

'We fixed up our latrines,' he later remembered, 'started gardens, houses and workshops, defeated the marauding monkeys, and settled in.'[75] It wasn't by chance that his list of improvements started with the latrines: Tagore and Elmhirst, like numerous other reformers in India – including Mahatma Gandhi – saw good lavatorial arrangements as symbolic of the healthy functioning of society. When Elmhirst arrived, villagers either defecated in the fields, risking spreading disease, or used latrines which were maintained by the lower castes, reinforcing social inequality. The Englishman had six buckets tarred and set inside newly built wooden huts, and he informed his students that from now on they must empty their buckets themselves, burying the waste in a trench, whose soil could later be turned over and used for manure. At the back of his mind was the integrated approach that Tagore advocated: here was an opportunity to promote sanitation, social unity and soil fertility all in one endeavour. But for a long time, the students refused to take part, some for religious reasons and others out of natural distaste. Tagore worried over this with Elmhirst, and then triumphed with him when, after days of reasoning, begging and demonstrating, Elmhirst told him of a 'red letter day in the history of our new institution' – two students had emptied the buckets themselves.[76] Soon they were ready to go out and instruct the villagers.

Elmhirst was an inveterate planner – just the kind of sidekick Tagore needed to counterbalance his visionary tendencies. He set about surveying the problems of the countryside under four heads: health, education, social welfare and the economy. Then he launched schemes to address each head. Within a few months, he was being aided in his efforts by an influx of other foreigner reformers. These men and women were drawn to Sriniketan by the novelty of Tagore's 'integrated approach', which offered a way to address not just one of society's ailments, but all at once, and by the unusual opportunity for experimentation permitted by Dorothy Straight's lavish funding. Economists, agriculturists and doctors, pedagogues and specialists in industry caught the train from Calcutta to the town of Bolpur, and then bumped along the rough road to Sriniketan on the school bus. They arrived rattled and dust-covered, but eager to begin applying their expertise.

Elmhirst assigned the new arrivals projects to which he thought them most suited. Working alongside a miscellaneous crew of locals, students and other foreigners, newcomers might find themselves in the barns experimenting with breeding drought-resistant cattle, or out in the fields constructing a water tank that wouldn't silt up. Or they could be sent to a nearby village to assist with road-building and well-digging; reviving traditional industries like weaving, tanning and pottery; or founding a producer cooperative or a cooperative bank. A young American nurse, Gretchen Green, opened up a dispensary at Sriniketan. Another American, Dr Harry Timbres, started a programme for malarial control.

In the past, Tagore had felt that his life of practical idealism had given him responsibility without companionship. In Leonard Elmhirst he found a co-conspirator. He walked often from Santiniketan to Sriniketan to talk over new ideas. Elmhirst, in dirt-grimed khaki shorts and sturdy shoes, and Tagore, in a pristine pale robe and sandals, made a striking couple as they toured the farm, stopping to gaze earnestly on hens, a half-completed workshop, a new manure heap. 'My whole heart is with you in the great work you have started,' Tagore told Elmhirst.[77]

There were tensions between the two idealists – particularly over the question of whether science was to be servant or master in the sphere of social improvement. When Elmhirst boasted to Tagore once too often about the productivity boost a new American tech-nique had achieved on a nearby farm, Tagore would chide him. 'We are not,' he said, trying to build 'the Kingdom of the Expert in the midst of the inept and ignorant.' The villages were in need of 'the living touch of creative faith' – not 'the cold aloofness of science which uses efficient machines for extracting statistics'.[78] Under the spur of Tagore's passion for holistic fulfilment, in the evenings and weekends Elmhirst instituted lectures and picnics, festivals and plays, even a travelling library – the first in Bengal – to ensure that social development at Sriniketan covered all bases.

The institute of rural regeneration blossomed through the early 1920s. Its integrated approach to social reform, remarkable in itself, is all the more remarkable looking back from the vantage point of the twenty-first century, since its example would go on to inspire the methods of the international community development movement that took off after the Second World War. Participants of this movement – aiming to cultivate the strength of communities in the developing world and in deprived inner-city boroughs – promoted all-round social welfare, encouraged local initiative, and used international scientific expertise and funds to increase the vitality of local life.[79] Even without foreseeing the long tail that Sriniketan would have, Tagore was satisfied with it in a way that he never quite was with Santiniketan. This was, he told Elmhirst, because the rural renewal project 'does not deal with abstractions, but has its roots deep in the heart of living reality'.[80] It turned out, unsurprisingly, that it was far easier to encapsulate ideals of village reconstruction in a practical form at Sriniketan than it was to fully embody a 'great meeting of world humanity' at Santiniketan.[81]

The institute for rural regeneration's third anniversary in 1924 was the high point of the endeavour, an evening of festivities that symbolized a fulfilment of Tagore's ambition to model locally rooted, internationally minded 'life in its completeness'. Eight hundred people turned up to celebrate, arriving by train, cart, bicycle and on foot. A large contingent came from Santiniketan – Indian teachers and students, foreign professors and pundits – as well as many locals, and a handful of British officials. It felt to Tagore as if his utopian community had become a place for the true meeting of East and West, as he had always hoped.

Elmhirst, sitting amid a pile of votive offerings at his mentor's feet, began proceedings by reciting the words which had been written by Tagore for the occasion: 'I offer this the invocation of union, ye who are distracted may we incline you towards one mind, one cause, one aspiration [. . .] let the divine powers in the universe be for our peace, which is for all, tranquillize whatever is terrible and cruel into the serene and good'.[82] These hopes were chanted back by the crowd, and then, as the sun sank and the stars came out, people wandered from activity to activity. Santiniketan students sang songs that had been composed by Tagore. Locals from the Santal tribe performed traditional dances. Beneath the trees, cross-legged groups gossiped, while, on the whitewashed wall of the cow barn, an educational film on controlling malaria was projected, followed by a shadow play. Tagore told Elmhirst gratefully, 'the beginning which you have made of this institution at a remote corner of the world carries in it a truth for which the men of today are groping in bewilderment.'[83]

*

By the mid-1920s, the whirlwind of activity that had surrounded the opening of the school and university at Santiniketan and the institute for rural regeneration at Sriniketan began to die down. Tagore became dissatisfied and restless. Santiniketan-Sriniketan's educational and agricultural arms weren't coming together into the unified blueprint for a better life that he had initially envisioned. Although he encouraged the school and university students to picnic at Sriniketan and take part in its projects, and to practise their sketching in the surrounding villages, they showed little interest in the state of the countryside. They preferred to eat in the comfort of their canteen and to sketch in the cool, mosquito-free sanctuary of the art department. The villagers involved in activities at Sriniketan showed an equal lack of interest in the academic activities at Santiniketan. The Scottish geographer Arthur Geddes, Patrick Geddes's son, who joined the community for two years, called it 'crab-like', because it was always walking 'to one side or other', led neither by the intellectual and creative concerns of Santiniketan nor by the practical and scientific ones of Sriniketan.[84]

Rather than pouring their energies into regenerating the surrounding villages, the students from Visva-Bharati petitioned Tagore to turn their university into a qualification-awarding body. They wanted to be sure that their studies would be useful to them when it came to competing for jobs in Calcutta and other cities. Tagore faced the classic quandary of the utopian educator: was it right to go on pushing students towards the ideal future social order that he dreamed of, or should he prepare them for the needs of the present? In 1926, he reluctantly yielded to his pupils' demands – hoping that in doing so he would at least make Santiniketan more widely influential. Visva-Bharati began an affiliation with the University of Calcutta, which did the actual awarding of the degrees. Although this pleased the students, Tagore found himself lacking the excitement he had once felt when thinking about his university. It no longer really seemed an alternative to the dominant social order, but a part of it. His interest in Patha Bhavana began to decline too. He could see that it was dominated by pupils from the urban elite, and it too was doing little to help the socially disadvantaged. And so his attention drifted away.

Tagore's institutions, which all lacked a strong infrastructure, twisted out of shape once his enthusiasm lapsed. Left to their own devices, Patha Bhavana and Visva-Bharati became more mainstream. Without clear leadership they also became fraught with argument. Scholars jostled for position, criticizing one another's work, leaving suddenly, complaining about the lack of organization and direction. Tagore was particularly distressed by the apparent loss of social idealism among some of the students. 'It hurts me very deeply,' he lamented, 'to find the best of our young minds indulging in a militant form of cynicism' that was 'destitute of all true vision [. . .] if my own inspiration fails them I shall ever blame my own feeble power.'[85] If students did not succumb to cynicism, they seemed to Tagore to veer too far in the opposite direction, becoming fixated on Mahatma Gandhi's nationalist civil disobedience campaigns. Tagore had been involved in these campaigns himself in the past – marching, lecturing, writing articles and composing patriotic songs – but he had been horrified when they deteriorated into sectarian violence. It seemed to him now that while people were living by such misguided values in India and around the world, nationalism and 'high sounding phrases like home rule, autonomy, etc.' were 'almost ridiculous'.[86]

He had already begun focusing his inspiration elsewhere – hoping, as always, that a new strategy, a new institution would bring him closer to creating a perfect society. It was in this spirit that he set up the fourth element of Santiniketan-Sriniketan in 1924, the school Siksha-Satra ('multi-purpose school'), exclusively for the use of local children.[87] This new school resurrected the ambition that Tagore had had long ago, while watching his own children play at Shelidah: to give villagers the education that would improve their daily existence and allow them to dream of ways of life beyond it. Students at Siksha-Satra studied maths and reading for an hour in open-air classrooms. They devoted the rest of the day to acquiring practical skills such as gardening, weaving, raising calves and canning food. They formed a scout organization – run on lines inspired by Robert Baden-Powell's scouting movement in England – which went out to do welfare work in the surrounding countryside.

Siksha-Satra was popular among the villagers, although most would send only their sons there, preferring to keep their daughters at home. Tagore told his friends that this school, rather than Patha Bhavana, was 'the Real School, the ideal school', and he hoped that it would become the model for India and further afield.[88] His sense of the superiority of his new institution would be vindicated when Gandhi – who visited Santiniketan-Sriniketan several times – adopted its approach in the 1930s as a model for a 'Basic Education' system for the whole of India.[89] Following Tagore, Gandhi's system promoted Indian self-sufficiency by making practical crafts, which were usually the preserve of the lower castes, central to his teaching programme in place of such 'elite' or 'colonial' skills as literacy and academic learning. (Gandhi did not, however, share Tagore's sense of the importance of promoting creative self-expression or knowledge about Western science, and he omitted both from his national curriculum.)

For a while, the work at Siksha-Satra was enough to give Tagore a sense that he had found his way back to the path towards creating the 'good place', modelling a new philosophy of living for the next generation. But other troubles began raising their heads. In 1924, Leonard Elmhirst left Sriniketan to marry and begin his own community in England. He and his wife Dorothy would continue to fund the institute for rural regeneration until 1947, but his departure plunged the project into disarray – 'rather a flock without a shepherd', as Arthur Geddes put it.[90] This underlined the tension between Tagore's ideal of village self-government and the reality of his work's dependence on foreign experts and capital. Tagore had intended to help villagers to liberate themselves from below, to rebuild what he called 'the lush green life of our ancient village community'.[91] Yet when it wasn't Tagore leading activities, it was an Englishman, an American or a university-educated Indian. Often, they failed to effectively share their ideas and projects with the locals, instead using the surroundings for their own experiments.

The difficulties over the community's leadership did not only stem from foreign influence. Tagore had set up Santiniketan-Sriniketan in an era of growing democracy – a democracy in which he, and most of the other key participants, believed. In practice, though, it wasn't easy for these elite reformers to reconcile their belief in equality with their inherited sense of privilege. This was an issue in many of the practical utopias that appeared after the First World War – the democratic ideals of the founders and their patrician instincts towards leadership were permanently at odds. Tagore, while paying lip service to egalitarianism, often behaved in an aristocratic, even dictatorial fashion. Community residents and local villagers were expected to greet him with a downward sweep of the hand, as if to take 'the dust from his feet'. The wife of the French professor Sylvain Lévi remembered that most communards believed that if someone stood up and disagreed with him the world would come to an end.[92] Intimidated by Tagore's fame and dignified bearing, few had the courage to go up and talk to him – let alone to call him out on his inconsistencies.

Santiniketan-Sriniketan as a utopia, in the way Tagore first envisioned it, remained a stubbornly abstract set of ideas that paralleled a much messier reality – one where the disparate projects already seemed to be pulling apart under the weight of their creator's own inconsistencies and the differing desires of their various participants.

Tagore spent hours in the treehouse that he'd had built at Sriniketan, which looked out across the farm, mulling over how to restore vitality to his enterprise. It was possible, he thought, that a closer relationship with government officials might give the institute for rural regeneration wider application – but he didn't want its independence corrupted by association with the Raj. The support of university research might allow the institute to refine its approach to rural problems more quickly and accurately – but Visva-Bharati had no science department, and the universities with agricultural expertise were too far away to cooperate with – and might also reduce his institute's freedom of action. In the end, Tagore comforted himself that the best he could do was to continue running his community as it was. He shouldn't fear his work's 'appearance of smallness', since, like a seed, it might yet 'overcome opposition and conquer space and time'.[93]

*

By the 1930s, Tagore was no longer in good health, and his mind turned more and more frequently to the question of how to secure his community's future. He was in his seventies now, and the short-comings of his personal approach to leadership had become unavoidably clear. Santiniketan-Sriniketan didn't have the stable institutional structure that would allow it to be self-governing on Tagore's death. And Tagore had no successor waiting in the wings: his son Rathindranath was a competent administrator, but no visionary; Leonard Elmhirst, the obvious candidate, had left to co-found a community of his own. Tagore struggled on at the helm of Santiniketan-Sriniketan, lonely and – as the Second World War hove into view and Gandhian nationalism flourished in India – more and more at odds with the direction of the world. He wrote plaintively to Elmhirst, 'For the first time in my life I feel that I am growing old.'[94]

Restlessness, which was a congenital part of Tagore's make-up, drove him abroad for protracted spells of travelling. After too long in his utopian stronghold he began to feel, as he'd said before, 'homesick for the wide world'.[95] He was a true internationalist. But he also hoped that on his travels he might discover a patron who shared his ideas, and would help him safeguard his community's future. In the countries he visited – Italy, Russia, Persia, Iraq, Ceylon – he failed to drum up new support. Instead, he came face to face with a very different social vision: militant fascism. Tagore was horrified to learn of the repressive methods being used to impose this totalitarian ideology – press censorship, the crushing of op-position parties, spies watching over populations, and the kidnapping and murdering of dissenters. 'It is a torture,' he wrote poignantly on his return to Santiniketan, 'for me to have to witness, in the last chapter of my life, the nauseating sight of maniacs let loose making playthings of all safeguards of human culture.'[96]

In India, too, Tagore's internationalist world view was being challenged – in this case by Gandhi's vision of national autonomy. Fundamentally, Tagore and Gandhi admired one another. It was Tagore who conferred on Gandhi the title 'Mahatma', or 'Great Soul'. Gandhi in turn called Tagore 'the great sentinel', because he guarded India against 'Intolerance, Ignorance, Inertia'.[97] Gandhi visited Santiniketan-Sriniketan to try to win Tagore over to his nationalist cause, but it quickly became clear that there were irreconcilable differences between them, in spite of their mutual admiration. Gandhi was a populist and traditionalist who saw the key to gaining Indian independence in mass civil disobedience. Tagore, too, hoped India would ultimately become independent. But he thought this would be a gradual process, one that had to be approached cautiously, and through the kind of progressive, elite- and expert-led multi-sided development that he was modelling at Santiniketan-Sriniketan. Tagore condemned what he termed Gandhi's 'cult of a selfish and short-sighted nationalism'.[98] As Gandhi's movement gathered momentum in India through the 1930s, Tagore was left nursing his internationalist vision for a new India in increasing isolation. Despite his lifelong efforts, the gulf between his ideals and the reality of human affairs seemed only to grow wider.

By his late seventies, having considered all avenues, Tagore came to the conclusion that there was only one possible way to ensure Santiniketan-Sriniketan's survival. Reluctantly, he wrote to Gandhi, asking him to take care of the community after his death, calling it 'a vessel which is carrying the cargo of my life's best treasure'.[99] Gandhi agreed to help. In spite of the men's disagreements, they shared the belief that India had a unique message of spiritual wisdom for the world, a message that could avert future wars. Even after the Second World War broke out, Tagore continued to cling to this idea. 'As I look around I see the crumbling ruins of a proud civilization strewn like a vast heap of futility,' he said of the West on his eightieth birthday in 1941; but he would not, he pledged, 'commit the grievous sin of losing faith in Man'. He would continue to dream of a new dawn, which would come 'from the East where the sun rises'.[100]

Tagore's death a few months later brought Santiniketan-Sriniketan's years as a practical utopia to a close. The community itself continued – after Indian independence in 1947 and Gandhi's assassination in

1948, it was taken over by the state. Today, Visva-Bharati is still home to several thousand students, and the institute for rural reconstruction continues to promote local arts and crafts.[101] But without Tagore's leadership, Santiniketan-Sriniketan's unity as a utopian endeavour unravelled. It was no longer a place striving to embody a single, radical social vision, but a series of independent institutions with little connection to one another beyond location. Tagore's energy, enthusiasm and romanticism had been essential to hold together its disparate projects, participants and ideas. Like other utopian leaders, he was that particular kind of visionary capable of bridging the contradictions between dreams and reality. The end of Santiniketan-Sriniketan's utopian phase was also the result of the passing of the historical conditions that had given rise to the community in the first place – colonial rule and the internationalist fervour that followed the First World War.

In its heyday, Tagore's practical utopia was a world standard for internationalist, communitarian cooperation, for holistic rural development, and for connecting the values that come from the inner spirit with day-to-day living. Gandhi drew educational ideas from it, and it became a touchstone for the community development movement. Santiniketan-Sriniketan came early on in the wave of practical utopianism that followed the First World War, and its ideas about living fully influenced many of the communities that would follow. It inspired Dartington Hall in England and helped shape Mushanokōji Saneatsu's Atarashiki Mura in Japan. It also influenced Sri Palee, a rural reconstruction community set up by the socialist educationist Wilmot Perera in Ceylon, where Tagore travelled to lay the foundation stone in 1934.[102]

Santiniketan-Sriniketan was at times fractious and inharmonious, shaken by problems of organization, finance and leadership. This didn't, however, prevent it serving as an influential test bed for social ideas, its experiments touching the world far beyond Bengal. It melded ideas from East and West, and joined together material and spiritual aspirations – if not in the minds of its entire population, at least in the minds of some participants and visitors. Touched by Tagore's vision of a spiritual and creative community-oriented way of life, those who spent time at Santiniketan-Sriniketan went on to influence Indian history, social reform movements and world philosophy.[103] The unitive ideals that Tagore's utopia projected for two decades and beyond are perhaps expressed best by his verses from *Gitanjali*:[104]

> *Where the mind is without fear and the head is held high;*
> *Where knowledge is free;*
> *Where the world has not been broken up into fragments by narrow domestic walls;*
> *Where words come out from the depth of truth;*
> *Where tireless striving stretches its arms towards perfection;*
> *Where the clear stream of reason has not lost its way into the dreary desert sand of dead habit;*
> *Where the mind is led forward by thee into ever-widening thought and action —*
> *Into that heaven of freedom, my Father, let my country awake.*

TWO

'A NEW MANOR WHICH MAY BE
THE UNIT OF THE NEW ENGLAND'[1]

Dorothy and Leonard Elmhirst's Dartington Hall

One weekend in the summer of 1935, with the sun shining on
Devon's gentle hills, Aldous Huxley sat hunched at a table in the
medieval courtyard of Dartington Hall. Glasses pushed high up the
bridge of his nose, he was at work on the book that would become
Eyeless in Gaza. It was a struggle to concentrate. A small boy sat at
his feet, stealing from the supply of figs Huxley had brought out
with him for the morning.[2] Children wandered in and out of his
peripheral vision, carrying hammers and nails and the planks of
wood they were using to construct a chicken coop. In the far corner
of the courtyard, a group of intellectuals, who in London might
have been relied upon to sit quietly over their reading, were sticking
pins into the face of his eminent zoologist brother Julian, experimenting with the newly fashionable art of acupuncture. On the old
tilt yard behind the Great Hall an entire ballet company, recent
fugitives from Nazi Germany, was rehearsing Kurt Jooss's latest
masterpiece. Rising above all these activities was the loud throb of
a tractor cutting a field of hay. Although Huxley was interested in
tractors, as in all novelties, he was beginning to realize that they
were a mixed blessing. But, like the free-range children, the
modernist dance and the scientific experiments, there was no
escaping them at Dartington. All these things stood for progress.

The writer looked up from his typewriter as the door of the hall opened. Dorothy and Leonard Elmhirst stood on the step: she crop-haired, wearing a sensible calf-length skirt and a string of pearls; he trim-moustached, Savile Row-suited, a shooting stick over his arm. They could have been taken for the traditional middle-aged English squire and lady, on their way to church, perhaps, or off to play whist with a neighbour. As they crossed the lawn, Leonard paused to show a child how to use a hammer and Dorothy's eyes rested with fascin-ation on the acupuncturists. But they didn't linger. They were going to take their place at the back of the lunch queue in the workers' canteen.

Nearly three decades later, living in the Hollywood Hills, Huxley would remember that day, and call the Elmhirsts' community 'one of the few places in the bedevilled world where one can feel almost unequivocally optimistic'.[3] Dartington was an experiment in living that was unique in Britain. Dorothy and Leonard, directly inspired by Tagore's practical utopia, wanted to found a community that aimed to promote cooperation and complete fulfilment. They had a second source of inspiration: the medieval village, which they idealized as a place of communitarian harmony, where daily life was richly interwoven with creativity, spirituality and economic work.[4] They aimed to modernize this medieval model, bringing in inter-national experts and the latest scientific theories. They also wanted Dartington to function as a test bed for ideas, inspiring people well beyond its physical boundaries.

The Elmhirsts' community was soon being feted in national and foreign newspapers.[5] It attracted crowds of visitors and influenced social reform projects in England, Denmark, Germany, America and elsewhere. Aldous Huxley took Dartington Hall as a model for his last novel, *Island*, written in 1962 – the only book he ever wrote about a utopia, and a work that he intended as a counter-balance to the pessimism of his *Brave New World*. For Huxley, Dartington Hall was proof that, in spite of two world wars and the loss of so many of the Victorian certainties that had framed his youth, his was an age that remained 'infinitely exhilarating'.[6] Thousands of others who passed through that medieval courtyard felt the same way.

*

It was Dorothy Whitney (who became Dorothy Straight after her first marriage and Dorothy Elmhirst after her second) who made this community possible. She was one of the few women to found a utopia in the years after the First World War, an opportunity that was open to her because of her inheritance from her family. Whitney money paid for the reconstruction of Dartington Hall's fallen roof, the sculpting of the overgrown gardens, the design and construction of modernist art studios, cutting-edge farm buildings and experimental, labour-saving workers' cottages. Whitney money supplied the salaries that drew intellectuals, labourers and artists to live and work in these new buildings; and funds for the school and the ballet and the scientific experimentation that Aldous Huxley found so impressive and so distracting. It was Whitney money that allowed Dorothy and Leonard to turn a run-down estate into a place that, one visitor suggested, would cheer up the war-weary world if it offered day trips for pessimists.[7]

Dorothy Whitney, born in 1887, was a child of America's Gilded Age – a time at the end of the nineteenth century when capitalists like John D. Rockefeller, Andrew Mellon and J. P. Morgan were getting rich on the back of the explosive growth of the industrial economy. William Collins Whitney, Dorothy's father, made a large part of his fortune through a monopoly over New York's railcars.[8] Like other so-called 'robber barons', he was unscrupulous, using bribery to secure control of the Metropolitan Transit Company and pocketing a large part of the dividends that were due to the shareholders.[9] He parlayed wealth into political influence, working tirelessly to get his friend Grover Cleveland elected president. When Cleveland got into the White House, 'kingmaker' Whitney was made Secretary of the US Navy. There were few men in America richer or more powerful, and few who enjoyed their position so much. His envious contemporary Henry Adams wrote that Whitney had 'satiated every taste, gorged every appetite, won every object until New York knew no longer what most to envy, his houses or his horses'.[10]

Under the glitter of all this wealth, though, lay a lonely childhood. William Whitney had little time for Dorothy. She had three siblings, but there was a ten-year gap between them and her, and they were at boarding school for most of her childhood. Dorothy's mother Flora, a busy socialite, died when she was only six. Her father remarried, but his second wife Edith died when Dorothy was twelve. Dorothy was passed from nurse to governess to companion with none of the steady affection that children need. Beneath a veneer of good manners and social ease, she became shy and introverted, never quite learning to trust the people around her – people who might, after all, only be attracted by her money. Later, she remembered melancholy hours spent rattling round 'a beautiful house in New York – a kind of Renaissance palace, with great salons and long galleries'.[11] From an early age she knew only too well that wealth was no guarantee of happiness.

In 1904 her father died of peritonitis, and Dorothy, at seventeen, was orphaned. The elite of New York and the gossip columnists who wrote about them began to describe her as the capital's 'Number One Marriageable Heiress'.[12] Dorothy had her formal coming-out ball two years later. Leading off the dancing in a Worth gown from Paris, her blue eyes bright, dark hair piled high on her head, she was the envy of many debutantes crowded into the hall, whose chief ambition was to make a good match. But Dorothy's conventional exterior hid an unconventional spirit. Since childhood, her father had once remarked, she had had a 'penchant for doing her own thinking', and she also had an unusual seriousness of purpose.[13] Instead of dreaming of husbands, she was wondering how she would ever escape her sense of not being a 'whole person' in this world of balls and parties.[14] She was already sure that her fortune of $8 million (over $200 million in today's currency) needed to be spent wisely, so that it could improve the world around her. Her life as a seeker of better ways of being – for herself and for others – had begun.

In the first decade of the twentieth century, a campaign for political reform was sweeping through America, with President Theodore Roosevelt and other progressive activists striving to reduce corruption in business and politics. William Whitney was a favourite target for these reformers, even after his death. When a scandal about the dubious legality of his monopolies broke in the press, Dorothy's guilt at the source of her family money propelled her into the first of a series of philanthropic causes.[15] She started by volunteering at settlement houses – buildings in deprived, immigrant neighbourhoods where middle-class reformers stayed and worked to remedy living conditions. Then she moved on to thinking about how she could improve the organization of the settlement houses themselves.[16] She was settling deeper and deeper into this work when she met her first husband: Willard Straight, an impoverished, charming diplomat and businessman.

Dorothy had written in her diary that she could only fall in love with a man of huge ambition, because she knew she would have a 'great longing to be part of his work'.[17] Here, all of a sudden, was a man who appeared to have such ambition. Straight told her that his highest hope was to create an 'American empire' – by which he meant taking political influence in Asia away from Britain, Russia and Japan, and putting it in the hands of those who were enlightened, liberal and allies of the United States.[18] Dorothy allowed herself to be distracted from helping New York's poor by Straight's zeal for liberating the oppressed abroad; it seemed to her an equally good outlet for her desire to improve the world. The pair married and left immediately for Beijing, where Straight was brokering loans for US banks – part of his plan to expand American power in Asia.[19] But it wasn't long before the Chinese Revolution of 1911 sent them home again.

After three years of marriage, Dorothy felt she had still not found a satisfactory way to make up for the sins of her father. She was a woman of remarkable energy and ability, who knew precisely what it was she wanted to address – the dominating world view of self-seeking greed – but she was, as yet, still not certain how she could do so. Her social work felt too piecemeal; the dream of an American empire was Willard's, not her own. Back in New York, she tried a new direction – working to change the intellectual climate. It was a book that suggested this step to her: progressive journalist Herbert Croly's *The Promise of American Life*.[20] Croly attacked capitalists like her father, men who exploited the weak to fill their own pockets. He argued that the elite needed to become socially responsible, and to devote themselves to turning America into a more united and democratic nation. Dorothy persuaded Willard that they should found a journal to support Croly's idea and inspire the elite to do their duty. At Dorothy's grand house on Long Island, the Straights convened a conference of the leading progressives of the time, including Felix Frankfurter, Walter Lippmann and Croly himself. In 1914, the first issue of their journal hit the news-stands. They called it *The New Republic*, after the rejuvenated democratic republic they hoped it would inspire.

The delight and satisfaction this project brought to Dorothy was short-lived. The First World War broke out and Willard enlisted, seeing a chance to advance his dream of expanding America's liberal influence. He survived the fighting, but was killed by the Spanish influenza pandemic that claimed over 3 per cent of the world's population. At the end of the worst war the world had ever known, Dorothy found herself with three young children to care for and no husband to support her in doing so. She rarely talked about her grief, then or later. Her private sorrow, like that of others who lost loved ones in the pandemic, was submerged by public mourning for the war dead – those who had died *for* something.

Dorothy tried to temper her grief by throwing herself into helping others. She began working with the Young Men's Christian Association, the women's trade union movement and a philanthropic organization called the Junior League. She busied herself with *The New Republic* and began yet another project, the New School for Social Research, a university (still running today) that aimed to offer ordinary labourers a high level of education and to investigate how the social sciences could be harnessed to social reform. As with other utopians of the age, Dorothy worked through the various avenues for reforming society from within before being driven to create a new social model of her own. Philanthropy, politics and journalism all came up short. She could not find an existing method of reform that satisfied her ambitions.

Dorothy began to educate herself, taking courses in economics, sociology and psychology at various New York universities, hoping that study might help her discover new solutions to the problems she saw in society. In the end, however, it wasn't education that helped her most. Nor was it the frenzied round of meetings, charity events and working dinners with the famous American progressives she now counted among her friends – Croly, John Dewey, Franklin Delano and Eleanor Roosevelt. It would take an unknown Englishman six years her junior to support her in reaching a positive social vision. Their shared vision would culminate in the founding of Dartington Hall.

*

In 1920, Dorothy responded to a knock on the door of her room at Cornell University. She was visiting to organize the construction of a hall to commemorate her husband. The impoverished twenty-seven-year-old postgraduate who entered, his appearance distinguished by little except his bristling moustache and rumpled suit, was Leonard Elmhirst. He had been writing to Dorothy for weeks, trying to convince her to donate to the Cosmopolitan Club for foreign students, of which he was president. Finally she had agreed to a meeting. She was polite but distant with Leonard, as she was with all strangers, listening with half an ear as he talked about the importance of promoting cordial international relations on campus in order to heal the fractures of the First World War. Gradually she warmed to Leonard's unguarded idealism, and to his straightforward Yorkshire manner. She allowed herself to be convinced to make a contribution, then put the episode out of her mind.

Leonard, on the other hand, could not forget the meeting. He went back to his lodgings and immediately set the encounter down in his diary: Dorothy, he wrote, was 'tall and slim, all in black except for a little sable fur around her neck and a very fetching hat'.[21] He had fallen in love. From that moment on he pursued her single-mindedly, writing letters to her daily, though he often had to send four before he received a reply. His irrepressible optimism served him well as he tried to break through Dorothy's reserve and her grief.

Leonard wrote to her about his childhood in Yorkshire, what it was like growing up as the second of a squire and parson's nine children.[22] He described Cambridge, how he had arrived at the ancient university in the fens as a gauche young man who wanted to become a parson just like his father. And he told her what happened when war struck. He hadn't been passed fit to join up by the army medics, so he went to work for the Young Men's Christian Association in India and then the army education corps in Dublin. His younger brother Ernest died at Gallipoli in 1915, and then his eldest brother William at the Somme the following year. Leonard lost his faith in the God who had done nothing to stop the slaughter of his generation, and he began to grow angry with the politicians and businessmen whose pursuit of power and material gain seemed to unnecessarily prolong the fighting. When he came back to England, he had given up the idea of becoming a parson, but he was still determined to improve the world. His friends at the time compared him to a quixotic 'knight errant', endlessly in pursuit of a holy grail whose nature seemed unclear, even to himself.[23]

At first Dorothy took little notice of Leonard's stream of letters, responding only cursorily, but he kept writing. Having exhausted his biography, he moved onto his ideas for post-war reform. Since the war, he wrote, 'the bottom of life had dropped out' and 'the old beliefs could not stand the test' of new times.[24] Leonard, Dorothy began to see, shared her feelings of disorientation in the post-war landscape, and she responded more often. In spite of her endless round of social work, she'd been sinking further and further into loneliness in New York. The grief that followed her husband's death had been increased by her sense that people weren't taking the First World War for what it was – a sign that society was headed in entirely the wrong direction. And here, finally, was someone else who had grasped this fact, and what's more was groping for a solution, for a way to replace personal gain with a philosophy of living that would allow the whole person to flourish. Dorothy began to find herself looking forward to his letters, disappointed if one didn't arrive for a few days. Leonard rarely let this happen.

What were the pair of them to do, they asked each other, when people were already forgetting about the millions of war deaths and returning to the old ways: man competing against man, nation against nation, chasing profit and political prestige? While Leonard continued studying agricultural economics at Cornell University, hoping to acquire the farming skills that would allow him to make a practical difference in the world, Dorothy continued her own search for answers. In 1921, she attended the Washington Disarmament Conference, the first arms control conference in history, as a delegate alongside philosopher John Dewey and writer H. G. Wells. But she saw little prospect of even these great men securing a more cooperative, peaceable world. Like everyone else, they appeared to her straitjacketed by the status quo, unwilling to do anything that would threaten the impetus of capitalist growth. Politicians, governments, treaties and conferences weren't the answer, Dorothy wrote to Leonard. But her scattered philanthropic causes did not feel sufficient either. To reform the world, it seemed to them both, a new model for how people should live was needed.

To Dorothy's astonishment, no sooner had they agreed on this in their letters than Leonard turned up on her doorstep. He had finished his course in agricultural economics. Would she give him the funds to help build a community in Bengal with Tagore? She was impressed by this demonstration of practical reforming zeal, so different from Willard's dreamy idealism. And in spite of some feeling of loyalty towards Willard's liberal imperialism, she was fundamentally more in sympathy with Leonard's aspirations to promote the international fellowship of all humankind. Dorothy had already been approached by Tagore on his university fundraising tour, but she had been put off by what she called the 'woolliness' of the poet's ideals, and by his institution's lack of organization and oversight by trustees.[25] Now, however, her faith in Leonard persuaded her to give him the money he needed. Leonard departed for India, planning to stay for five years, and immediately began to write to Dorothy with jubilant descriptions of his work.[26] Santiniketan-Sriniketan was the refuge from the world of economic competition that they had been longing for, he said: a place where spiritual and creative values were just as important as material ones. For Leonard, this community was the holy grail for which he had long been searching.

'Leonard your life is a great one,' Dorothy replied enviously from America. 'The life of ideals in action!' Her life, on the other hand, remained depressingly 'passive' and 'unexpressed'.[27] She was writing from her bed. Existential angst, and the overexertion she habitually deployed to escape it, had exhausted her. The doctors warned that unless she rested fully, she was in danger of a nervous breakdown. Preoccupied with her health, Dorothy was shocked when the next letter from Leonard came not with news of Sriniketan, but with a proposal of marriage. He told her it was time for them to turn their own ideals into reality – to start a community of their own. 'We've played with our dreams long enough.'[28] The tone seemed more one of a business proposition than a serious romantic offer – if utopia-building could be considered a business. She was too old for him, she responded, and their different nationalities and her children would make a marriage unworkable. She even went so far as to persuade the American nurse Gretchen Green to go out to India as a potential substitute wife.

But Leonard wouldn't be put off. He was unmoved by Green. He continued writing letters to Dorothy, sketching out futures for them both in explosions of scrawled handwriting.[29] Her children, he said, were far from a problem – children were the best 'pioneers and experimenters' in social reform.[30] The first thing they would do when they were married would be to start a school, which would form the centre of a community demonstrating a better way of living. Instead of the race for material gain, he wrote, the community would be underpinned by a spirituality like Tagore's – a non-denominational religion that didn't require clergymen, ritual and doctrine, but which ran through life in the form of 'music, drama, dancing, colour and freedom'.[31] Instead of a hierarchy dependent on money and power, it would be a place where everyone's views would be listened to and respected equally – a true democracy. To Dorothy, it was as if Leonard were articulating the deepest desires of her heart, describing how she might learn to live as a whole person while helping others to do the same. His dream was too like her own for her to resist.

In 1925, they were married. Leonard was thirty-two and Dorothy thirty-eight. The wedding was in the garden of Dorothy's house on Long Island. Only a few close friends and relatives attended, along with Dorothy's numerous household staff. The bride kept anxious watch on her children; Whitney, Beatrice and Michael, aged thirteen, eleven and nine, had mixed views about the prospect of a stepfather and a move to England. But they all seemed happy enough as the ceremony began. Dorothy left out of her wedding vows the usual promise to obey her husband; she was determined to preserve a separate sense of herself in this marriage. Leonard fell in willingly with his bride's choice. 'If I was 100% man she'd be too masculine for me,' he wrote to his brother: 'capable, vigorous, farsighted, a statesman in her way and one of those thoroughly international women that only America produces. But I'm not, and she sweeps me off my feet.'[32]

*

'The most beautiful place you can find in England will not be too
beautiful for your school,' Rabindranath Tagore wrote to Leonard
on hearing of the couple's plans to start a community of their own.
'Why not look for a site in Devon? I still remember my visit with
delight.'[33] The poet had visited the West Country on his first trip to
England, staying with his sister-in-law in Torquay. The Elmhirsts
followed his advice and began looking in south-west England. The
land agent Leonard hired was delighted to find a client who wanted
to buy and not sell; the English aristocracy had been in financial
trouble for several generations and, following the hardship of the
war, country houses had flooded the market.[34] While Dorothy took
leave of her New York friends, Leonard sat through the first and
only driving lesson of his life, bought a car, visited a land agent and
set off with a list of forty-eight properties to inspect.[35]

At the end of the winding driveway that led to the second estate
on his list, he found, as he wrote to Dorothy, the ideal setting for
their modernized version of the medieval village – a place where
'the handiwork of nature joined with the reverent hand of generations of men'.[36] He immediately opened negotiations to buy.
Dartington Hall's 800 rolling, fertile acres, half circled by a bend
in the River Dart, were paradise compared to the inhospitable
country of his Yorkshire youth, or to the dry, flat land that surrounded
Santiniketan-Sriniketan. As soon as Dorothy arrived in England he
took her to visit, boasting as they crossed the medieval courtyard
that they were on royal land, granted by Richard II to his half-brother,
the famous jouster John Holland, in 1384.

As they stood in the huge, dilapidated banqueting hall, Leonard's
evocation of archers sharpening their arrows before a hunt was lost
on Dorothy, who saw only a roofless ruin overgrown with ivy. In
spite of Leonard's passion for scientific methods, she would always
be the more realistic one in their marriage. They watched a few
pigs rootle in the corner of the hall, then took a tour of the rest of
the estate, which comprised several farms and hamlets as well as
extensive woodlands. Leonard expanded on the possibilities he saw
in every building and field, while Dorothy noted missing roof tiles,
broken windows, orchards overgrown with nettles. What oppressed
her above all was the absence of people. There were only seventeen
residents on the entire estate – hardly enough to populate a single

thriving farm, let alone a world-changing model community.[37] It was nothing like what she'd been imagining from Leonard's glowing descriptions. And it was nothing like the English country houses she had read about in Henry James's novels, or visited on her grand tour of Europe as a girl. She went to the local church the next day. Although she, like her husband, had lost her Christian faith in the war, it was somewhere she could be alone – and she wept bitterly.[38] But she had made a pact with Leonard, and decided that they must press on.

Six months later, the hammering and sawing of mass restoration was under way across the estate. Dorothy and Leonard held a five-day meeting with the estate workers and the handful of like-minded friends who had agreed to join the community. They had decided that the first step in their programme would be to start a school, not least to provide for Dorothy's children.[39] The chaotic gathering to determine its outline was chaired by Dorothy's friend and mentor Eduard Lindeman, an eminent American academic who had come over from the New School for Social Research to help with planning.

Everyone agreed that rote learning, exams, the cadet drill and the cane of the traditional school had to go – these approaches had fuelled the competitive, nationalistic mindset that led to the First World War. But beyond this, they could agree on little. Lindeman, who specialized in group-led adult education, held forth on how they needed to create an environment in which pupils learned to be democratic citizens by governing themselves. Leonard interrupted him with stories about Santiniketan-Sriniketan, where students were free to go about and learn from the world around them. Wyatt Rawson, one of only two trained teachers in the room, told Leonard that Tagore's idea was already a well-known educational theory: what John Dewey called 'learning by doing'.[40] At this, Leonard began to backtrack, saying he didn't trust theorists; the modern world was 'book-ridden' and their social experiment would progress better if it stuck to practical examples.[41]

Before Rawson could reply, Lindeman raised a hand to restore order. Did the people in the room who hadn't yet spoken have any suggestions? Dartington was meant to be a democracy, after all. Most of those present, long-standing estate labourers, shook their heads. They were still confused about why they had been summoned to the discussion in the first place. In the world to which they were accustomed, it was for the squire and lady to make the decisions, and everyone else to obey. Dorothy was silent for a different reason. She was battling a sense of horror at the situation in which she found herself. Their conservative neighbours had been openly hostile to her since she arrived, rejecting her for her New York clothes, her 'socialist' ideas and her big American car. She had just given birth to Ruth, her first child with Leonard, but she still felt she barely knew her husband, or anyone else in the country for that matter. The English, she told Lindeman privately, 'rarely ask questions and don't seem to care what one feels'.[42] The ideal of group self-government, which had seemed so clear in her correspondence with Leonard, felt nearly impossible in the reality of this divided room.

Despite all this, Dorothy was clinging to the dream that had brought her across the Atlantic. Rousing herself, she began soothing ruffled tempers, a skill she had perfected while chairing philanthropic committees in New York. Surely, she said, the point of Dartington was to pose the question of how to live well – not to put forward any single dogmatic answer? Their community would be about democratic living, and about an existence that treasured all the parts that made up man: the spiritual and creative, the social and practical, the need to earn a daily wage. Beyond this, anything could happen. The estate could and should be home to all the ideas under discussion, and thousands more besides. She was as reluctant as Tagore to commit to a blueprint. This refusal of any single manifesto or plan for Dartington would turn out to be a critical intervention: it set the pattern – or the lack of pattern – for all that was to follow.

*

The school's first seven pupils – five of them local, two from America – arrived at the estate in September 1926.[43] They joined Dorothy's three children in beginning an education unlike any other then available in the world. Since the student accommodation hadn't yet been built, they stayed with the Elmhirst family in the hall. The opulent surroundings, rich food and servants were a stark contrast to the spartan life of the traditional English school. This wasn't the only distinctive feature. In place of a headmaster, the students were told that they would have to decide everything themselves in democratic meetings.[44] Instead of being taught subjects by teachers in classrooms, they were to pick their own self-directed projects from what was happening across the estate – whether that meant mending motorbikes, gardening or raising chickens.[45]

There was no pattern, no routine to the students' education. In the course of one early week, there was sewing (for boys as well as girls), dancing, chorus-singing, boxing and a physiology demonstration on a dead chicken by a poultry expert, Professor Gustave Heuser, who was visiting from Cornell University.[46] Another week, Leonard took those who wanted to learn history for a ramble among local ruins, lecturing extemporaneously as they walked, and then encouraging the children to give their own talks on their findings. This was 'experience replacing textbooks', he and Dorothy agreed approvingly when they discussed the outing.[47] Later, Dorothy took eight children on a walking tour in the Welsh hills to see a solar eclipse.[48] It was as much a novelty for her as for the students – this was the first time in her life that she had handled day-to-day expenses herself, and to cope she took to noting down each penny spent in a diary. But she was glad, at last, to be doing something practical. She wrote to a friend in America that although the school had only a handful of pupils, 'they present as many and as interesting problems as if we had a hundred' – adding to this double-edged observation, reassuringly, 'how encouraging and splendid it all is'.[49]

For most of that first term, the school lived from moment to moment. Schemes for the day were decided as and when a group of bored children collected in front of an Elmhirst or another teacher. Gradually, everyone became accustomed to this haphazard approach to teaching. The children grew better at choosing what to do by themselves. When the first summer holiday arrived, and Dorothy and Leonard paused to evaluate their progress, they were exhilarated to realize that the founding element of their community, the school, seemed to be a success. They congratulated each other, and the growing number of idealists who had gathered to help them, saying that they had given the 'bullet headed Britishers' a demonstration of how to educate children in a new way, one that would make them pioneers of a brave new world of cooperation and self-fulfilment, rather than the foot soldiers of capitalism.[50] The pupils themselves were just as caught up in the excitement. Dougie Hart, one of the first students, remembered that time as 'like being with a big group of friends'. He got only a 'little bit of education', but that was made up for by the more important lesson of 'love and respect for the community'.[51] Many years later he would return to teach at the school himself.

How did the estate appear to those on the outside? Already, Dartington was the source of fascination that it would remain in subsequent decades. Local gossips speculated that it was a nudist colony or a communist hotbed.[52] News of the Elmhirsts' refusal to give lessons in Christianity snowballed into rumours that black masses were being said in the medieval hall, Leonard chanting to the devil beneath an upside-down cross.[53] Lines were drawn, loyalties declared, and significant numbers of locals joined together in opposition. The Dartington parish council, the Women's Institute, the cricket club and the village hall all refused to have anything to do with the estate.[54] J. S. Martin, the rector of the church that stood just beyond Dartington's gates, warned his congregation of the Elmhirsts' 'evil'. But the couple pressed on. 'I am afraid we see very little of the neigh-bours,' wrote Dorothy with characteristic understatement to an American friend, 'but for the time being we are concentrating on building up a community life among ourselves.'[56] Now that the school was under way, she and Leonard were beginning to look to the other strands that would make their community a complete utopia, a place where men and women could achieve that full self-realization that the conventional world with its reactionary pastors, conservative squires and regimented school-ing did not allow.

*

As a boy in Yorkshire, Leonard had seen farmers struggling to survive while competing with the cheaply produced goods that were being shipped in from overseas. Some sold their land, while others hung on long enough to be temporarily rescued by the government subsidies that came with the First World War.[56] In the early days of Dartington, Leonard focused on how agriculture could make the community self-sufficient, as he imagined had been the case in the villages of the Middle Ages. But he quickly realized that this would not fit in with his desire to offer farmers in England and beyond hope for the future, so he fixed on an alternative framework: as well as modelling a life of holistic fulfilment, Dartington should be a test bed for ideas and practices that would help wider society. Cornell University's agricultural department, along with his experience at Sriniketan, had given Leonard a firm idea of how this ambition might be achieved. A series of demonstration units or model farms would show locals that by combining large-scale industrial efficiency and scientific expertise, livestock and crops could still be made to pay.[57] To accomplish this at Dartington, he turned for assistance to the international cast of agricultural experts whom he had met in America and in India.

As at Sriniketan, the experts came. They were attracted by Leonard's open-minded zeal and Dorothy's generosity and passion. Professor Gustave Heuser oversaw the construction of a factory farm for chickens, an innovation that wouldn't become mainstream in Britain until the 1950s.[58] Dr C. E. Ladd, Heuser's colleague at Cornell, established an agricultural research department with a modern laboratory – an idea which the British government would take up, but only twenty years later, when it launched the National Agricultural Advisory Service to help farmers after the Second World War. Christian Nielsen, a Danish farmer with an impressive background of agricultural training in Denmark, Scotland and England, set up a farm with huge barns, high-yielding breeds of cattle, tractors instead of horse-drawn ploughs, and large fields where the tractors' efficiency could be shown to best advantage.[59] These innovations, which would become cornerstones of later twentieth-century agriculture, were virtually unknown in Devon at the time, their processes strange and as yet untested.

The local farmers observed the proceedings with barely concealed scorn, either laughing over the latest folly of their new neighbours, or fuming because the Elmhirsts had poached their best workers with offers of greater autonomy and higher wages.[60] But those at Dartington were too busy to be concerned with outside judgement. The estate resounded with the clatter of experimental machinery and the buzz of foreign voices arguing over whether the sturdy local cow breeds or the high-strung Danish imports were the most productive, and speculating about the revolutionary effects of their work.

*

Dorothy praised her husband's energy, his 'power to stir people to something beyond themselves'.[61] But she was a New Yorker born and bred, and her interest in farming was limited. She admitted to Leonard that she preferred the picturesqueness of traditional 'unscientific farming' where 'eggs are discovered in the hay' to the industrial look of his modern chicken barn and tractors.[62] She could understand the importance of economic regeneration, and how Leonard's demonstration units would lead to that, but her own vision of a fulfilling community life revolved around the ideal of creative expression. For her, creativity was akin to religious worship, an act that should be part of the day-to-day, and which would bring everyone closer to each other as well as to the divine. When the local vicar chided her for not going to church, she told him that it wasn't in the formal rituals and dogma of Christianity that man found 'the unity and harmony that his soul is forever seeking'; that could only be found in art.[63]

And so, while Leonard was writing to agricultural experts, Dorothy was seeking out dancers, musicians, potters, painters and sculptors, and inviting them to the estate. Sometimes she offered grants and salaries, sometimes bed, board and a studio, and sometimes nothing but the chance to carry on their work in the lively surroundings of the community she and Leonard were building. She told all of them that their role should be to create great art themselves and to ignite the creativity of others. By their very presence, they would aid the spiritual progress of the community.

Where Leonard was bluff, easy-going and indiscriminately sociable, Dorothy was shy by nature and negotiating a foreign country with a rigid but opaque class system. She found it difficult to break out of what she called her 'hard icy core' and into intimacy with Dartington's participants.[64] While love of humanity was one of her defining characteristics, her efforts to treat people as equals could come across as awkward and condescending. She was, as one Dartington teacher wrote, cocooned in the 'unreality generated by money'.[65] Employees complained of her excessive efforts to make them feel equal to her

– going last through doors, taking the worst chair and the worst cut of meat – which only drew attention to the gulf between them.[66] They would have been more comfortable if she took certain privileges as a matter of course, the way Leonard did.

Dorothy would never be entirely at ease with the manual labourers and domestic staff, but her overtures of friendship to the artists who flocked to the estate at her invitation were often better received. She became close to a potter, Jane Fox-Strangways, who set up a studio on the estate. Fox-Strangways organized exhibitions featuring all the products being made across Dartington, emphasizing that creativity could be expressed in anything from an elegantly thrown pot to a highly polished boot or neatly typed letter.[67] Dorothy also took to Mark Tobey, a soft-spoken, spiritually minded American who would later gain international fame for his densely textured abstract paintings. Driven all her life by the desire for some unspecified kind of enlightenment, she found succour in the drawing classes Tobey gave, in which he pinned up huge sheets of paper on the walls and asked students 'to experience the whole being making marks with chalk to music'.[68]

A third close friend was the expressionist dancer Margaret Barr, who ran a professional dance troupe at Dartington in a newly built theatre, and also worked with amateurs on the estate and in the surrounding villages, aiming to produce art that was relevant to ordinary lives.[69] With titles like *The People*, *The Colliery* and *The Factory*, her performances depicted struggles between downtrodden workers and cigar-smoking capitalists – figures who might have stepped directly out of Dorothy's childhood. Dorothy was delighted by all this. She wrote to the personal secretary who was still looking after her affairs in America that Barr 'has all of us dancing, workmen, apprentices, and even the children in the village school'.[70] In spite of her shyness, she was for the first time approaching the fulfilment she had always dreamed of. She had never felt entirely herself in her philanthropic work in New York. In the alien surroundings of Devon, she had found her natural home: in spiritual communion with art and artists, and in sitting up with Leonard after supper, listening to the sound of young laughter ringing around the courtyard long after ordinary children would have been sent to bed.

*

When Leonard had first glimpsed Dartington Hall in 1925, it had seemed in terminal decline, like so many of Britain's large country houses. Only four years later, several hundred workers emerged onto the grounds each morning from newly built cottages on the estate and from the nearby hamlets. They walked together along muddy lanes, discussing the schoolchildren's raid of the tool shed, or the strange design of the modernist chair that the carpenters were constructing. They might pass an artist swaddled in shawls at an easel, up since five to capture a herd of bullocks grazing in the morning mist. When they had started at Dartington, these labourers would have stared or laughed, but they'd become used to the ways of artists, and now merely doffed their caps. At the hall they broke into smaller groups, heading off to one of the many enterprises that crowded all the available buildings.

Textile production and carpentry jostled for space with the cider press and the scientific laboratory. Beyond the boundaries of the estate, more acres of land had been acquired to meet the demands of the experimental farms, to provide wood for the mill and space for new orchards. During the day each worker set his or her own pace, breaking for lunch in the canteen. Most finished early so as not to miss out on the many pastimes. There were two rival drama groups, lessons in dance and in mime, and a spiritual study circle reading its way through Eastern religious texts. If the workers were practically minded, they could learn accounting, plumbing or typing. And if they didn't like organized entertainment – which was true of many people drawn to Dartington – there was the Dart for swimming, and endless conversations that rambled on until late in the estate's main courtyard.

News of this unusual existence soon appeared in the local newspapers, in the national broadsheets and on the BBC. While the hostility of the Elmhirsts' neighbours continued, Dartington began to be heralded by progressives across the country as 'The New Rural England'.[71] By 1928, reports of its activities had crossed the Atlantic and were being discussed in the *New York Herald Tribune*. Rabindranath Tagore wrote to Leonard, praising his achievements. In 1930 he came from Bengal for a month's visit, and suffered pangs over how much easier his own utopia-building would be if he had had the Elmhirsts' resources.[72] It was rare, by this period, for a week to pass without a fresh consignment of visitors being dropped by train at the nearby station of Totnes: people like the young political scientist George Catlin, who, as he told the Elmhirsts, was eager to embrace an alternative to the modern 'malaise of ambition, pushfulness and urban rush'.[73]

Dorothy and Leonard found themselves showing around politicians in search of inspiration – Labour MP 'Red' Ellen Wilkinson, Alfred Striemer, a German government economist, and Rexford Tugwell, sent over by Dorothy's friend Eleanor Roosevelt to search for remedies for America's rural poverty.[74] Leonard's favourite visitors were significant British landowners like Lord Trent and Christopher Turnor, who allowed him to demonstrate his latest agricultural inventions and gave him hope that more of Britain's acreage would soon be under similarly scientific cultivation. Dartington was also a site of pilgrimage for the iconoclastic headmaster A. S. Neill, who ran Summerhill School on lines even more liberal than the Elmhirsts' own school; bohemian artists like Roger Fry and Vita Sackville-West; and those from a younger generation, including Stephen Spender, W. H. Auden and Aldous Huxley. The estate was toured by a group of Christian 'brothers' and 'sisters' from the utopian Bruderhof community in central Germany, curious to see the practicalities of another idealistic social experiment.

Yet as Dartington grew, the very size and diversity of its activities seemed to work against the communal principles Dorothy and Leonard had intended it to demonstrate. The Elmhirsts tried hard to maintain a sense of unity and democratic collaboration, but this was no easy task. Leonard compared Dartington to a biological organism which, as it grows, splits into differentiated parts and is unable to maintain its original unity.[75] To reverse this process, the Elmhirsts began holding a weekly estate meeting in the hall, meant as a forum where everyone could air their views. They also encouraged all employees to contribute to a daily news-sheet, *News of the Day*, hoping to keep everyone abreast of developments on the estate now that people could no longer be updated in informal, face-to-face conversation. But many of the labourers felt shy about putting forward their opinions when there were intellectuals and artists about.[76] They might have strong feelings, but they hadn't been trained to articulate them with references to ancient mythology or the latest journals, and it was rare that they felt confident enough to put themselves forward. One worker from the gardens department, G. H. Thurley, complained that *News of the Day* was just as elitist as the newly established BBC: both claiming to be democratically inclusive, but both dominated by the ruling classes.[77]

For Leonard in particular, the solution to the problems Dartington faced was always to be found in science. He conducted a questionnaire about the experience of community members on the estate and sent the results to Sir Frederic Bartlett, Cambridge University's first professor of experimental psychology. On the basis of the responses, Leonard asked for Bartlett's advice on how to create a better community. More generally, he asked how man could be offered 'a oneness of life as he leaves the family and an ever increasing boundary to that oneness until it includes the whole of mankind'.[78] The scientist's understandably bewildered reply was that with his 'perhaps deplorably empirical habit of mind' he found 'the greatest difficulty in envisaging' what such a question even meant, or how it related to the questionnaire – but he guessed that the Elmhirsts wanted to know how to make individuals feel part of their community.[79]

In spite of Bartlett's bemusement, he found the practical idealism of Dartington an exciting alternative to theories and laboratories. He sent a list of suggestions about how to improve the community – as did many of the other British and American social scientists who were consulted by the Elmhirsts. Bartlett thought that to maintain vigour and unity, the estate should make overtures to 'neighbouring social communities' through 'games contacts, aesthetic contacts, discussions contacts, administrative contacts'.[80] Others had more outlandish suggestions, including the eugenically tinged scheme of psychologically profiling applicants who wanted to join the estate. The Elmhirsts tried many of these ideas, even briefly experimenting with psychological assessments of the schoolchildren. But the social unity they yearned for wasn't forthcoming. The advice they received was too theoretical, too detached from the day-to-day difficulties of helping people live in harmony together.

Leonard channelled his worries about community spirit into ener-getic infrastructural improvement, hoping that if he created the perfect physical environment, social unity would follow. He built a hydroelectric station on the Dart to make the estate more self-sufficient; laid on mains water to show that a rural life could also be a luxurious one; added new roads to be used by the official estate transport system (a bus and a couple of cars), along with the tractors, travelling library service and one-truck fire service that were now in use. Cottages and departmental buildings mushroomed across the estate's many acres, designed by whichever architect the Elmhirsts happened to be friendly with at the time – the Arts-and-Crafts-influenced Rex Gardner, then Louis de Soissons, the planner of Welwyn Garden City, who was followed by the modernist Swiss-American architect William Lescaze.[81] Friends, baffled by Dartington's aesthetic disorder, asked why the Elmhirsts couldn't just pick one designer and stick with them? Leonard declared that it was impossible, because how could they find someone who specialized simultaneously in 'children, cows, chickens and wage earners'?[82]

Dartington had become a town in miniature, turning Leonard and Dorothy into something more like municipal administrators than participants in a creatively, spiritually and socially fulfilled collective. With endless decisions to be made about management, the only moment they were alone together each day was as they saw to their morning correspondence, sitting at desks set at speaking distance from each other, and for the few minutes they spent listening to the BBC news in the evening. Their relationship was less close than it had been in the early days, but they were firmly united by their passion for their social experiment.

In spite of their almost frenetic busyness, it was the Elmhirsts themselves who posed one of the greatest obstacles to community spirit at Dartington. They had talked of creating a utopia that was 'a group working together' – even of modelling a reformed version of social democracy where power was fully in the hands of the people.[83] But when it came to giving up their own power and handing over control of the estate to the residents and employees as a whole, they found themselves paralysed by worry. Surely 'the common folk' would 'make a mess', they told one another.[84] They saw the artists, labourers and schoolteachers as too detached from the overarching sense of community that they had been working to establish. The habit of self-government was something that had to be learned. In this the Elmhirsts resembled Tagore: while championing democracy

in theory, they never made it clear how they thought it should be brought about.

Their clear-sighted friend William St John Pym warned Dorothy and Leonard that their effort 'to square communistic theories with the possession and enjoyment of great wealth' was 'eating your cake and having it'.[85] And Pym was right: the Elmhirsts were living a contradiction. While their labourers pursued frugal lives in experimental cottages that often malfunctioned, they lived in luxury, with Dorothy's collection of modernist art by the likes of John Piper, Graham Sutherland, and Ben and Winifred Nicholson hanging on the walls of their wing of the hall.[86] The Elmhirsts were part of a constellation of rich, Anglophile American landowners including the Baillies (Dorothy's relatives) at Leeds Castle and the Astors at Cliveden House. They hosted intellectuals, artists and social reformers from London and abroad, and had a leading garden designer, Beatrix Farrand, shipped in from the United States to oversee the landscaping of their grounds. And although their children were educated in the same way as the rest of the students at the school, they were also cared for by a private nanny; she was just one in a household staff that included four gardeners, two chauffeurs and a haughty butler, Walter Thomas, who had previously been employed by the Marquess of Bute.[87]

Pym suggested that it would be less hypocritical if the Elmhirsts abandoned their utopian aspirations completely and made 'a bold bid for normality' – taking up hunting, shooting, going to church and paying calls on the local gentry.[88] But Dorothy and Leonard showed little consciousness of the contradiction. This was not, perhaps, extraordinary, since their position was one shared by elite progressives across the country and, to some extent, across the world.[89] They supported democracy, but didn't trust 'ordinary' people to rule and didn't want to give up their traditional privilege, so the only solution was to put up with the dissonance that came from preaching one way while living another. For most outsiders, the Elmhirsts' lifestyle did not detract from the fact that they had built an astonishing, near-revolutionary social alternative: 'a new Manor,' wrote one commentator, 'which may be the unit of the new England'.[90]

That summer of 1929, two of Dorothy's friends visited from

America, the theatre producer Maurice Browne and puppeteer Ellen van Volkenburg. Together they organized a production of John Milton's masque *Comus*, partly chosen because of its author's republican sympathies. It was the biggest and most lavish artistic undertaking the estate had yet seen, with Dorothy and Leonard among the huge cast of amateurs who took on roles, artists carving the players' exotic masks, and musicians and dancers contributing to the ornate richness of the production. The play was staged on the lawn in front of the hall and drew a huge audience, estate labourers sitting cheek-by-jowl with visitors from London on wooden planks laid out on the grass.[91]

After the performance, excitement kept the Elmhirsts up late, talking to one another eagerly while still in their costumes. Communal creativity had 'lifted us out of ourselves', they agreed.[92] It had brought them together with different classes, sexes, ages and nationalities, just as performances in the church or churchyard had done in the medieval village. This was what they had been working for. Although there were social tensions, and the tightly knit democratic community they had originally conceived of had been considerably loosened, the performance of *Comus* seemed to them proof that Dartington could still be everything they had dreamed of in their early letters: a cooperative endeavour that demonstrated that the good life wasn't defined by material gain. Leonard said that it was a true utopia – 'a glimpse of what might be'.[93] The Elmhirsts didn't know it, but this was the high point of the estate, the calm before the storm.

*

The American stock market crash came a few months after the staging of *Comus*, triggering the worldwide Depression that would tip millions into unemployment and poverty. Looking around urgently for salvation, people latched onto the demagogues who had been hovering on the margins of politics, preaching belligerent nationalism throughout the 1920s. By 1929, Mussolini in Italy and Stalin in Russia already wielded huge influence. In the early 1930s, Hitler swept to power in Germany. These leaders raced to militarize their countries as fast as possible, in part because they saw territorial expansion as a way to distract their citizens from economic

hardship at home. As they started building battleships, stockpiling shells and preying on weaker neighbours, it became increasingly clear that the world would soon be shaken by another international conflict.

Britain wasn't immune to the turbulence. During the Depression, more than a fifth of people in some counties were out of a job. The streets of central London teemed with disgruntled protestors. A group of unemployed men from the northern town of Jarrow walked 300 miles to the capital to petition parliament for help – to little avail. Communists brawled with the black-shirted supporters of Oswald Mosley's British Union of Fascists. Dorothy wrote to her secretary in America that she had a sense of 'living on the edge of a volcano'.[94] It was no longer enough for Dartington to continue its inward-looking exploration of community-building. Unless she and Leonard could turn the estate into something that engaged actively with the world outside its walls, what they had created risked being nothing more than 'a rich man's phantasy'.[95]

Leonard believed the best way to increase Dartington's influence was to formalize its running, so its example could be more easily imitated by others. This institutionalization went a long way to preserving the Elmhirsts' community in the long term; it was the vital organizational step that Tagore had failed to take with Santiniketan-Sriniketan. Leonard and Dorothy consulted with lawyers and then set up a company, Dartington Hall Ltd, with a board of directors who would look after the estate's commercial departments – the many industrial and agricultural enterprises they had established over the years. Alongside this, the Elmhirsts formed the Dartington Hall Trust, a charity with a large endowment that would oversee the school and the arts – the parts of the estate that weren't intended to make money.[96] Leonard was chairman of both company and trust. Although Dorothy was a trustee, she was content to let her husband take the leading role officially, just as she had been to let Willard Straight front *The New Republic*. Her influence in shaping both organizations was great, but she preferred for the most part to exercise it behind the scenes. In public, she called Dartington 'Leonard's plan'.[97]

The Elmhirsts' new strategy was to pass the day-to-day running of the estate onto managers and experts, in the hope that this would increase the efficiency and the impact of their projects. In 1931, a flamboyant socialist teacher, W. B. Curry, was given responsibility for the school (unusually for a socialist, he was the owner of two Rolls-Royces, a Bentley and the Hispano-Suiza that later featured in the film *The Third Man*).[98] Chris Martin, an orderly minded young man just down from Oxford University, was put in charge of streamlining the arts department. The commercial ventures came under the direction of W. K. Slater, a dispassionate, accounts-obsessed scientist who began his tenure by sending out a flurry of memos warning employees that if they didn't turn a profit they would be sacked.

Those who had been involved with the estate since the beginning mourned the change in priorities. Dartington had deteriorated from an 'attempt at living in a group' to something 'more conventional, national and orthodox', in which 'you are free to do anything save fall below your costings keep'.[99] But for the Elmhirsts, it wasn't enough any more to create a community where participants could feel satisfied in the life they were leading. Times had changed, and Dartington needed to change to respond to them, reorienting itself in a way that would help strengthen British society as a whole. The way to do that, they felt, was by speaking the language of that society: the language of economic success. Dartington's engagement with capitalism at this point in its existence sets it apart from the other practical utopias of the period, most of which continued to critique the dominant economic system by steadfastly refusing to engage with it. The potential for this engagement had been inherent in the Elmhirsts' utopian vision from the start: they hoped to create not only an ideal community, but a test bed for ideas that could be adopted by people beyond its boundaries – people who did not necessarily want to change their entire way of life. This dual ambition is one of the reasons why the Elmhirsts' community had a wide impact on the outside world.

Despite Leonard's determination and W. K. Slater's strict bookkeeping, few of Dartington's businesses broke even in the 1930s. They had been set up as scientific demonstration units, sheltered from economic necessity, but now, during a decade-long Depression during which few people had the money to buy extra goods, they were suddenly being expected to turn a profit. It was all but impossible. Nonetheless, the community remained a productive, innovative place. Its experiments inspired outsiders, and it continued to attract those who wanted to turn theories into practice – even if these people tended to be less radical in their aspirations than those who joined in the 1920s.

By 1933, the commercial units of the estate had 850 employees among them.[100] These units included a sawmill and a furniture workshop that processed the estate's wood, a cider press that used up the apples from the orchards, and a textile factory powered by a water wheel. The potter Bernard Leach – recently returned to England from Tokyo, where he had befriended Mushanokōji Saneatsu, founder of the utopian community Atarashiki Mura – was invited by the Elmhirsts to start a small pottery factory. Each of these projects made sense as a test bed for new methods of production, or as a way to make the estate self-sustaining. But the attempt in the 1930s to force them into profitability led to one disaster after another. Dartington's flock of factory-farmed chickens was decimated again and again by disease. The fruit grew mouldy on the trees. No one wanted the cider produced from the orchards – it was too unfashionable to export and the local farmers made their own. Leach turned out to be less keen on organizing a ceramics factory than on working on pieces at his own pace. His business and every other commercial unit haemorrhaged money.

Part of the problem was Leonard's impatience. He was always changing his mind about the way units should be run before he had time to find out whether his first approach had worked. He was also, like Tagore, magnificently bad at choosing employees. One persuasive Irishman, Heremon 'Toby' Fitzpatrick, convinced the Elmhirsts that small, water-powered looms were the perfect way to decentralize industry and create rural jobs, and that Dartington was the best place to demonstrate their effectiveness. He spent weeks at the Elmhirsts' expense researching looms in isolated valleys in Wales, but the water-powered factory that he built at Dartington could not reliably turn out fabric at all, let alone fabric that could be sold at a profit.[101] Even so, the ever-optimistic Leonard tried to persuade Gandhi to come and learn from it on his tour of Britain.[102] Leonard's passion for endless experimentation was part of what made Dartington such a vibrant place, but such experimentation was fundamentally incompatible with running a large-scale, economically successful business.

Leonard became increasingly frustrated, so much so that he began to distance himself from Dartington, turning his attention elsewhere. For the first time, he began to doubt the usefulness of the community he had worked so hard to create. In 1929, he had helped set up the International Association of Agricultural Economists. By the mid-1930s, he was seeing agricultural economics as a truly 'objective and dispassionate discipline', and the study of it became a replacement for Dartington – in the sense that he began to identify it as the best 'universal blueprint' for the improvement of mankind. It was agricultural economics, he wrote, not community living, that he hoped 'statesmen, bankers, industrialists, housewives, town and country planners' would adopt.[103] His chairmanship of the organization meant that he started taking frequent trips away from the estate. These periods of absence were lengthened by his involvement in founding the think tank Political and Economic Planning, which aimed to produce another kind of social blueprint, this one for regenerating Britain through centralized planning.[104] As the political situation worsened, the two organizations pulled Leonard's attention further and further away from Dartington. He now believed he could do more good lobbying in London than he could by tilling fields in a secluded corner of Devon.

*

Dorothy's response to the deteriorating international situation was entirely different. Although she agreed with Leonard that the estate should be economically successful, in her view it was the community's inner life rather than its outer life that most urgently needed reforming. Dorothy had always been restless in her search for meaning and purpose, moving from philanthropy in New York to supporting her first husband in Beijing to setting up Dartington with Leonard. Now she decided that it was the absence of spiritual structure that was to blame for the estate's failure to provide a satisfactory alternative to fascism or communism. What the community – and she herself – lacked was any 'philosophy or religious idea which gives meaning to the whole'.[105]

A solution seemed to materialize on her doorstep in the form of a visitor, a young man named Gerald Heard, who had shared a tutor, Goldsworthy Lowes Dickinson, with Leonard at Cambridge, and had been a distant acquaintance of the Elmhirsts since the mid-1920s.[106] Heard would go on to found a utopian community of his own in the United States – Trabuco College. But at the time of his visit in the early 1930s he was still working as a science commentator for the BBC, and writing books about science, evolution and history. He had come to take a tour of the estate's activities, about which he had heard so much at the dinner parties of his progressive friends in London. Dorothy gave Heard tea. She discovered that, like her, he was eager to discover a new spiritual system by which to live. Heard was further along the path than she was: he had already devised his own faith – a pacifist religion for modern times, he explained, that was based on meditation, good works and asceticism.

Dorothy was entranced. This, she felt, was what she'd been looking for. Heard enlarged on his ideas: the engine of his faith, he told her, he called the 'generating cell' – a group of believers who met regularly and helped one another to achieve connection with the 'general will' of mankind. Eventually, thousands of these cells would encircle the world, creating such intimate, telepathic connections between people of all nationalities that another war would be an impossibility. Dorothy insisted that Dartington be the site of Heard's first generating cell.

Heard began taking the train down from London most weekends to lead group meetings. On Sunday afternoons in the oak-panelled room beside the main hall, Heard and Dorothy would congregate with one of the schoolteachers, Margaret Isherwood, the artist Mark Tobey and a handful of other workers and visitors, all people who, like Dorothy, felt in some ways at odds with the world. Heard and Tobey were homosexual in a period when this was illegal. Isherwood was uncomfortable with her status as a single woman. Dorothy, an independent-minded woman in a patriarchal society and a believer who had lost her Christian faith, longed for a new way to understand herself and society. The generating cell became a place where people could explore identities outside the mould of straight, male and practically minded that dominated at Dartington and in wider society.[107] Participants were drawn to a spiritual system in which, as Heard described it, the 'partial and incomplete self is united with all others in a unity, sanity, self-forgetfulness and communion'.[108]

Dorothy was delighted with Heard's method of scrutinizing the world's religions, from Quakerism to Buddhism, and pulling out the elements that would best assist in developing mankind's spiritual interconnection. During some meetings the group discussed the psychology of Carl Jung and Sigmund Freud; during others, they listened to American jazz on a record player, making notes on how it made them feel.[109] But some people on the estate were critical of the generating cell. Often these were men with conventional social identities who felt little need for introspective spirituality. For W. B. Curry, the school's individualist, agnostic headmaster, Heard's promotion of spiritual groupthink was dangerously akin to the 'semi-mystical ideas of fascists'.[110] After attending a few generating cell sessions, Leonard complained that Heard's faith was 'running away from social duties' and 'too empty and too much like uplift'.[111] For such critics, the search for spiritual meaning was less important than contributing tangibly to improving society. It was an indicator of Dartington's tendency towards a patriarchal model that, in spite of the spiritual interests of the circle around Dorothy, it was Leonard's bluffer, more practical and outward-looking style of social reform that set the overall tone of the estate.

Nonetheless, Dorothy was fully committed. She tried to pare down the rest of her weekly estate duties – the relentless round of meetings, interviews, lunches, teas and evening engagements – so that she could spend time alone in meditation and reading. She knew that the coming weekend would bring a fresh meeting with Heard, a man who shared her quest for a new spiritual system. Heard, too, was enthusiastic about the generating cell's progress, and about Dartington as a whole. In one of the journals he wrote for, the *Architectural Review*, he said that the community was the first 'complete, purposive, fully conscious social organism', and should be used as a blueprint for reconstructing the world.[112]

* * *

Both the Elmhirsts had diverted their energies almost entirely from the day-to-day running of Dartington to focus on other projects. But while Dorothy was preoccupied with the generating cell and Leonard was absorbed by his associations and think tanks, Dartington retained a utopian energy, drawing in idealists intent on doing things differently. The managers that the Elmhirsts had put in control of the estate's various departments began steering it in new, outward-looking directions. The commercial units continued to be unprofitable, but the scientists who were attached to them had found some success by shifting their attention away from the estate. They set up a cattle-breeding centre that, inspired by a trip Leonard had taken to Soviet Russia, introduced a form of artificial insemination that would later be taken up across Britain.[113] They also began the nation's first soil-fertility analysis service, which the Ministry of Agriculture took up and expanded, in 1939, into a soil survey of the whole country.[114]

At the same time, W. B. Curry was transforming the school into something of a private empire, ruling it from an airy new modernist home called High Cross House, designed by William Lescaze. Under Curry's forceful leadership, the school became so popular that its student population rose to 200. Parents sending their children to Dartington included intellectuals like Bertrand Russell and Aldous Huxley; the artists Barbara Hepworth and Ben Nicholson; the left-wing publisher Victor Gollancz; and the architect Ernst Freud (Sigmund Freud's son). They also included progressives from further afield, such as a wealthy Zoroastrian meteorologist from India, K. J. Kabraji, who was a keen follower of Tagore.[115] The school had become an institute for the international progressive elite. This was, in part, a triumph: the estate's ideals were now being broadcast widely. But at the same time it signalled the fragmentation of the unified, locally rooted community that Dartington had once aspired to become.

The new head of the arts department, Chris Martin, had also put Dartington on the international map. He replaced the first generation of estate artists with the refugees who were fleeing in increasing numbers from totalitarian regimes in Europe. Kurt Jooss settled in with his entire ballet school from Essen, including twenty dancers, twenty-three students and the stage designer Hein Heckroth. During their tea breaks, they gathered in the main courtyard and discussed their alien surroundings with other displaced artists from the Continent – among them the Viennese sculptor Willi Soukop, the founder of the Bauhaus Walter Gropius, and Rudolph Laban, a leader of the German expressive dance movement.

Many of the local labourers began to avoid the courtyard. This wasn't only due to their discomfort at the cacophony of foreign languages and the sophisticated flamboyance of these artists' dress and manner, but also due to their resentment over the way in which the artists were treated. Carpenters and agricultural workers, heading back along the lanes to their homes in the dusk, grumbled that while they were being told by managing director W. K. Slater that they would lose their jobs if their departments failed to make a profit, the equivalent of their whole year's salary was being frittered on a single night of ballet.[116]

The atmosphere at Dartington had always been intense, verging on fractious, but without the Elmhirsts actively holding things together, tensions began to mount. Arguments brewed between those who wanted the estate to make a profit and those who prioritized the community's unity and non-materialistic ideals. Experimental artists like the painter Cecil Collins were criticized for the incomprehensibility of their work. Labourers who came to one of Collins's exhibitions complained that it contributed nothing to the life of the estate, since it was impossible for most people to engage with it — and that, as no one even seemed to be buying the paintings, it was an economic failure as well.[117]

Meanwhile, the sales department was condemning W. B. Curry for letting the schoolchildren put off customers by throwing stones at cars. The school was costing the estate a thousand pounds a year in bribes to the press, manager James Harrison protested, bribes which were essential to stop the publication of 'sensational tit-bits' that would damage the reputation of the whole estate.[118] He was referring to the fact that girls and boys shared accommodation and swam together naked in the river; that one of the housemothers was addicted to morphine; and that Curry permitted sexual relations between his pupils, and if asked, gave them advice on birth control.[119] Curry, in turn, told the managing director that he was allowing the estate to be sucked into the capitalist mainstream. And he complained to Chris Martin that no payment was made when school chairs were borrowed by the arts department for their performances, and that the musicians who taught his pupils seemed to consider education a 'mere by-product' of their own private work.[120]

A breaking point came when Curry had an affair with one of the school's housemothers, Marsie Foss, and began living with her before he had divorced his wife Ena. The estate divided into opposing camps about this behaviour, which was highly unconventional in the 1930s.[121] For some, it was Dartington's duty to protect the freedom of its participants, however they chose to behave. But it seemed to others that unless communards could behave in the kind of exemplary fashion that would convince outsiders of their community's ideals, they should be summarily ejected. At an estate meeting that was so full that many people had to stand, the headmaster argued that it was more crucial than ever to uphold individual freedom of action when that freedom was exactly what the fascists were eroding overseas.[122] The Elmhirsts were won over by his arguments – and also by the fact that they didn't want to be diverted from their own pursuits by having to take responsibility for the school again. Others were unconvinced. Heard read the affair as proof that Dartington was doomed to be 'a society without agreed moral principles', and that both it and his generating cell were a failure.[123] Soon afterwards, in search of more radical ways to promote international pacifism, he migrated to America.

While Dartington's participants argued, the prospect of another war began to loom. In 1936, after Italy had marched into Abyssinia and the Spanish Civil War had begun, a debate was held on the estate to discuss whether Britain should be re-arming and preparing to fight the fascists, or whether it should hold to its position of non-intervention. The non-interventionists won by invoking the awfulness of the First World War. But in 1938, Hitler annexed the whole of Austria, triggering the terrifying realization that there might be no limit to the dictator's ambitions. Standing on the sidelines, it suddenly seemed, might not even be an option.

All over the estate in the summer of 1938, groups gathered in hushed conversation. Labourers, artists and teachers, Devonians and foreigners forgot their differences, united by fear. Who would be Hitler's next victim? When would the British government decide to stop appeasing the Führer and fight? Was it already too late for the country to arm itself? Those who had listened, rapt, to the Elmhirsts talking in the early days about how Dartington would bring about world peace, tried to engage Dorothy and Leonard in the discussion. How should they be safeguarding the community? Shouldn't

Dartington be helping the country to prepare for the approaching conflagration?

But when the workers knocked at the door of the Elmhirsts' wing of the hall, it was only to be told by the butler Walter Thomas that Leonard had gone up to London for an emergency meeting of Political and Economic Planning. Dorothy, while still on the estate, had withdrawn from its day-to-day life. She had been shaken when Heard left for America in 1937, but had discovered a new, more forceful guru in the actor and director Michael Chekhov (nephew of the playwright Anton, and an exile from Soviet Russia), who had opened his Theatre Studio on the estate. He was a spiritually minded foreign artist – the very type who, as the English labourers on the estate complained, Dorothy always expected to lead her to some great revelation.[124] Dorothy had enrolled herself in Chekhov's classes, and was spending six hours and more a day dressed like her fellow students in a long blue gown and suede slippers, following the intense regime of role-play, acting, lectures and spiritual exercises that Chekhov promised would teach them how to communicate 'inner realism'.[125]

When prime minister Neville Chamberlain returned from meeting Hitler in 1938 with the declaration that he had secured 'peace for our time', few at Dartington believed him. The estate was close to the coast, and only twenty miles from the naval dockyards at Plymouth. They knew it would be on the front line in the case of invasion. The refugee artists whose lives had already been upturned once by dictatorship were understandably anxious, and they began to look for safer refuges. Chekhov announced his impending departure for America. To everyone's astonishment, Dorothy said she was going with him.

On the eve of leaving, she gave a speech to the estate's participants in the Barn Theatre. Wringing her hands nervously – in spite of her training with Chekhov, she hadn't mastered her shyness before the workers – she said that she could not, even at such an apocalyptic moment, give up the personal discovery of 'a different dimension from ordinary life' to which 'the Master' had led her.[126] She promised that she was only going with Chekhov in order to finish her training as a drama teacher for the benefit of Dartington – that she would be back soon.[127] Yet it was clear to everyone, from her

husband down to the estate's longest-standing odd-job man Herbert
Mills, that Dorothy wasn't really going away in service of their
community. She was following her guru and her restless urge for
enlightenment. Whispers ran along the rows of seated workers as
they cast sideways glances at Leonard. What would become of
Dartington if Dorothy didn't return? What would happen if her
money stopped coming over the Atlantic? Was her departure a sign
that their community had failed?

Dorothy wrote to Leonard from Connecticut in the spring of
1939, saying that being part of Chekhov's Theatre Studio was an
ideal existence, 'the perfect pattern for monastic life, a group without
restriction of age or sex, intent upon a task, and under the direction
of a great leader'.[128] But only a few months later, in September,
Hitler invaded Poland. Within two days Britain declared war on
Germany. This changed everything for Dorothy. She decided that
this was no longer the time for spiritual quests or monastic living.
Real-world action was called for. And she still believed the best
place for real-world action was Dartington Hall. She hastened back
to Devon to stand with her husband and her fellow utopians in the
defence of democratic freedom.[129] The war that drew Dorothy and
Leonard together again also drew the community at Dartington
together, providing a common purpose that was far easier to understand and to act on than the ideal of a life of complete fulfilment.

*

From the autumn of 1939, Dartington's inhabitants put aside their
pacifist leanings and joined in the war effort. Dorothy toured the
country giving patriotic lectures, while Leonard returned to Bengal
to try to help the government mitigate the effects of a severe famine.
The estate's hall, school buildings and experimental cottages were
used to house evacuees from schools in London and Plymouth, as
well as many other visitors – foreign refugees, wounded airmen,
and intellectuals and artists seeking relief from Blitz-torn London.
Dartington's fields grew potatoes and carrots for the towns and its
forests supplied the army with timber. National shortages were so
severe because of German submarine activity in the seas around
Britain that even the community's weakest commercial units began
to make a profit for the first time.

With the end of the war came the establishment of the first welfare state in Britain, under Labour leadership. The new government shared the Elmhirsts' hope of promoting people's holistic well-being, and began to take an unprecedentedly active role in education, the arts and social improvement. The participants of Dorothy and Leonard's community contributed directly to some of its initiatives: advising civil servants on how to run soil surveys; leading a national Arts Enquiry that emphasized the importance of universal access to the arts; and showing civil servants around the estate as an example of community planning. Michael Young, one of Dartington's pupils and later one of its trustees, helped write the 1945 Labour election manifesto. In the 1950s, with the Elmhirsts' financial help, he also set up the Institute for Community Studies (now the Young Foundation) – part of the same international community development movement that Santiniketan-Sriniketan fed into. The degree to which the Elmhirsts had gained mainstream acceptance was shown when, in 1946, Clement Attlee offered Leonard a baronetcy, largely as a reward for his war work in Bengal. But Leonard refused the honour, writing that as his life's work had 'lain in the main among country people', his acceptance 'would neither be easy for me to explain nor easy for my friends to comprehend'.[130] He was more comfortable with the role of a visionary outsider.

In many ways it seemed as if Dartington's ideals had become part of the new status quo. State educators adopted more progressive, child-centred values. The government launched the National Agricultural Advisory Service to help farmers adopt scientific methods. The Arts Council was set up to sponsor artists and widen access to the arts. The notion of social planning – designing communities to promote the all-round welfare of their inhabitants – became a national touchstone. While the Elmhirsts' social experiment was not, of course, the trigger for these changes, its example foreshadowed and helped to encourage the establishment's embrace of them. The story of Dartington illustrates how even marginal idealistic communities can – given sufficient creativity, and the backing of connections and wealth – find their way into shaping the mainstream. In part, the widespread adoption of so many of the ideas pioneered in the Elmhirsts' community brought to an end

Dartington's utopian phase – its period of offering a social alternative to the mainstream. The estate was no longer a magnet for those with radical hopes for reshaping society. Instead, it was part of the establishment.

Dartington has survived to the present day, supported by its company-and-trust institutional structure and by its endowment.[131] Over the course of the second half of the twentieth century, it struggled to define its purpose. It became a place of vaguely liberal, creative relaxation – offering lifestyle shopping, venues for weddings and conferences, and courses in anything from opera singing to spoon carving. With the exception of Schumacher College, an environmental sustainability teaching centre that was founded in 1991, the estate was no longer a hotbed for social change.[132] The Elmhirsts saw the passing of that idealistic zeitgeist that had, in the 1920s and 30s, fanned the hopes they had exchanged in their early letters into a community that attracted the foremost painters, psychologists, novelists, farmers and architects of their time. Nonetheless, up until Dorothy's death in 1968 and Leonard's in 1974, the couple continued to support Dartington. As Leonard had told Dorothy five years into their experiment, 'the risks that we have taken up to date – with money, with goods, with lands, most of all with people – they appal and frighten me', but 'are we to throw up our hands and say, no, the possibility of making mistakes is so great, of damaging a human life so serious, that we should quietly retire from the scene?'[133]

THREE

SELF-REALIZATION IN
THE MOUNTAINS OF JAPAN

Mushanokōji Saneatsu's Atarashiki Mura

On a damp evening in 1919, the famed Chinese author and scholar Zhou Zuoren arrived at Atarashiki Mura ('the New Village'), situated on a remote plot of land in southern Japan. For months, Zhou had been reading about the creation of this community in imported newspapers and journals. Finally, he had braved the long journey from Beijing by ship, train, bus and carriage to see it for himself. The community's leader, Mushanokōji Saneatsu, led him into the unlit village through darkness and drizzle.[1] Zhou knew Mushanokōji as a writer who had won an enthusiastic following across Japan by extolling a hedonistic lifestyle of 'self-love'. The man's transformation from Tokyo aesthete to this weather-beaten, muddy-footed farmer living in the middle of nowhere at once astonished and impressed him.

Over the next four days, Zhou accompanied Mushanokōji and the other New Villagers as they planted sweet potatoes and weeded their fields, raised chickens and tended sheep. He admired how, after the communards had put in the minimum number of hours of manual work needed to keep their community going, they all turned to their own individual pursuits – be it painting pictures of pumpkins, writing and printing novels, or listening to *Carmen* on the gramophone. When it was time to leave, Zhou told his hosts that he felt he had, for the very first time, been 'experiencing life in a genuine way' – with the physical and the intellectual, the individual and the communal brought together in a harmonious whole.[2] Back in Beijing, Zhou dedicated himself to publishing and lecturing on this new model of living. His efforts inspired many – not least among them a young Mao Zedong, who dreamed of building his own New Village at the foot of Mount Yuelu in southern China.

Mushanokōji's vision of the 'good place' offered something radically different to the mainstream in Japan. The New Village championed pacifistic internationalism, trying to fuse traditional Japanese ways of living with new ideas from abroad, and to create links with foreign thinkers. At a time of rapid industrialization, with many people working long hours in factories for subsistence wages, the community sought to interweave economic labour with communality, leisure and creativity, offering a more rounded and fulfilling way of life. 'As long as there remains one single person who toils for bread alone,' wrote Mushanokōji, 'then it is a sign that the world is incomplete.'[3] In a country permeated by an ethos of self-sacrificing service to the collective, Atarashiki Mura was a community in which self-realization was prioritized. Mushanokōji's emphasis on individualism was in stark contrast to many of the other utopia-founders of the era, who blamed self-seeking for the First World War and concentrated on promoting cooperation. But he was operating in a very different context, reacting against a culture of public duty and extreme social obedience. For the New Villagers, focusing on personal fulfilment was an act of radical rebellion, and an essential part of building the perfect world.

Through the 1920s, Atarashiki Mura excited the enthusiasm of thousands, most of them urban elites. Some admired the village from afar, while others left their homes, occupations and social circles to join the community, or began similar experiments of their own in imitation of it. Japan in the first half of the twentieth century is often remembered for its ultranationalism: its occupation of Manchuria, its alliance with Nazi Germany and fascist Italy, the Rape of Nanjing – the mass killing and ravaging of citizens and soldiers in the capital of Nationalist China – and the bombing of Pearl Harbor. But the story of Mushanokōji Saneatsu's practical utopia shows how the same melee of international influences, the same anxieties about disorder, war and revolution, gave rise to another and more liberal form of ambition: a vision of Japan based on the values of individual freedom, self-expression and international peace. Mushanokōji and his followers tried to construct an alternative path for society. Resisting populism, fascism and militarism, they pointed towards a better world.

*

Mushanokōji was born in 1885, and grew up in a country that was deliberately and dramatically reconfiguring itself. For the preceding 250 years, Japan had been controlled by the Tokugawa shoguns, a series of feudal rulers who pursued a policy of strict isolation. But in 1853, the American government used warships to force the country's ports open to trade. This triggered a political crisis: the shogunate collapsed and in 1868 the position of emperor, which had been deprived of any real influence for more than two centuries, again became the source of ultimate authority. Emperor Meiji, who acceded to power at this point, had a single, driving ambition – to modernize Japan.

A favourite slogan, 'Enrich the country, strengthen the military', captured the Meiji regime's intent: to industrialize, to update the army and navy, and to expand Japan's borders.[4] A second slogan, 'Japanese spirit, Western technology', summarized its approach: yoking the nation's traditional ethos of public service to modern methods borrowed from Europe – from empire-building to the use of cutting-edge technology in factories. Within a few decades the Meiji vision had been vindicated. Japan achieved such a quick transition from an insular, feudal, agrarian society to a cosmopolitan, industrial and imperial one that many Europeans began trying to emulate what they called Japan's 'cult of efficiency', admiring in particular how the Japanese placed the common good above the personal good.[5]

But in wrenching Japan out of its isolation and plunging it into an era of internationalist modernity, the Meiji regime had provoked social dislocation and unrest. Millions of people migrated from villages to towns, and from towns to cities. In the space of less than a generation the populace transitioned from peasants loyal to their feudal lords into an urban proletariat demanding the democratic rights they saw being enjoyed by the working class in other countries. Their discontent fuelled protests, strikes, riots and the assassination of several politicians. At the same time, Japan's new openness to foreign influence meant that the next generation of elites – including the young Mushanokōji Saneatsu – were becoming increasingly curious about the liberal, individualistic culture of the West. They wore European dress, listened to jazz, went to cinemas or to cafes where they avidly discussed affairs abroad, from the campaign for women's suffrage in Britain to modernism in Paris and psychological experiments in Vienna. Their passion for new ideas and modes of behaviour further disrupted their country's traditions.

Japan joined the First World War as an ally of Britain and France, but it played only a minor role in the fighting, convoying Australian and New Zealand troops across the Indian Ocean and sending naval cruisers to protect the west coast of Canada. While the European imperial powers were distracted by battles on the Western Front, Japan took advantage of the vacuum left in the Far East to expand its trade and empire. The country emerged from the conflict with a buoyant economy and with greater international influence than ever before. But its new power and prosperity increased its internal turbulence, creating yet more ideological dislocation and social inequality. The government feared that the widespread turmoil might lead to a Russian-style revolution. It focused still more intensely on transforming Japan into a centralized, industrialized, militarized imperial state.

Japan, in the early twentieth century, was disorderly, rapidly evolving, an unstable mix of native tradition and foreign innovation. The government tried to control Western influence, embracing its technological advances but rejecting its individualistic tendencies. It emphasized a traditional civic ideology based around loyalty to the family, the nation, and above all to the emperor – even running courses in 'moral training' in primary schools to reinforce this system. But some young intellectuals like Mushanokōji, having glimpsed alternatives abroad, did not want to spend their lives conforming, obeying and serving. Nor did they think that the Meiji regime's industrialization and bellicose nationalism were necessarily what was best for Japan. It was their thirst for an alternative way of living that fuelled the creation of Atarashiki Mura.

*

Each year, on the anniversary of her husband's death, her white face powdered even more meticulously than usual, Mushanokōji Naruko bent down in her formal kimono in front of the family shrine in Tokyo to repeat for her two young sons, as solemnly as if she were intoning a prayer, the last words that her husband had spoken before he died.[6] Of Kintomo, her eldest son, he had said, 'This child will grow up to be a government minister at least.' But it was for Saneatsu that he had reserved his most hopeful prophecy. 'If he is raised well, he will become the greatest man in the world!'[7]

As the son of Viscount Mushanokōji Saneyo, a prominent figure in government circles, Saneatsu was raised to believe that service to the imperial state was to be prized above all things. He was only two years old when his father died of tuberculosis. The family fell on hard times financially, but his mother emphasized to her children that their circumstances didn't matter as long as they remembered they were *kuge*: aristocratic servants of the emperor. She told Saneatsu and Kintomo that they, like their father, must distinguish themselves as diplomatists, scholars, barons of industry – as anything, in fact, that fulfilled the Confucian value of public service.[8]

While Mushanokōji Saneatsu's family expected him to achieve magnificent things, he was from boyhood free-spirited and not at all sure that he could fulfil these expectations – or even that he wanted to. He was too curious, too questing, too open to other ways of being to submit to a lifetime of self-denying public service. The ideals of freethinking and free-living that were flowing into Japan from abroad fascinated him. So too did his country's rapid social transformation. People were no longer remaining in their home villages, tied for life to an inherited occupation and an inherited place in the social hierarchy. They were migrating into towns and carving out their own paths in life. These changes seemed to contradict the beliefs in duty and tradition with which Mushanokōji was being inculcated at home. From a young age, he dreamed of a future for himself as something other than a loyal, obedient and patriotic citizen.

At the Peers' School in Tokyo, the exclusive establishment catering solely to the sons of the *kuge* and the imperial family where Saneatsu and Kintomo studied, the consensus was that there were two possible paths to greatness: academic or athletic.[9] Within a few years, Mushanokōji knew he wasn't going to succeed at the first. His failure to excel in the newly imported Western curriculum was made all the more painful by the success of his brother Kintomo, who was the first student to graduate from the Peers' with top marks in every subject.[10] The second path, too, seemed to be ruled out for Mushanokōji. As five of his seven siblings had died in early childhood, his mother was determined that his smaller-than-average frame should be shielded from the rigour of the school's samurai-inspired athletic training regime.

Confined to the sidelines, Mushanokōji watched longingly as his fellow students competed in archery, fencing, horse riding and martial arts on the field beside the 'Review Mound' – so-called because Emperor Meiji had once stood there to inspect the school-boys. To combat the growing sensation that he was failing in the great destiny his father had foretold for him, Mushanokōji escaped into fantasy. Hands dug into the pockets of the woollen jacket of his uniform, he strolled up and down between the formal flower beds of the school's garden and dreamed of becoming a general, a statesman, even the ruler of Afghanistan.[11] He began to set these fantasies down on paper, and soon he was composing long, elaborate stories, each with some new version of himself as the protagonist. Privately, he began to wonder if there might not be a third path to greatness – through art – but he hadn't the confidence to mention this aloud. He knew his family would not favour the idea: art, he could just hear them chiding him, was not true public service.

Later in his life, Mushanokōji would say that there was never a clear border for him between the fictional worlds he wrote about and the real-world utopia he would go on to build. He described them as his 'twin children'.[12] He was part of a long tradition of writers-cum-utopians, like Rabindranath Tagore and the nineteenth-century French philosopher Étienne Cabet (who wrote the utopian socialist novel *Voyage en Icarie* and then led his followers, the Icarians, to found two experimental communities in America). A fictional utopia is a thought experiment. A practical utopia is an experiment in living. But both approaches are ways of questioning the status quo, their visions gesturing powerfully towards other ways of being.

When Mushanokōji was eighteen years old, his cousin Tei joined his family's household from the new industrial powerhouse of

Ōsaka.[13] Mushanokōji's dreams of glory were quickly overshadowed by another obsession. Love descended like a haze, clouding his thoughts and making daily life miserable, for Tei was already betrothed to a wealthy Ōsaka businessman. She was to marry him as soon as her education was complete. In the summer of 1903, Mushanokōji took himself off to the Miura Peninsula in an attempt to escape his fascination. The region was a traditional holiday spot for fashionable Tokyoites, but Mushanokōji's host – his reclusive uncle Kadenokōji Sukekoto – was far from fashionable. After suffering a series of financial setbacks, Kadenokōji had retired to live alone on his sole remaining estate. He worked in his fields in the daytime and spent the evenings studying sacred texts and discussing them with Christian pastors and Buddhist monks. His eclectic spirituality set an example for his nephew, who would also spend his life gathering ideas from diverse sources.

At first the urbane Mushanokōji was baffled by his uncle's mode of life. He tried copying the ascetic, vegetarian Kadenokōji – rising early, taking long walks on the seashore, raking manure over the fields. But he found himself sitting for hours on the beach, immune to the salty perfume of the tide and the beauty of the clouds shifting over the distant island of Oshima, thinking only of his cousin.

Sensing his nephew's unhappiness, Kadenokōji suggested he look for guidance in the New Testament. Mushanokōji had absorbed the conservative patriotism of his mother's circle in Tokyo, which disdained Christianity as a Western cult. His first inclination was to brush off the suggestion. But when he finally took up the book out of boredom, he was astonished to discover a hero who wasn't the respected pillar of society he expected. Christ was courageous, uncompromising and, more than anything else, an outsider. 'This fellow is really wonderful,' he wrote in his diary – feeling that here, at last, was a great man whose example might actually be worth following.[14] Mushanokōji didn't convert to Christianity, but from then on he began to believe, against the injunctions of his upbringing, that people should obey the moral drive that came from within, even if it made them behave in ways that were at odds with society's expectations of them.

Mushanokōji made a second life-changing discovery that summer when he found the works of Leo Tolstoy on the shelves of his uncle's library. Tolstoy's spiritual and philosophical treatises *My Religion* and *The Kingdom of God Is Within You* had very recently been translated into Japanese.[15] The Russian writer, aristocratically born like Mushanokōji himself, vehemently criticized capitalism and the class system, which he believed encouraged the exaltation of a few at the expense of the masses. Mushanokōji found himself nodding along as he read Tolstoy's critiques. It was easy enough to pick out the parallels between the rigid hierarchy of Tsarist Russia and the inflexible social system of Japan. The abolition of feudalism under Emperor Meiji meant that the Japanese were now theoretically free to choose their own occupation. But most people's paths in life were still set by the classes into which they were born – from the privileged *kuge* down to the *burakumin* ('untouchable caste') at the very bottom.[16]

Perched in his uncle's library, Mushanokōji went from one book to the next, enthusiastically absorbing Tolstoy's ideas for an alternative way of living: an egalitarian 'religion' based on everyone adopting a life of poverty, abstinence, self-discipline and universal love. Mushanokōji was awed to read about the estate Tolstoy had set up at Yasnaya Polyana – where the writer lived in a community with his peasants, dressing in a smock, eating modest vegetarian food, and working the land. Here was a man who lived by his ideas, who had a thought and then translated it into reality. Tolstoy, Mushanokōji later wrote in his autobiography, 'proved to be a miracle-cure for my sentimental hangover [. . .] I would remain a Tolstoy convert forever.'[17]

*

Mushanokōji returned to Tokyo wanting to live as a Tolstoyan humanist and a Christ-like 'great man'. The immediate effect of his (selective) interpretation of Tolstoy and Jesus was to convince him to reject the Japanese social model of self-sacrificing public service. He decided instead to focus on self-realization through writing. In his final years at school, he became the leader of a quartet of literary friends, which included Kinoshita Rigen, an academic prodigy; Ōgimachi Kinkazu, who was retaking his final year for the third time; and the hedonistic Shiga Naoya, a luxury-loving dandy who adored Western dress. The boys would gather during lunch in a camellia-covered arbour in the school's gardens to discuss their poems and stories. After school they would decamp to one of the group's homes to continue their discussions of the writers who inspired them. Since they were being educated in the Western mode – in line with Emperor Meiji's curriculum reforms – they favoured foreign authors over Japanese. Their heroes included Johann Wolfgang von Goethe, Ralph Waldo Emerson and Walt Whitman.

As they read out extracts from their writing, Shiga often interrupted to show off the pictures of various inamoratas he carried in his pocket. But Mushanokōji had forsworn love since his disappointment over Tei. At these moments he would take out his own treasured photo – one of Tolstoy – and hold forth on the higher ideals by which he hoped to live.[18] At this stage Mushanokōji was thrashing about like many adolescents, picking up on all sorts of ideas largely because they challenged the status quo. But his discovery of Tolstoy's advocacy of social equality and universal love had made him genuinely wonder about the state of his country. Even in the confines of the aristocratic 'greenhouse', as he now called it, of school and home, news reached the students of demonstrations and marches taking place up and down the country.[19] During Mushanokōji's duller lessons he took to reading the socialist journal Heimin Shimbun ('The Commoners' Newspaper') under the desk. The publication was banned by the government, who feared its subversive support for working-class rights, but it continued to circulate clandestinely. Mushanokōji hoped it would teach him how the lower orders lived.

With growing horror, he read about the poor farmers forced to go hungry because of the ever-higher taxes imposed by the government to fund modernization; of the strikes of the urban proletariat over terrible factory conditions; of tragically early deaths in the slums of Tokyo and Ōsaka. Like all Peers' students, Mushanokōji had been educated to celebrate his government's feats of modernization: they were told again and again about the hundreds of Western experts imported to advise on mining, banking, education and armaments; the thousands of miles of telegraph wires and railways installed across the country; the construction of an ever-larger merchant navy; the support being given to companies that were adopting Western technology and helping to transform Japan into an industrial nation.[20] But now he discovered there was a downside to all this great industrial progress, an underbelly of despair which his privileged existence had prevented him from seeing.

When the school day ended, Mushanokōji began to skip the group's usual literary discussions to walk Tokyo's backstreets. He wanted to get a sense of the state of Japan with his own eyes. For the first time in his life he really noticed the cost of economic development – the sludge-filled canals, the deafening grind of machinery that emanated from dark basement workshops, the recruitment posters pasted on telegraph poles calling labourers to the textile mills and factories. All this, he thought, had been invisible to him. Now that he had seen it himself, he wanted to act. But what could he do to redress the pervasive ugliness and misery all around him?

Heimin Shimbun argued for socialist revolution. Looking at the young children trailing home from their factory shifts in the dusk, Mushanokōji felt that the newspaper had a point: something drastic needed to be done. But – like Tagore and the Elmhirsts – he had been brought up to think of himself at the top of a preordained social hierarchy. He couldn't quite believe that the best route to improving social conditions would be for him and the rest of his class to give up their wealth, their grand houses and fine things.[21] If they joined the masses in their daily drudgery, who would be left to lead society on to better things?

Yet if socialist revolution was not the solution, what was? Clearly, Mushanokōji thought as he wandered the slums, the government was on the wrong track. There was no point promoting industrial progress and earning Japan status on the international stage if the effect was to make ordinary people suffer. He wanted to work out a grand plan of action of his own, a way to make life equal and fulfilling for all. Inspired by Tolstoy's ascetic lifestyle, he moved out of his family home into a hut in its garden, where he lived in a space the size of a few tatami mats, wearing simple clothes, eating as little as possible, and refusing to light the stove even when the temperature dipped below zero.[22] Like many conscience-stricken members of the elite before and after him, Mushanokōji thought that through such self-deprivation he would at least be sharing the pain of the labouring classes.

The seal was set on the young man's alienation from the Meiji regime when, in 1904, the government took the country to war with

Russia. The Meiji leaders saw the world as divided into colonizers and colonized, and they wanted to ensure that Japan stood among the first group. Their attempts to gain territory in the Far East had already led to war with China in 1894 – a conflict Japan had won with ease. Now, Japan's efforts to wrest influence from Russia in Korea and Manchuria brought about another war. By this point, Mushanokōji was an ardent devotee of Tolstoy's pacifist internationalism.[23] He couldn't stand the thought of the pointless slaughter being carried out in the name of national loyalty. His hatred for the Russo-Japanese War intensified when two young students who were lodging in his family's house were conscripted into the army and killed shortly after. 'The news upset me so much,' he wrote in his autobiography, 'that my loathing of the war – and of all wars, for that matter – became total.'[24]

In 1905 the war with Russia ended – Japan had won, using pioneering techniques like massed infantry attacks on defensive positions, and its victory altered the balance of power in East Asia. Japan had acquired primacy in Korea and economic and political influence in Manchuria. It was well on its way to building a substantial empire, and the vast energies the government had poured into industrialization and modernization were seemingly vindicated. Mushanokōji felt alienated from the majority of his schoolmates and teachers, who had become more fervent than ever in their militant patriotism.

The next year, aged twenty, Mushanokōji and his friends graduated from the Peers' School (even Ōgimachi Kinkazu managed it on his fourth attempt) and all enrolled at Tokyo Imperial University, the training ground for government officials. Within a year of starting his course in social science, Mushanokōji decided that he could never work for the state. His revulsion at its industrial policies and its expansionism was too great. While his brother Kintomo began to race ahead in the diplomatic service as a good *kuge* should, Mushanokōji dropped out of university. After long discussion with his friends, he came to the conclusion that the most honourable course of action would be to devote himself to writing. At least this way, he told his distraught mother, he wouldn't be doing any actual harm to others, as he might in government service. Privately, he hoped that he would actively manage to do some good – by working out and sharing a social philosophy that would make people's lives a pleasure rather than a burden.

*

Mushanokōji spent his twenties in a manner typical of young men on the literary make the world over: developing his authorial voice, cultivating friendships, peacocking at exhibition openings and theatrical first nights. To begin with, he was uncomfortable with how out of touch this new life was from the suffering of the masses: he was doing nothing to improve the social blueprint. But the intense joy of his liberated, bohemian existence soon muffled concern with reforming society – at least temporarily.

The conventional path to literary success in early twentieth-century Japan was to win the attention of the *bundan* – an insular, clique-ridden community of a thousand or so writers, critics, translators and publishers based in Tokyo. Mushanokōji was well placed to achieve this. He already had his family home as a place to live and write, and moderate financial support from his mother. With his three closest friends from school and various others, he found it easy to start a literary coterie and set up a literary magazine of his own.

He and his friends began calling themselves the Fortnight Group, and in the evenings they would gather at the new, European-style cafes in Tokyo's fashionable Ginza district.[25] Drinking coffee, they discussed what unique characteristic would distinguish their group's prose from that of rival coteries. Shouldn't their selling point be writing about altruistic philanthropists in the mould of Tolstoy and Christ, one friend asked – the kind of social reformers that Mushanokōji had so admired at school? But Mushanokōji, guiltily aware that his choice of a career in writing had little to do with social activism, said that Tolstoy's books had started giving him headaches.[26]

Mushanokōji told his friends that he had discovered a new hero: the Belgian playwright and philosopher Maurice Maeterlinck, an author whose philosophy chimed with the Fortnight Group's desire to find a distinctive framing idea. Maeterlinck argued that before you could think about loving your neighbour, you had to learn 'to love yourself with a love that is wise and healthy, that is large and complete'.[27] Unlike Tolstoy, Mushanokōji said, Maeterlinck was no killjoy; he saw lust, sex and pleasure-seeking as essential, even moral, components of human experience. What the coterie must do, Mushanokōji continued, was to adapt Maeterlinck's doctrine of self-love into a literary philosophy. The Fortnight Group would conduct themselves like individualistic, European moderns – living for their own pleasure – and they would write about the process, exploring the 'latitude, longitude and depth' of their own natures.[28] No one in the *bundan* had celebrated the joys of self-love before; the writing it approved of tended to glorify service to the family, state and emperor. Their approach would, Mushanokōji said triumphantly, be revolutionary. This new philosophy of hedonistic egotism was the second of the two strands that Mushanokōji would eventually weave together to form his utopian ideology, combining it with the socially minded influence of Tolstoy and Christ.

Mushanokōji adapted quickly to the Maeterlinck-inspired world view, abandoning his spartan hut and moving back into his comfortable family house. He filled his rooms with prints by artists whose independent lives he idolized: Vincent van Gogh's crooked, brightly coloured scenes of the south of France; Auguste Rodin's shockingly realistic sculptures; Paul Gauguin's women in the South Seas (he especially loved the story of Gauguin rebelling against his career as a clerk to go and live the artistic life in Tahiti). Mushanokōji spent his mornings at his desk writing short stories that were, for the most part, thinly veiled accounts of his own experiences. In them, he proudly laid out his new manifesto: 'I only love myself. Everyone else, even my parents, my brother, my master, my friends, my beloved, are enemies to my growing self.'[29] He began work on an elaborately self-referential book in which a writer, worried about his unpopularity, writes about his fear of his critics in the third person.[30]

In the evenings, the Fortnight Group were to be found at Tokyo's most avant-garde events – at the New Theatre, for example, when Ibsen's *A Doll's House* premiered. While Mushanokōji retained a Tolstoyan simplicity of dress, alternating between a dark European suit and a sober kimono, his friends went all out in their flamboyance: Shiga Naoya sported the latest Western fads, experimenting with spats or walking with a cane; Satō Haruo – who was translating Oscar Wilde – wore a velvet suit and red fez, or a bowler hat and flowing cravat.[31] When they had all taken their seats in the theatre, it was as if a circus had descended. Afterwards, over saké at Café Printemps – renowned for its beautiful waitresses – they exchanged literary gossip and discussed Russian novels, German philosophy and, most of all, the writing they were doing about themselves.[32] The coterie's life was an echo chamber: writers writing about writers writing about writers.

Mushanokōji's early publications were greeted by the *bundan* with dismissive reviews. There were accusations that he was an 'aristocratic brat'; that he was worse, even, than the Lady of Shalott – she, sitting up in her tower looking into her mirror, was at least watching the ordinary people labouring on the ground, while Mushanokōji only looked at himself.[33] The Fortnight Group's magazine struggled along with a minuscule circulation. But then Mushanokōji had the idea of pooling resources with two other small magazines run by writers educated at the Peers' School. The result was a new, more distinctively voiced and confidently run magazine called *Shirakaba* ('White Birch'), after the trees that abounded in both Russian and Japanese literature. It took Japan by storm. Mushanokōji was one of the magazine's directing editors and main contributors, as well as its spokesman. His literary reputation was made, and he blossomed into a magnetic, self-confident leader. There were few other cultural figures in Japan in this period who were as influential.[34]

Mushanokōji set out the *Shirakaba* agenda in one of its earliest issues. 'I only understand myself. I only do my work; I only love myself. Hated though I am, despised though I am, I go my own way.'[35] Mushanokōji was voicing a vision for a radically different social ideology, the same vision that would eventually fuel his practical utopianism. Alongside showcasing Western individualism in stories and poetry, *Shirakaba* promoted Western aesthetics. It featured photographs of paintings and sculptures by the Impressionists, post-Impressionists and Symbolists, and essays about Western artists' heroic efforts at self-liberation. *Shirakaba* spoke to the spirit of the times. The journal appealed to the young men and women across Japan who were caught between the tradition of social service and the Western ideas they had learned at school and read about in books and in the foreign news.[36] While the Japanese government wanted to take from the West only the technology and science that would increase its power, retaining traditional hierarchical values, *Shirakaba* offered a different solution: reject all the old values and embrace the new. The majority of literary magazines of the period had a monthly circulation that limped along in the hundreds, but issues of *Shirakaba* were being bought in their thousands.[37] It quickly became a symbol of Japan's new international outlook.

Enthusiasm for the journal snowballed into a nationwide movement: young people across Japan organized *Shirakaba* lectures and reading groups, and committed to living by the journal's ideas.[38] The cult of self-love became so popular that the government began nervously rewriting school ethics textbooks, hoping to stave off the pleasure-seeking individualism that it feared would undermine loyalty to the state.[39] In the newspapers, conservatives protested that Western ideas were destroying Japan's social cohesion, and that traditional, nativist values of piety and loyalty had to be revived. Mushanokōji no longer concerned himself with criticism. If he hadn't yet become 'the greatest man in the world' as his father had prophesied, he had at least succeeded in making a mark on his country.

Like many other idealists of the age, Mushanokōji was always a restless thinker, cycling through phases and passions. Amid the adulation for himself and for *Shirakaba*, he had largely forgotten about his ambitions to promote social change. But he was still developing the qualities that would serve him as a utopian: confidence in rejecting mainstream thinking; the ability to attract a following of like-minded people; and skill at promoting an ideology.

In 1912, after composing several stories about men 'starving for women', he married Miyagi Fusako, who helped run the all-female literary magazine *Bluestocking*.[40] Four years later, tiring of the frenetic pace of Tokyo life, the couple relocated to the hamlet of Abiko, twenty-five miles outside the capital. Here, they formed an artistic commune with several other *Shirakaba* members, including Shiga Naoya, and Bernard Leach, who would later join Dartington Hall.[41] Leach introduced Mushanokōji to the work of William Morris, the nineteenth-century founder of the Arts and Crafts movement, who idealized the notion of a community of artists living and working together. Beside a long, reed-bordered lake with magnificent views of Mount Fuji, Mushanokōji's days drifted by in a rarefied haze of writing, tennis-playing and discussion.[42] 'Literature,' he would assert, 'must be concerned with human life but it is not necessary for it to be concerned with society.'[43] For the moment, art alone was enough to sustain him. But in the background, a sequence of events had been taking place which would put an end to his detached aestheticism.

*

In 1912, after half a century in power, Emperor Meiji died. His funeral cortège, drawn by the traditional white oxen, processed from the imperial palace to the imperial mausoleum on the outskirts of Tokyo. The streets were spread with sand and lined with hundreds of thousands of mourners. Before the emperor was settled in his grave, the country was jolted by the news of two more deaths. General Nogi Maresuke, a bearded, medalled hero of the Russo-Japanese War who had been the head of the Peers' School, reacted to the emperor's demise by killing his wife and then committing suicide in an old samurai tradition that had long been outlawed: *junshi*, or 'following your lord to his death'.

The response to the triple fatality revealed a fundamental division in Japanese culture. Traditionalists, mostly of the older generation, were near-hysterical in their admiration for the general's self-sacrificing loyalty. Here, they said, was the highest form of morality. But young progressives, including the followers of *Shirakaba*, were horrified at this sign of their country's 'backwardness'. The general's act, wrote Mushanokōji in his journal, was one 'that could be praised only by the warped intelligence of men who have been nurtured on thought shaped by a warped age'.[44] The debate was the first salvo in a rising social confrontation.

The new ruler, Emperor Taishō, suffered from mental ill health after a childhood bout of meningitis. He took little part in government. The statesmen who ruled in his name between 1912 and 1926 oversaw a period of liberalization that became known as the 'Taishō Democracy'. This process was largely driven by the demands of the people, who wanted control taken out of the hands of the emperor and elite and handed over to representatives of the working classes. Urbanization, industrialization and the adoption of foreign-style labour movements had given the Japanese proletariat a loud voice. Demands for social equality issued from a dizzying range of quarters: societies of journalists and teachers; socialist, anarchist and labour organizations; women's, students' and tenant farmers' movements.

When the First World War began, working-class unrest only increased. Japan played a limited military role.[45] Instead, it seized on the instability of wartime as a chance to take over German colonial territory in the Pacific – the Caroline, Mariana and Marshall Islands – and to expand its influence in China. Japanese industrialists tightened their grip on the Asian markets in arms, shipping and textiles. The resulting economic boom increased the divide between the elite and workers. As the war dragged on there was an uptick in strikes, demonstrations and marches, some of these leading to riot and murder.

Mushanokōji rejected the claims of the working class, but he himself was being spurned even more severely by the *bundan*. As the leading spokesman of the *Shirakaba* school of self-love, he found himself singled out as a scapegoat for the ongoing social turmoil. What could be more irresponsible at a time of war, critics from the *bundan* asked, than this young *kuge*'s continuing promotion of self-regarding hedonism? The writer Akagi Kōhei published a stinging article condemning Mushanokōji for his writing style – 'like heavy, sluggish treacle' – but even more so for his 'weak sense of ethics'.[46] Before the war, Mushanokōji might easily have ignored such criticisms, but now he found himself beginning to doubt the adequacy of Maeterlinck's doctrine of selfhood and social irresponsibility. He did his best to rebuff his detractors by starting work on an allegorical anti-war play, *A Young Man's Dream*, but for the first time in his life, writing about his principles did not seem to him enough.[47] He believed now that action was necessary.

Mushanokōji was thirty-one when Rabindranath Tagore arrived in Tokyo.[48] It was 1916, and Tagore was on the lecture tour of Asia and America that followed his Nobel Prize. Tagore was greeted by thousands of admirers, by journalists and photographers with flash-bulbs. But when he began to lecture on the dangers of industrialization, militant nationalism and emulating the West, going so far as to accuse the Japanese of becoming 'slaves' of the nation-state, his listeners grew restive. What Tagore did not understand,

they whispered to one another, is that these so-called dangers were
the very things transforming Japan into a world power. Mushanokōji,
an avid Europhile, agreed with his countrymen that Japan still had
a great deal to learn from the West. But when he read a review of
Tagore's talk in the newspaper, he was deeply impressed. Here, he
thought, was an aristocrat and writer who had turned away from
mainstream society, just like himself – 'honest and elegant, a poet
in the true sense of the word', as Mushanokōji put it, 'a person I
would have liked to meet face to face for a leisurely discussion'.[49]
What was more, the poet was also trying to persuade the world of
his ideals. Mushanokōji was inspired.

But it was not until the national upheaval of 1918 that Mushanokōji
would turn to the idea of building a community of his own. In July,
a group of housewives in the fishing village of Uozu staged a protest
against the dramatic increase in food prices, a consequence of
wartime inflation. This sparked off the social discontent that had
been building for decades. Protests and riots spread from village to
village and town to town, until over a million people were involved
– 2 per cent of Japan's total population attacking shops, rice dealers,
police posts and government buildings. It was the largest episode
of mass domestic rioting in living memory.

For six months, Mushanokōji feared that revolution was upon
Japan, and that he and his class would lose everything, like the
aristocrats of revolutionary France or the elite in Russia in 1917.
Martial law and harsh censorship slowly restored order, but the
upper classes could no longer be complacent about their position.
Mushanokōji knew that neither he nor society could continue as
before. Some form of democratic revolution was going to come, he
wrote, 'whether we like it or not. The only question is whether it
will be peaceful or violent.'[50] His role in life, he now believed, was
to ensure that the revolution would be peaceful.

Mushanokōji surveyed his friends' responses to the tumult. The
Shirakaba movement had been fragmenting since the start of the
war. Shiga Naoya was withdrawing into his private literary world.
The author Arishima Takeo had taken up socialism, which
Mushanokōji continued to reject. Meanwhile, *Shirakaba* writer-
potter Yanagi Sōetsu, along with Bernard Leach, began developing
a new left-wing movement called *Mingei*, or 'People's Art', which

celebrated ordinary people's everyday aesthetic expression.[51] The *Mingei* approach didn't appeal to Mushanokōji any more than socialism. It championed traditional, communal Japanese art over the modern, individualistic Western art that he admired. Mushanokōji realized he had to find his own way of combining what was good from Japan's past – social stability, strong local communities – with the beneficial effects of modernization and international influence, and, in particular, Western-style individualism.

The solution came to him as he was pacing his garden in Abiko one afternoon, turning over the diverse array of approaches to social reform that he had considered so far. He was thinking of Tagore's advocacy of the union of Eastern and Western culture; of the exemplary life of Jesus Christ; of the books that he had read by William Morris, who extolled the beauty and dignity of creative labour in medieval guilds; and those by Edward Carpenter, who advocated a simple life of sandal-making and market gardening. Mushanokōji recalled the intense enthusiasm for Tolstoy that had consumed him before he had been won over by Maeterlinck. Now that he had returned again to the question of social reform, it struck him that the pacifistic egalitarianism of Tolstoy had been the solution all along.

Before the great Russian died in 1910, Mushanokōji remembered, he had promoted social change not just through his writing, but practically, by building a community for the peasants on his estate at Yasnaya Polyana. Was that so different, Mushanokōji asked himself, from the semi-communal existence he and his friends had been leading at Abiko? It wasn't too great a leap to imagine setting up a fully fledged community of his own: one that was built on the Tolstoyan model, bringing agriculture and cooperative living together. But his New Village would be different. It would in corporate the other influences that were close to his heart – Tagore and Christ and the Victorian socialists like Morris and Carpenter – and even Maeterlinck. 'It is work nobody else but I can do,' Mushanokōji would write: 'To create a new society; to make a model of utopia.'[52]

*

During the final months of the First World War, Mushanokōji launched a recruitment campaign for his new community in the pages of *Shirakaba* and of *Mainichi Shimbun*, one of Japan's major newspapers. He described the utopia he wanted to build as a place where 'all the world's people will fulfil their own destinies, and where the individuality residing in each of them will be allowed to blossom fully'.[53] At Atarashiki Mura, residents would live together in peace and harmony. There would be no competition, no class tension, and the functions of intellectual elite and manual labourer would be effortlessly amalgamated. One of the overriding questions posed by Mushanokōji's utopian plan was how the ostensibly opposing doctrines of individualism and cooperation would mesh together. Mushanokōji, just like Tagore, was a man with a vision rather than a rigorously logical thinker, and he smoothed over this tension with an optimistic maxim. 'First let us give life to ourselves, then we can make ideas blossom, and then we shall be able to gather the fruit by linking comrades together.'[54] Once the community began, he thought, the correct relationship between these two doctrines would emerge organically: by living in a transformed society – an egalitarian village – each individual would grow, develop and achieve personal transformation.

Mushanokōji went on to lay out the practical details of the community. Atarashiki Mura would be built in the remote countryside, safe from the social unrest, aesthetic horrors and government control of Japan's towns. Its inhabitants, the New Villagers, would pool all of their resources and buy a farm; they would then divide up the work of running that farm between them, receiving housing, clothing, food, education and healthcare in return. They would spend the rest of their time – which would be plentiful – in self-cultivation and enjoyment. Over the next ten to twenty years, Mushanokōji told his readers, the community would build a library, gallery, theatre, concert hall, school and hospital. All of the luxuries of Tokyo would be available, with none of the rush, ugliness and tension of metropolitan life. Like the other utopians of his age, Mushanokōji believed that his model community would stand as a guiding beacon in the development of a new world order. It would induce change not through violent revolution, but through inspiring a peaceable international wave of New Villages. The unnecessary struggle between classes and nations would come to an end.

After the success of *Shirakaba*, Mushanokōji expected his clarion call for New Villagers to bring in a stream of eager volunteers. But there was a wide gulf between those willing to adopt – or read about – an aesthetic philosophy, and those ready to embark on a completely new way of life. Only a few volunteers came forward – five escaping from factory work and domestic service, and two of Mushanokōji's artist friends, the art critic Kimura Sōhachi and the painter Nakamura Ryōsei.[55] To make matters worse, there was a slew of discouraging articles in the press, with critics calling the plan 'a publicity stunt' from a writer known to be frivolous and attention-seeking.[56]

The most painful criticism came from Arishima Takeo, who had once been a stalwart *Shirakaba* supporter, as well as Mushanokōji's close friend.[57] 'Your plan to embark upon social reconstruction is, I believe, noble,' Arishima stated in an open letter to Mushanokōji that was printed in the newspapers. But the community, he went on, was bound to collapse under the 'desperate tyranny of the capitalist mainstream'. As a fervent socialist, Arishima's chief accusation was that Mushanokōji was failing to engage with class consciousness. Along with many other socialists and communists in Japan and further afield, Arishima believed that class struggle was the only mechanism by which true social change could be effected. The struggle between classes would never just 'go away', as Mushanokōji seemed to believe. Setting up a utopian community, even one with left-leaning ideals, smacked to Arishima of bourgeois privilege and ivory towers.

Mushanokōji was shaken. For the past decade he had been riding high on a wave of popularity. He had allowed himself to believe that he was the mouthpiece for young, progressive Japan. Now he saw this was not the case. People had refused to join his latest venture; old friends were publicly sniping at him. But Mushanokōji continued anyway. At heart he was a true utopian: criticism only strengthened his belief that he was right and everyone else was wrong. The response his articles had received, he told himself, just showed how badly Japan and the rest of the world needed his enlightenment. He broke with the *Shirakaba* coterie and launched a rival monthly magazine devoted to his ideas, which he named after his community: *Atarashiki Mura*.

Mushanokōji thought up an ingenious method of raising funds, which allowed the community to come into existence. He decided to offer two types of membership to his New Village. 'Type-one' members would live in the community itself, and contribute as much money as they could to its coffers – but there would also be 'type-two' members, who could subscribe from afar, paying a minimum of one yen a month. They could make further donations and visit whenever they liked. Type twos would enjoy all the moral and ideological excitement that came with being part of a utopian community, without having to alter their day-to-day lives. The ploy worked brilliantly. Within a few weeks, Atarashiki Mura had acquired over 160 type-two members. Mushanokōji finally had the capital he needed to start constructing Japan's first New Village.

*

It was on a night in September 1918 that Mushanokōji had what he called his 'revelation': he dreamed of a thriving community nestled in the remote mountains. On waking, he decided that this was a vision of Hyūga, the mountainous province in the island of Kyūshū far in the south of Japan. The dream had to be auspicious – even if it may have been triggered by the visitor he'd had from the region the day before.[58] Hyūga was about as remote as it was possible to get from Japan's main industrial centres, which seemed an ideal location for the New Village to begin. It would, Mushanokōji wrote, be an escape from the 'fixed, twisted and unreasonable order of contemporary society', a society of exploitative employers, suffering workers and parasitical elites.[59] Hyūga was also the home of the nation's mythological founder, Emperor Jimmu. If one great civilization had started there, Mushanokōji reasoned, surely there was no better birthplace for a second.

Mushanokōji, his wife Fusako and his handful of type-one New Villagers set off to look for a site in Hyūga. There were sixteen of them now, some with heavy trunks and others with no more than a battered rucksack. All were in their twenties, apart from a couple of small children and Mushanokōji and his wife, who were now in their early thirties. It was a long, circuitous journey by train, carriage and boat to the south of Japan. On the way, the group stopped off at Kyoto, Ōsaka and Kobe to rally additional support. Crowds of people turned up to see Mushanokōji. Many of them were enthusiastic readers of *Shirakaba*, and when they heard the passion in his voice as he spoke about what the New Village would achieve, how he was about to bring to Japan the joys of self-expression, independence, pacifism and internationalism, they rushed to sign up as type-two members. Mushanokōji decided that the lukewarm response to Atarashiki Mura in Tokyo had been misleading; outside the capital, there was a real hunger for change.

Through the window of the train and then the stagecoach, Mushanokōji watched bustling towns give way to villages, villages to hamlets.[60] The parcels of farmland grew smaller and smaller as they reached the blue mountains of Hyūga. Between the tiny rice fields carved out on the steep terraces above the road, farmers moved sure-footedly along precipitous footpaths, while women crouched outside their homes, weaving or basket-making as they watched their children. It all made a great change from the haughty ladies posing for one another outside the cafes in Ginza, with their Western dresses, cigarette holders and fur stoles. Mushanokōji began to think he was making a journey back in time, a journey to a better, older Japan. Like Tagore and the Elmhirsts, he idealized his country's history (or at least, its less hierarchical and self-sacrificing elements). Like William Morris, he had come to see the harmonious village community as the noblest part of the past. Traditionally, he was sure, cooperation and creative fulfilment had always been valued above material gain – and now he was close to bringing those days back to life.

But when Mushanokōji and his followers tried to purchase a plot of land, they ran into difficulty. The people they approached were backcountry-dwellers, living in small, dark homes with beaten-earth floors, subsisting on a diet of barley gruel and pickles.[61] Several with land for sale rejected the would-be buyers for their 'foreignness'. Mushanokōji tried to explain his vision in the same words he had used in Kyoto, Ōsaka and Kobe – but to the landowners the idea of a group of intellectuals from Tokyo in the field next to theirs, attempting to redeem global humanity by farming, was so bizarre that it seemed unhinged. They looked away, shuffling their wooden clogs uncomfortably. Faced with their blank incomprehension or outright fear, Mushanokōji found his flow of rhetoric drying up.

Finally, as winter was drawing in, the group found land with a

willing seller, near the small village of Kijō. This site was so remote
that there were no neighbours to object, and no other buyers who
would consider a purchase. To Mushanokōji, it was paradise. The
twenty-five gently sloping acres of grass, farmland and woods were
encircled by the wide, slow flow of the Omaru River. To the
north-west, the plot was protected by high, densely forested mountains whose tops were shrouded in mist. It was like walking into
the landscape of an *ukiyo-e* print, he said to his companions; later
he recalled that 'the scenery seemed not to be of this world. A
haze lay about, from which numerous hills appeared to float like
islands.'[62] The seller informed him that the site had once been the
location of a feudal castle, although the wooden structure had long
since rotted away. It would become a stronghold again, Mushanokōji
thought, a place to nurture his community in safety. He told his
followers that the setting was sure to 'produce a legend', and that
legend would be their community.[63] The New Villagers immediately
began constructing the two huts that would shelter them through
their first winter. On 14 November 1918, three days after the
First World War Armistice was signed, they moved into their new
quarters.

*

That first winter was miserable. Only a city dweller could have
thought it was a good idea to move to the remote countryside in
November. Farming was all but impossible, the soil too cold and
hard to dig. The temperature plummeted below freezing. Snow fell,
but there was no time to appreciate its ethereal beauty since everyone
was too busy trying to survive. How would they stay warm? What
would they eat? Already supplies were running low. There were two
small towns ten miles distant – Miyazaki and Ishikawachi – but to
get to them the New Villagers had to cross a high, treacherous
mountain pass on foot. For the cosmopolitan idealists sent to fetch
sacks of rice – most of them used to accessing anything they wanted
within ten minutes in Tokyo – the shops, hospitals, post offices and
stagecoach posts of the towns felt as far away as the moon.

   Inside the two chilly, jerry-built huts, harmony soon fell apart.
The lack of privacy and the extreme isolation bred bickering and
quarrels. Mushanokōji's wife Fusako – a small, delicately built woman

fond of dressing in fine silk – was one of the leading malcontents. Other utopian communities of the era, including Dartington Hall and the Bruderhof, were run by couples with shared ideals, but Atarashiki Mura was a one-man show. Day after day, Fusako told her husband she wasn't cut out to be a peasant. Their straw futon was a nest of fleas, their clothes stank, there was never a chance to wash properly with warm water and soap. And while they were rotting in the countryside they were losing touch with culture, with the latest trends in fashion, in the news, in literature and art. Surely, she said, these were the very things that made life worth living? How was holing up in these dirty huts supposed to improve exist-ence for themselves or the rest of society?

Mushanokōji, who was himself suffering acutely from every diffi-culty his wife listed, didn't know how to respond. Even worse than her complaints, from his point of view, was that he wasn't writing. He forced himself to sit down at his desk at the end of each difficult day, but nothing came. He told himself angrily that Tolstoy had produced both *War and Peace* and *Anna Karenina* while living at Yasnaya Polyana. But the lonely, snowbound landscape of Kyūshū oppressed rather than inspired him. So did the unhappy presence of his fellow villagers. He felt responsible for their suffering. Listening to the crackle of the fire in the stove and the snow pattering on the thin mud-and-wood walls of the hut, he began to think that the New Village had been a mistake.

Spring revived Mushanokōji's optimism. He called a meeting. The communards crouched in front of him outside their huts, a thin column of cooking smoke coiling up behind them into the still-cool air. Mushanokōji cleared his throat and told them that their life at Atarashiki Mura had been lacking in structure. But he had devised a plan.[64] Before next winter, they would build more accommoda-tion, turning their two huts into a proper village; and they would transform their overgrown acres into productive farmland. The days must now start with six hours of physical work – the same number that Thomas More set out in his book *Utopia*. This, Mushanokōji asserted confidently, would be a pleasure rather than an obligation. Did the Victorian writers like John Ruskin and William Morris not promise that 'good labour' – work that was self-directed – fulfilled in a way that labour for others never could?[65]

Since this gem of wisdom from England was greeted with little excitement by his shivering listeners, Mushanokōji hurried on with the practicalities. His plan for structure and discipline was far looser than the other, more collectivist utopias in this period: after those first six hours, the rest of the day would be entirely devoted to self-realization. Every person would do what they felt suited them best. He, for example, would write, along with a little painting. And they, he asked his audience – what would they like to do? His question was met with silence. The New Villagers continued to watch him, apparently waiting for some kind of revelation. He felt a twinge of annoyance. Now that they were here in Hyūga, these 'brothers' and 'sisters' (their agreed term of address) were supposed to be a group of equals, living in cooperation but working towards individual ends. That was the theory, what they'd all agreed on before the long journey south. And yet the New Villagers continued to look on him as if he was their *sensei*, the master with all the answers. They were stuck in the past, unable to wrench themselves free from unthinking obedience to anyone above them in the social hierarchy.

Mushanokōji remembered the social doctrine of yet another Victorian – Matthew Arnold – who wrote that humankind had a natural 'aristocracy', an elite endowed with superior gifts who should lead society.[66] This chimed with the lesson that had been drummed into him since childhood: that as a *kuge* he was born to govern. Should he acquiesce to this idea? Appoint himself the community's formal leader since he was its de facto leader already? It would certainly make things easier. But Mushanokōji had founded the community to promote individual self-fulfilment and freedom. The Atarashiki Mura he had dreamed of was a utopia of equals, and he was determined that it should stay that way now it was becoming a real place. He ended his talk quickly. From today, he said, all community decisions would be made democratically. The only rule would be: 'Do not issue commands, and do not act upon commands.'[67]

*

The New Villagers began to farm in earnest, heartened by the change of season and Mushanokōji's renewed enthusiasm. But the work was far from easy. Much of their land was thick with weeds, and the first task was to cut down or rip up the dense vegetation. The founding members of the community – men and women both, but mostly men – had little capacity for strenuous physical work, and next to no experience of agriculture.[68] They had imagined Atarashiki Mura as a cross between a university and a literary salon. Mushanokōji, after all, was famed for his love of pleasure. Men like Kawashima Denkichi, Mushanokōji's houseboy and an aspiring author, and Himori Shinichi, a high-school dropout who would go on to become a famous actor, had joined the village in the expectation of pursuing their aesthetic development – they weren't ready to wield a hoe in the fields for six hours a day.[69]

Before the smallest domestic task could be achieved there was always a squabble. At the very moment when the firewood needed to be carried in or the rice prepared for supper, at least one person – often more – would be sure to be bent studiously over a calligraphy brush or one of Tolstoy's novels, excusing themselves with a curt: 'I'm busy working on my art'.[70] Persuading people to farm was even more of a challenge. Everyone loved the idea of eating rice they had grown themselves, but no one actually wanted to do the growing. Farming rice isn't easy. It involves hours of backbreaking work, standing knee-deep, numb-footed in the mud: digging irrigation ditches and ploughing and fertilizing the paddies; flooding them nine inches deep with river water; and painstakingly planting out the tender rice shoots. Mushanokōji had to lead every stage of the hard labour himself, drawing on the memories of his brief period of agricultural labour with his uncle, and on what he could glean from the activities of neighbouring farmers. His kimono tucked up, his muscles aching, his forehead bathed in sweat, he straightened up to rub the calluses on his once-white hands.

Returning to the huts at dusk, Mushanokōji couldn't help but smile ironically at the memory of his *Shirakaba* friends so casually comparing themselves to pioneering farmers. 'With much sweat and toil,' Arishima Takeo had written, the coterie 'began to plough the virgin soil. The soil was hard. Weeds proliferated unchecked.'[71] In Mushanokōji's life, the metaphor had become a reality, and now he knew how little resemblance the act of writing bore to farming. But by the time the rice was planted at the end of spring, he was prouder of his fields than he had been of any of his stories. Mushanokōji walked among the newly built huts, admiring the paddies on the upper slopes and, on the lower slopes, the young crops of wheat, barley and sweet potatoes. Close to the main buildings, chickens and sheep nosed about in newly constructed pens. Work had begun on a communal canteen. Mushanokōji thought that it was all so much more tangible than getting a collection of essays into a Tokyo bookshop; so much more satisfying than lounging about in Ginza and merely talking about how people ought to live.

But the field work exhausted everyone, and after wolfing down their evening rice, dizzy with tiredness, they immediately fell asleep. Where, Mushanokōji asked himself, was the 'truly human life' of creative fulfilment he had promised?[72] Without that, the New Villagers were little better off than beasts of burden, or the workers in the factories in Tokyo. In the late afternoons he began to coax his tired followers to write and paint, to make pottery and music. As they gradually became accustomed to the toll of physical labour, he met with some success. Most people took up at least one creative activity.[73] In later years, Mushanokōji would try to ensure that these artistic endeavours had a communal aspect to them, by organizing village plays, or a gallery where paintings could be hung for all to admire; even setting up a printing press for publishing low-cost *mura no hon* ('books of the village') and the journal *Atarashiki Mura*.[74]

When the rains set in that first summer, Mushanokōji found to his great relief that he too was able to express himself creatively. It was like the bursting of a dam. Mushanokōji composed novels, stories, essays and plays. He dedicated one book, *The Happy Man*, to Bernard Leach, hoping that the English potter would spread the news of Atarashiki Mura to the West. Mushanokōji wrote the story as the literary counterpart to the physical New Village. A good, wise man, known as 'the Teacher', arrives at a village that is in disarray. Ignoring the hostility of the older generation, he wins a following of young people with his philosophy of equality, simple living and benevolence. 'When state policy and truth are at odds, which should we follow?' asks a disciple. 'Truth, of course,' the Teacher replies.[75] His main message, which he preaches from the temple that his disciples help him build, is that the happiest man of all is 'the man who lives for his brethren and can die for them'.[76] Now that Mushanokōji had established his utopian community in reality, he wanted to preserve and pass on its legend in prose.

Despite the easy harmony of *The Happy Man*, conditions at Atarashiki Mura remained difficult. There were money shortages, and worse, food shortages. When people began complaining of hunger, Mushanokōji pointed out the beauty of the crops growing in their fields – a paradise, he said, that they had created with their own hands. 'Rather than envy those who live in luxury,' he chided the New Villagers, 'we should be happy to have escaped their fate.'[77] A second difficulty was governance. In an effort to maximize democracy, the New Villagers had decided that money for community projects should be allotted proportionately based on votes at the weekly village meetings: if a project secured only a quarter of votes, only a quarter of the available funds would be invested in it.[78] The result was that vital large-scale improvements, such as building a serviceable road through the steep mountain pass, were never achieved, because people would not vote for hard, unpleasant work. Without this road, the villagers were locked in for days on end throughout the rainy season, surviving on a diet of wheat porridge.

The rain pelted down all through that first summer, and mud rose to coat every available surface, inside the village huts and out. There were arguments over whose turn it was to cook the communal meal, a thankless task that no one enjoyed since there were never enough ingredients to cook with. Meals were often delayed, and sometimes missed entirely. There were quarrels and illicit affairs. Mushanokōji and his wife weren't exempt – they both took lovers. While there were, by now, more private huts for people to live in, the village was still too small to conceal infidelity. The population of Atarashiki Mura was increasingly divided: on the one side were those totally dedicated to performing the chores required for its practical survival; on the other, those for whom self-gratification always came first. Nonetheless, the two groups rubbed along, with Mushanokōji encouraging them to see each other's point of view. 'The individuality residing in each of us must be allowed to grow fully,' he told the communally minded. He warned the excessive individualists that 'they mustn't allow the promotion of their own individuality to infringe on others [. . .] to harm the destiny or just demands of others merely for their own pleasure, happiness or freedom.'[79]

As the founder of the village, 'Brother Mushanokōji' bore the brunt of people's discontent. He was too much of a dreamer, complained New Villager Kurata Hyakuzō sourly. He always concealed truth beneath a layer of fantasy: 'My brother has the gift of forging reality according to his views.'[80] When these criticisms were aired, Mushanokōji would leave the communal dining hut to stand beneath the stars in the humid darkness. He contrasted the rustling silence that surrounded him to the traffic of Tokyo and the harsh cries of hawkers peddling aubergines and morning glory from dawn to dusk. He reminded himself that great works of art were never created easily – and here, surely, he wasn't merely pioneering a better world, but was creating his own greatest work of art.

Autumn arrived. Several of the villagers were already shaking their heads regretfully and taking their leave. They said that the reality of Mushanokōji's dream was too much like hard work. The first to go were the two married couples with children, whom Mushanokōji, with an eye to the longevity of his community, had been particularly keen to keep. He had promised them peace and privacy to pursue self-fulfilment, they complained, but Atarashiki Mura was a hothouse of bickering. Their rooms were permanently damp, their children sick all the time. It was nothing like the paradise he had painted. Mushanokōji consoled himself with physical labour, carrying in the huge sheaves of rice from the drying racks in the fields. The people who had left, he decided, had been too conventional to be true pioneers.

With the harvest completed, the New Village had managed to survive an entire year. The local peasants might still shun it. Tokyo intellectuals might sneer. The leader of the Japanese Communist Party, Yamakawa Hitoshi, might write of the community that 'even if an oasis survives for tens of thousands of years, it will never make the desert bloom'.[81] But Mushanokōji believed the village was proving all its critics wrong. Atarashiki Mura would inspire a new world order. It had been a challenging beginning, but the New Village was slowly coming together. He began composing a new poem as he worked: 'Fire from a single match / is capable of kindling everything flammable in the world.'[82] He wasn't alone in his optimism. The New Villagers who had persisted through that first year were just as convinced that their example had the power to inspire lasting change. 'I felt strongly,' recalled one Shiro Seshimo, 'that we were going to create a new world.'[83]

*

There would always be a rapid turnover of participants at Atarashiki Mura, with more than a hundred people coming and going in the first four years. It was a difficult life. In many ways, as the poetry and paintings preserved from this time show, it was also a beautiful, peaceful one, close to nature.[84] But the community continued to attract urban intellectuals rather than farmers, people who struggled to adapt to the manual work and harsh rural conditions, and few lasted long. Those who left the village after a short time were not necessarily turning their backs on its ideals. The *Shirakaba* follower and schoolteacher Kobayashi Tatsue, who joined the community for a few months in 1918, could still be found extolling its virtues – 'nurturing the self, respecting individuality, loving beauty and seeking peace' – on his deathbed in 2000, aged 104.[85]

As the community's reputation grew – spread by passing visitors, by newspaper articles and the journal *Atarashiki Mura* – new arrivals began turning up from all over Japan. While Mushanokōji had not exactly created the utopia he had dreamed of, where people pulled together easily at the same time as pursuing their individual aesthetic projects, he had established a place where idealists of many backgrounds lived and worked alongside one another. Nowhere else in Japan would you find members of the *Shirakaba* movement sharing living quarters with teachers, students and labourers; people from wealthy backgrounds – like Nakamura Ryohei, who sold his house and land and brought a substantial amount of capital with him when he joined the village – working in the rice paddies alongside members of the lowly *burakumin* class.[86] The community attracted participants from across the political spectrum. Among them were the left-wing Awaya Yuzo – who would continue to promote social change after leaving the village to become a member of Parliament – and the right-wing extremist Sagoya Tomeo, who would gain notoriety for his attempt to 'improve' Japan by assassinating its prime minister in 1930.[87]

While the New Villagers were drawn by the idea of a new way of living that combined self-realization with communality, they were equally attracted by the community's dedication to international cooperation. This was highly unusual in a country that had been closed off from foreign influence for over two centuries, and which had entered into international engagement largely from the point of view of securing a competitive advantage and building an empire.

'Of course it is not capitalism, nor is it socialism,' Mushanokōji wrote of Atarashiki Mura. 'We have a third way: humanism, world brotherhood.'[88]

After the first year, the New Villagers found life slightly easier, as they learned the rhythms of farming and cooperation. They rose early to feed the animals and worked in the fields while it was still cool. After breakfast, and two more hours of work, they broke off to swim in the river or play tennis. From four they worked for three further hours, then it was time for their own private pursuits.[89] The number of permanent residents rose to thirty-two in the second year, and to thirty-seven in the third – including six children.[90] The passing of time was marked by the seasons, by minor improvements to the infrastructure, and by the dates chosen by Mushanokōji as annual feasts: these included the birthdays of Tolstoy, Rodin, Jesus and Buddha – a signal of how internationally oriented the community remained in spite of its rustic day-to-day life.[91] The local peasants, who had for the first year continued to regard their new neighbours with intense suspicion, gradually got used to their peculiar ways. They even began looking forward to the community's anniversary meals, and to the plays that the New Villagers staged in the open air.[92]

In this more settled and tranquil period, Mushanokōji's attention turned to evangelizing. Like Santiniketan-Sriniketan and Dartington Hall, Atarashiki Mura was supposed to inspire a peaceful revolution that would ripple out across the globe. He channelled his energies into composing vivid, persuasive articles for *Atarashiki Mura*. On sunny afternoons, he settled down outside his hut, the grass prickling through his kimono, and wrote the essays, stories and reports on village life that he hoped would entice the world beyond the mountains to the New Village.

Mushanokōji's writing attracted old friends, including *Shirakaba* novelist Shiga Naoya, to the New Village. Shiga admired the spectacular scenery of Kyūshū, his eyes wandering from blue sky to mountain peak to wide, green river, and to the people labouring picturesquely in the fields. He decided he must get all these details into his next story, and made a donation to the community's upkeep. But after only a few days living at the village Shiga could not imagine putting up with its discomfort for any longer.[93] It was the idea of Atarashiki Mura rather than the reality that provoked widespread enthusiasm.

By 1929, the number of type-two, non-resident subscribers had climbed to 800. Various social experiments started springing up across Japan in imitation of the community. Arishima Takeo, the *Shirakaba* writer turned socialist who had initially been so critical of Mushanokōji's utopian plans, decided to transform his estate in Hokkaidō into a cooperative, tenant-owned farm. Itō Isao, who lived at Atarashiki Mura for a few years, went on to establish his own series of model villages.[94] A group of young reformers set up a 'Community Loving Society', a short-lived association that aimed to reconstruct the whole of Japan along agrarian, communal lines.[95] The newspapers reported on a 'New Village craze' in tones ranging from anxiety to jubilation.[96]

Ripples from Atarashiki Mura were spreading out across East Asia and beyond. Two Koreans already living in Japan, Yi Shi-hwa and Jeong Jeon-gyu, joined as type-one members in 1920, and spread news of the community to their friends back home.[97] The septuagenarian English poet and socialist Edward Carpenter, whose writing had influenced the young Mushanokōji, wrote to his friends in Tokyo to ask about goings-on in Kyūshū.[98] The community also had admirers in China. Sino-Japanese diplomatic relations were tense in this period, due to Japan's colonial ambitions in Asia, but this didn't prevent a lively exchange continuing between Japanese and Chinese intellectuals. They visited one another, wrote essays on their experiences abroad, studied at each other's universities, and imported one another's journals. The thick-moustached, bespectacled Zhou Zuoren, a direct contemporary of Mushanokōji, had been a long-time follower of *Shirakaba* and had also begun reading *Atarashiki Mura*. So impressed was he by Mushanokōji's descriptions of the New Village – a community overcoming class divisions and combining communal labour and individual leisure – that he arrived to investigate it for himself.[99]

Mushanokōji was delighted: that Zhou should have travelled all the way to Atarashiki Mura seemed to him proof that his vision of world brotherhood would soon become a reality. As well as introducing Zhou to the life of the community, he discussed with him Eastern and Western social ideals – among them those of Leo Tolstoy and Rabindranath Tagore, whom Zhou had heard lecture at Peking University.[100] Zhou, on leaving, said that he was going to import the New Village model to China.[101]

Back home, Zhou published a spate of articles promoting Atarashiki Mura's philosophy. 'These days,' he declared enthusiastically, 'even though we still dwell in the old world, in this one small corner one can glimpse something of a miracle.'[102] His reports were seized on by young Chinese idealists eager to overcome class divisions. They organized New Village associations in Beijing and outside Shanghai. As the New Village movement's chief intellectual mentor in China, Zhou found himself inundated by visitors wanting to learn about his experiences at Atarashiki Mura. These included Chen Duxieu, founder of the Chinese Communist Party, and Mao Zedong, who went on to lead the Communist Revolution in 1946.[103] Zedong was inspired to write an article that pointed to the New Village as an ideal model of socialist living, and he dreamed of organizing a 'mutual aid group' who would build a New Village of their own.[104] Although he never took the practical steps to create this village, the people's communes that he would establish across China in the 1950s – agricultural collectives with shared ownership and labour – would carry traces of the New Village model.[105]

Mushanokōji was highly gratified by this 'New Village craze'. He felt that his community was beginning to change the zeitgeist, convincing people at home and abroad that there was an alternative to hierarchies, to industrialized life and to state-backed militarism. He encouraged his fellow utopians to begin learning the recently invented universal language Esperanto under the guidance of New Villager Kimura Sōhachi, so that they could participate fully in forging the harmonious new global order.[106] He announced in *Atarashiki Mura* that he hoped to 'increase type-two membership to ten thousand within a year and to one million within a few years'.[107] To commemorate Zhou's visit, he wrote a poem celebrating internationally minded individuals working together.[108]

> No matter where you are from
> Even if our countries are at odds
> As long as we are friends, all will be well
> Let's work together, let's help one another
> For the sake of humanity.

*

By 1923, Mushanokōji Saneatsu had been living in Atarashiki Mura for five years. Despite the community's success, he was starting to feel restless. Like Tagore, like Dorothy and Leonard Elmhirst, he had an active, questing nature that was ill-suited to a long period of quiet, rural life. He was now in his late thirties and did not want to spend the rest of his days in rustic isolation – no matter how significant his presence was as an example for others.

Then came the news that Arishima Takeo – the *Shirakaba* writer who had been inspired by Atarashiki Mura to establish a cooperative community of his own – had committed suicide. The act was driven by his conviction, as a *kuge*, that all elite-led social reform was doomed to failure – that real change must come from the proletariat.[109] Mushanokōji was distraught at the death of his friend, a man whose struggle to reconcile a *kuge* upbringing with social idealism had been so like his own. The suicide reawakened his long-held uncertainty about exactly what role – if any – the elite should have in an egalitarian utopia. It was the same question that Tagore and the Elmhirsts struggled with in enacting their own social visions, and a challenge faced by democratically minded elites across the world in this period. Was Mushanokōji's position at Atarashiki Mura still too prominent? In spite of his efforts to make the village a democracy, was he undermining the community through his very presence?

While Mushanokōji was worrying over this, his wife Fusako announced that she was divorcing him and leaving Atarashiki Mura. In itself, her departure caused no great surprise or upset to anyone, least of all her husband. Mushanokōji was already living with his lover, Ishikawa Yasuko, who was pregnant, while Fusako had moved in with another New Villager.[110] Yet the defection was still a blow. Divorce was considered a disgrace in interwar Japan, and Fusako's departure gave rise to a spate of critical articles about Atarashiki Mura. These evoked the same problem faced by Dartington Hall when the school's headmaster divorced: the tension between defending individual freedom of action and maintaining the community's reputation in order to continue attracting members and supporters from mainstream society.

Fusako's departure gave Mushanokōji the sense of an era coming an end. This feeling was compounded by the Great Kantō Earthquake of September 1923, the worst natural disaster Japan had ever experienced. Half of Tokyo was reduced to rubble by tremors, and the firestorms that followed swept through the city and incinerated acres of buildings.[111] The headquarters of *Shirakaba* were destroyed. Over 100,000 people were killed.

Devastating earthquakes – like those in Lisbon in 1755 and in San Francisco in 1906 – are often interpreted by people who experience them as an apocalyptic warning that they have been living in the wrong way.[112] The Great Kantō Earthquake was no exception. Many in Japan read it as a divine punishment meted out to them for their egotism and materialism. Emperor Taishō issued an edict urging his subjects to return to a 'sincere and strenuous life' devoted to the family and the imperial state.[113] There was a nationwide campaign to strengthen the Confucian philosophy of public service. In an upsurge of xenophobic nationalism, vigilante groups began patrolling the streets. They murdered several thousand Koreans, Chinese and other foreigners, whom they accused of treacherous acts, like poisoning wells. When these stories reached Mushanokōji in Kyūshū, he felt that the tide of history had turned against him. In place of enlightened individualism and pacifist internationalism, the whole of Japan seemed to be embracing the superstition, self-sacrifice and militant patriotism that he had striven against for two decades.

Over the next three years, Mushanokōji's desire for personal change took an ever-firmer hold. He still believed in his utopia's ideals. But he was weary of day-to-day life in the community: the constant draining of his intellectual energies into field work, the thankless, emotionally exhausting job of resolving villagers' squabbles. He missed the simplicity of his earlier existence as an aesthete in Tokyo, and began to spend more and more time travelling to the surrounding towns, recruiting type-two members. In 1926, Mushanokōji decided that he could do more to further the Atarashiki Mura philosophy if he left the community for good. He moved first to Nara, a town halfway between the New Village and Japan's capital, and then back to Tokyo, where he resumed his old habits – mornings of writing, seeing new plays, launching another magazine, and whiling away the evenings in cafes.

Mushanokōji's departure did not lead to a dramatic break in the life of Atarashiki Mura. The idealists left in the community continued to farm, paint and write as before, and to hope that their 'good life' would inspire people outside their mountain stronghold. After an interval away, Fusako rejoined the community; she would remain central to it for the rest of her life. Mushanokōji went on supporting the village from afar, transferring from type-one to type-two membership. He championed New Village ideals in his writing and helped the village financially, dedicating the majority of his literary royalties to funding it. (It would take until the 1960s, when its residents began to farm chickens on a large scale, for the community to become financially self-sufficient.[114]) When, in 1938, a new, government-sponsored dam on the Omaru River was scheduled to flood half of Atarashiki Mura's acres, it was Mushanokōji who rallied the type-two members to buy new land for the community near the town of Moroyama, thirty-five miles from Tokyo.[115]

But while the bucolic life of Atarashiki Mura continued in much the same way through the late 1920s and into the 1930s, the world around the community changed rapidly. In 1926, Emperor Taishō was succeeded by Emperor Shōwa. Taishō democracy gave way to totalitarianism and ultranationalism. Prompted by the change of leader and the severe global Depression of the 1930s, Japan became a place of censorship, tight policing and rigid orthodoxies – all imposed in the name of promoting social harmony at home and expanding the empire abroad.

*

In a dramatic volte-face, Mushanokōji devoted himself to the new regime. He had always had a weakness for new ideals, for new formulas for how people should live; he soaked up the spirit of his generation and then articulated it in its most radical form. In his youth, the zeitgeist of his contemporaries had been pro individualism and liberal internationalism. Now that he was in his fifties, militant patriotism was the order of the day. And Mushanokōji, still searching for improved social models, seized on it with both hands.[116] Part of him missed his moment in the sun, his time of being relevant as a writer and utopian – since he'd moved out of the community, people had paid far less attention to his opinions. During the Second World War, he used his literary talent and reputation to support the Japanese state's invasion of more Chinese territory; its withdrawal from the League of Nations; and, finally, its push to develop an Asian 'co-prosperity sphere' (a euphemism for Japanese empire).[117]

At the end of the Second World War, Mushanokōji was named a war criminal for his support of the militarist government. His books were banned and he was excluded from public office, and even from public transport. In 1951 he was formally reinstated into society, but he remained withdrawn from most social engagement. His popular image became that of an old man remarking blandly, 'How beautiful congeniality is', as he painted childlike pictures.[118]

Despite Mushanokōji's personal turn towards militant patriotism, the community he founded, and the idealists who lived there, remained dedicated to its original principles. Mushanokōji had contributed towards this steadfastness of vision when he founded Atarashiki Mura by distilling his ideals into a clear manifesto – a feat that few other utopians of the age achieved. The 'spirit of Atarashiki Mura' was printed on the back of each issue of the *Atarashiki Mura* magazine and it was, and still is, displayed prominently beside the community's meeting hall, making it easy for communards to adhere to it. If people followed its recommended model for living, the last point of the manifesto ran, 'then the world we desire will come to be without struggle between nations and classes. We will do our utmost to achieve this goal.'[119] The community's endurance was also the result of its small size – which meant it did not fragment like Santiniketan-Sriniketan and Dartington Hall – and its success in developing a system of genuinely democratic decision-making.

When the Shōwa government began suppressing all ideas and modes of life that did not serve its bellicose nationalism, Atarashiki Mura was forced to be less evangelical. Nonetheless, the community continued to attract people from across Japan, becoming a haven for those who would not or could not conform to the new regime: freethinking idealists, dispossessed farmers, bankrupt traders and the occasional convict on the run. The New Villagers went on with their lives, more quietly and unobtrusively than before, but still hoping that their example would inspire others.

Atarashiki Mura continues to this day, although it feels more like the relic of a past dream than an active experiment in social reform.

It occupies a few tranquil acres beside a small railway line on the outskirts of Tokyo. There are currently less than a dozen New Villagers, most of them over the age of seventy. Showing impressive vitality, they continue to farm on a small scale and to display their paintings of flowers and vegetables in a communal art gallery – although weeds grow high between the houses, around the aged chicken sheds and in the orchard. The most prominent features of the village are a meticulously tended museum that commemorates Mushanokōji Saneatsu, and the mausoleum where he was interred on his death at the age of ninety-one in 1976. Even after Mushanokōji's ideas changed in the late 1930s, those who lived in the New Village remained conscious of their debt to him as chief progenitor, proselytizer and financial benefactor of their community.

Atarashiki Mura inspired people across Japan and abroad, fuelling the creation of other communities, rural regeneration centres and even utopian fiction.[120] Like all practical utopias, it was in one sense quintessentially local – small, and rooted in the soil – but at the same time it fed to an impressive degree into global networks of ideas and actions. Its influence is still visible in the social experiments of the late twentieth and early twenty-first centuries. In 1995, the Kobayashi Tatsue Peace and Handicraft Folk Hall was opened in Japan as a centre for local democracy and the celebration of the arts, marking the ninety-ninth birthday of ex-New-Villager Kobayashi Tatsue.[121] The cooperative farm Comunidade Yuba – set up in Brazil in 1926 by a Japanese emigrant inspired by Mushanokōji and Tolstoy – continues to provide a refuge where agricultural work is combined with art and ballet.[122] Participants in China's 'new village development initiative', who opened two rural reconstruction institutes in 2003 and 2004, hark back to the example of Mushanokōji's Atarashiki Mura.[123] So, too, does the artist and filmmaker Ou Ning who, in 2011, established a self-governing artistic community, a 'microstate', in the Chinese village of Bishan.[124]

Atarashiki Mura was a rare undertaking in Japan. The community reacted against the views of the majority, rejecting centralization, industrialization, militarization and the sacrifice of the individual to family, state and empire. These values, the New Villagers felt, could never lead to social and personal fulfilment, so they created a place where that fulfilment could be found. They drew together strands of idealistic thinking from Japan and India, Russia and Belgium, France and England to forge a social model unique in itself: one in which self-love could be combined with communal responsibility, creative fulfilment with material well-being, and national tradition with an openness to global wisdom.

FOUR

THE FOREST PHILOSOPHERS
OF FONTAINEBLEAU

G. I. Gurdjieff's Institute for the
Harmonious Development of Man

The town of Kars crouches on a high plateau in Transcaucasia, surrounded on all sides by red-grey mountains. For hundreds of years it was a way station on the trade routes to the Caucasus, Georgia and Tabriz, attracting a stream of merchants, adventurers and refugees. On its narrow, crooked streets, churches stood beside mosques, tea rooms opposite hammams, and mud-floored hovels in the shadows of pillared mansions. 'Probably nowhere else in the world can so great a variety of stocks, languages, and religions be found huddled together,' wrote the Irish traveller James Bryce, passing through in the late nineteenth century.[1] Its polyglot population of Christians, Muslims and Jews, Georgians and Armenians, Azerbaijanis and Turks was united by the tenacious frontier spirit necessary to face down the snowbound winters, the scorching summers and the desolation of the surrounding landscape.

In 1877, Kars ceased to belong to the Ottoman empire and became a part of Russia. Tsar Alexander II, a man usually preoccupied with peaceful reform (he was famed for emancipating his country's serfs), succumbed to a rare bellicose impulse and invaded his neighbour. Kars' Russian conquerors immediately started making 'improvements'.[2] Workmen entered the central mosque and, in order to transform it into a Russian Orthodox cathedral, painted Cyrillic inscriptions on its slab walls and began building a bell tower. Russian administrators schemed to open up the town by constructing wide boulevards. A swarm of opportunists descended on Kars, hoping to gain from this moment of change. They included a middle-aged Greek named Yiannis Georgiades, whose dreamy character had led his businesses as a cattle grazier and then as a carpenter in Alexandropol to fail. He travelled west to change his luck, bringing his Armenian wife Evdokia, a cartload of household goods and five small children.[3]

The move from the backwater of Alexandropol to cosmopolitan Kars transformed the life of Georgiades' eldest son George Ivanovich Gurdjieff.[4] This dark-eyed, dark-haired eleven-year-old – already distinguished from his siblings by his curiosity, love of attention and determination to go his own way – found his horizons suddenly opening. His parents persuaded him to audition for Kars' newly founded cathedral choir. The director, Dean Borsch, detected in Gurdjieff a talent for music and took him on, singling him out for private academic tutoring. Eagerly embracing this education, Gurdjieff conceived a passion for two subjects in particular, religion and science, both of which would shape his thinking for the rest of his life.

In his teens, Gurdjieff's wilful independence came between him and his studies. He discovered the pleasures of leading his chorister classmates astray, persuading them to skip practice in favour of smoking and gambling in the shelter of the half-constructed cathedral bell tower. If they refused to join him, he would duck out of school in the mid-afternoon on his own, and walk across Kars to the quarter where townsfolk congregated around charcoal braziers. Gurdjieff, though young, often led the conversation there – describing what he'd learned at school as vividly as possible in the hope that it would capture his audience's imagination as it had his. The attention of the mostly illiterate crowd inspired in Gurdjieff a desire to teach. At the same time, he discovered a passion for women, choosing as the first object of his desire the daughter of the local vodka manufacturer – a girl who, conveniently enough, was also able to cater to another new-found passion: drink.

Religious pilgrims often turned up in Kars, including followers of Sufism, Yazidism and various Christian sects. These gaunt figures trudged between holy places with a bag and a staff, telling miraculous stories to the locals in exchange for food and shelter.[5] Gurdjieff was drawn to them, feeling that they represented a model of real-world faith he hadn't encountered in the confines of the cathedral. By contrast, the Orthodox sermons he heard seemed cut off from life – little more than 'children's fairy tales'.[6] He began to experiment with this lived form of spirituality, watching for day-to-day manifestations of the otherworldly. Soon he was adding instances of clairvoyance and telepathy to his talks with the townsfolk. A favourite anecdote was of how, one afternoon, he had heard a young Yazidi boy crying out for help, and discovered that a magical circle had been traced around him in the dirt, trapping him inside.[7] For Gurdjieff, there was always a slippage between spiritual insight, earthly reality and the realm of the imagination. The three were interrelated, and the occasional lapse of factual accuracy was less important than the pursuit of spiritual truth.

Gurdjieff decided that it was his destiny to become a holy man, someone who could lead others in the question of how to live. This vocation, he believed, required a profound personal investigation of spirituality. Eventually, he concluded that he needed to evolve a complete spiritual system of his own, one that made sense of his now-eclectic set of enthusiasms: for science; for paranormal events that defied scientific explanation; for exploring different faiths; and for pleasure-seeking. It was obvious to him that he was not going to work out this system on the streets of Kars. He took to the road, joining the pilgrims in their search for enlightenment.

In later life, Gurdjieff revelled in reliving his twenty-year journey through the Caucasus and Central Asia. His written accounts blend real experiences with clear exaggerations, which are, perhaps, meant to be taken as parables. His travels took him through a shadowy late-nineteenth-century world of fakirs and yogis, remote monasteries and ashrams, obscure tribes and isolated sects.[8] He paid his way, he claimed, by selling carpets and 'American canaries', which were really sparrows he dyed yellow.[9] He was led blindfolded to visit the monastery of the legendary 'Sarmoung Brotherhood' in remote Asia; then there was an expedition across the Gobi Desert where everyone wore stilts to avoid sinking into the sand and one man was gnawed to death by a wild camel.[10] While his true itinerary is impossible to reconstruct, what is certain is that Gurdjieff ended his travels a fully fledged mystic, eloquent about a spiritual system of his own devising, which he called the 'Fourth Way'. This system combined the 'way' of science with three different spiritual traditions – the 'ways' of the yogi, the fakir and the monk – to produce a new and modern philosophy by which to live.

The Fourth Way would become the foundation for a community of spiritual seekers, the Institute for the Harmonious Development of Man, which Gurdjieff would establish in the forests outside Paris in 1922. Where other utopians in the interwar years worked to create self-governing communities that reflected the democratic impulse of the age, Gurdjieff channelled another strand of the zeitgeist: the ideal of redemption by a single 'great man' or 'master'.[11] Notwithstanding this difference, the institute spoke to many of the same concerns as other contemporary communities: it was a place where, its inhabitants believed, a new, enlightened pattern of living would emerge, providing total fulfilment for its adherents and preventing another war. Gurdjieff's community was marked out by its lived internationalism, with participants drawn from across Russia, Europe and America living by tenets inspired by Gurdjieff's travels in Asia. Its syncretic spiritual system suggested a way forward for those puzzling over how advances in science could be combined with religion in a way to promote human progress. The community offered an alternative to the social hierarchies of the outside world, since all communards, regardless of rank or class, shared the same lifestyle. During the decade that it lasted, the Institute for the Harmonious Development of Man drew the interest of distinguished intellectuals, scientists, writers and artists; and its example went on to inspire diverse spiritual communities and organizations across France, Britain, the United States and South America.

*

In the early twentieth century, Russian society was on the verge of breakdown.[12] While aristocrats danced and conversed in French in Moscow's mansions and St Petersburg's palaces, on their estates in the countryside hard-labouring peasants were scraping by on a diet of bread baked from tree bark. The serfs may have been liberated in name, but people were starving, and growing increasingly impatient in their demands for voting rights and for the ownership of the land they worked. At the same time, tension was mounting around a new race of entrepreneurs who were building factories, mines and dams across Russia. They were bringing industrial progress to the country, but a lack of regulation meant their enterprises introduced manifold new ways for the proletariat to suffer.

In 1905, there was an attempted revolution: strikes, military mutinies and peasant protests swept the country. Though this failed, it was impossible for the elite to continue ignoring the widespread discontent – yet many of them were still too fearful to contemplate the realities of reform. Unable to control the process of society's modernization, they took refuge in refashioning themselves spiritually instead. Occultism and theosophy, seances and table-turning became as popular in the early twentieth-century salons of the wealthy as Marx was in the cafes of the proletariat. This was prime recruiting ground for a holy man in search of disciples.

After his travels in the East, Gurdjieff arrived in Moscow in 1912, determined to spread his spiritual ideas. He was in his forties now, and had acquired the striking, singular look that marked him out as a guru: as one observer described him, 'a shaven dome, an unlined swarthy face, piercing black eyes, and a tigerish moustache that curled out to big points'.[13] Each evening he would commandeer a restaurant table, or even the whole of a small cafe, for the purpose of holding a spiritual meeting. He rejected the exotic clothes and settings many mystics used to attract followers, on the basis that he was more authentic wearing his old black coat and astrakhan hat. He directed proceedings with a confidence bordering on arrogance: I don't need you as disciples, his manner seemed to say; it is you who must impress me. This ended up being the perfect way to gain the trust of the nervy Russian elite. The aristocratic composer Thomas de Hartmann attended one evening where all Gurdjieff did was eat and drink an inconceivable quantity of food, scarcely speaking at all and leaving his fellow diners to pick up the bill. Gurdjieff's silences, his aura of assured mastery, left his fellow diners certain that there must be something to his spiritual ideas. Hartmann soon afterwards became one of Gurdjieff's most devoted disciples.[14]

The usual subject matter of Gurdjieff's gatherings was his 'system': a metaphysical fusion of elements borrowed from Tibetan Buddhism,

Sufism and esoteric Christianity, Jewish mysticism and behaviourist psychology. Gurdjieff's explanations for how these various elements related to each other were often difficult to follow, an obscurity amplified by his idiosyncratic, strongly accented Russian (he had grown up speaking the regional Greek dialect of his father, and never lost his thick accent in other languages), and by the freedom with which he scattered references to occult paraphernalia – the ennea-gram, the law of octaves, the table of hydrogens . . . But the aim of his teaching always came back to the larger truth he was trying to convey, which was that people needed drastically to change how they were living.

. Gurdjieff always wanted newcomers to grasp a first important lesson: that Western civilization had thrown people out of balance, causing their intellectual 'centres' to outweigh their emotional and physical 'centres', and turning them into 'unconscious machines'.[15] This desire to balance humankind's outer and inner development was a central concern for many idealists of the age, echoing the vision of a 'complete life' pursued at Santiniketan-Sriniketan, Dartington Hall and Atarashiki Mura. Once Gurdjieff was sure his listeners had understood this point – and they often did quickly, since the notion of being stuck in a world of unpiloted machines made perfect sense to aristocrats disturbed by proletariat protesters running amok in the streets – then he moved on to his second lesson. This was that his system was one of the few ways people could learn to reconstruct themselves as harmoniously integrated wholes. The Fourth Way would leave them fully conscious and in control of their own des-tinies – and it would also contribute to the creation of a more orderly, peaceful world.

Gurdjieff explained that he had devised the Fourth Way by drawing together modern Western science with three ancient methods of spiritual enlightenment he had discovered on his travels in the East: 'the way of the fakir', who subdues his body through pain; 'the way of the monk', who refines his feelings through devotion; and 'the way of the yogi', who cultivates his intellect through study.[16] His system, he said, would balance out people's intellectual, physical and emotional centres, so that none took precedence over the others. If they followed it, they would progress through various stages of consciousness until they became 'genuine, natural men'.[17] Gurdjieff warned his audience that grasping the Fourth Way theoretically was merely the preliminary step: achieving balance or 'reawakening' required years of 'conscious labour and intentional suffering'.[18] And, since no one could waken themselves alone, those who wished for enlightenment must join a group, a group which would be supervised by 'him who knows' – a teacher whom they must obey absolutely.[19]

To listeners already accustomed to Tsarist absolutism, it was not much of a leap – it was comforting, even – to follow Gurdjieff, embracing another kind of autocratic system. Many of the aristocrats who gathered at Gurdjieff's cafe table or in his rented rooms felt their place in society crumbling, their beliefs, traditions and wealth threatened by industrial modernity and the demands of the proletariat. They craved guidance, confidence, security, and a way to quell what seemed to them the growing chaos of society. The Fourth Way system offered all of these things: as one new disciple put it, it was an 'ark' promising safety 'at the time of the flood'.[20]

Within a short period Gurdjieff had won thirty loyal supporters, and a larger, more dilettante following in both Moscow and St Petersburg. His disciples included teachers, engineers, doctors, guards officers and profession-less aristocrats, an eccentric barrister called Rachmilievitch and a Finnish psychiatrist, Leonid Stjoernval, who was so besotted with his new teacher that he believed him to be Christ in his second coming.[21] Gurdjieff was particularly pleased to win over Julia Osipovna Ostrowska – a Polish woman twenty years his junior, who became his wife.[22] Equally gratifying was the eager discipleship of de Hartmann, whose ballet *The Scarlet Flower* had been one of the first that Serge Diaghilev produced in Moscow, and of de Hartmann's wife Olga, a great-granddaughter of Kaiser Wilhelm I. With followers from such a wide range of milieus, Gurdjieff was convinced that his spiritual system would soon reach into all parts of society; that a spiritual revolution had begun.

From 1912 to 1917, 'the Master', as Gurdjieff was called by his followers, travelled between Moscow and St Petersburg, guiding his group's progress and honing his own system as he did so. 'Shocking' his followers into wakefulness became one of his favourite teaching methods.[23] This strategy might mean furiously berating pupils who failed to remember one of his adages. 'His entire body would shake, his face grow purple and a stream of vituperation would pour out,' one victim remembered.[24] Or it might mean forcing pupils to do things they wouldn't ordinarily contemplate: confessing to the group the worst act they had committed, or donating a thousand roubles to the Fourth Way.[25] Sometimes a shock called for a complete change of lifestyle: one government official was ordered to choose between carnal relations and the Fourth Way.[26] Through these shocks, Gurdjieff meant to shake his followers out of engrained habits and unbalanced patterns of thinking, teaching them to distinguish what he called the '*real* I' – their authentic selves – from the multiple forces that they had been unconsciously allowing to direct their lives.[27] It was the way of the fakir and the way of the monk at once – emotional pain that demanded a show of devotion, which, if properly carried out, would result in becoming 'one's own master'.[28] This, for Gurdjieff, was always the ultimate aim.

An early coup for the Fourth Way came in the conversion of the established spiritual authority P. D. Ouspensky, whose books on mysticism included the acclaimed *Tertium Organum*, which, like the Fourth Way, attempted to reconcile science and the supernatural.[29] After attending one of Gurdjieff's meetings, this serious-minded Russian told Gurdjieff that the Fourth Way surpassed every one of the spiritual models he had encountered before, and that he was going to dedicate himself to it from then on.[30] Ouspensky would be a vital help to Gurdjieff in getting his practical utopia under way. Immediately he began translating Gurdjieff's impassioned rhetoric into his own, more measured explanations of the Fourth Way, which proved vital in widening the system's appeal.

The growing success of the Fourth Way was in large part due to the turbulent political times. People had been 'shaken out of their usual grooves', as Gurdjieff put it, by the 1905 attempt at revolution.[31] When the First World War began, this destabilizing of the status quo only continued on a larger scale. People were drawn as never before to new systems and new ideas, and more and more of them turned up at Gurdjieff's talks, which combined spiritual theory with pronounced pacifist ideals. 'A conscious man refuses war,' Gurdjieff told his audiences. 'Mutual destruction is a manifestation of men who are asleep.'[32] For many at this moment, there was something intoxicating about what Gurdjieff offered, the idea that

1. Rabindranath Tagore surrounded by students at Visva-Bharati, Santiniketan, 1929.

2. Open-air learning, as prescribed by Tagore, 1920s.

3. Modelling modern farming methods at Sriniketan, 1920s.

4. Students cultivating vegetables at Sriniketan, 1920s.

5. Tagore delivering a welcoming address to Mahatma Gandhi and his wife Kasturba at Santiniketan, 1940.

6. Tagore and Leonard Elmhirst at Dartington Hall, 1930.

7. Dorothy and Leonard Elmhirst at Dartington Hall.

8. (*bottom left*) Dorothy Elmhirst (*left*) with Julian and Juliette Huxley (*seated*), experimenting with acupuncture.

9. Margaret Barr's 'Funeral and Wedding', performed
in Dartington's main hall in 1931.

10. Group on Dartington Hall's terrace, 1930s. Back row, left, are Cecil and
Elizabeth Collins. Michael Young sits behind the table with a cigarette.

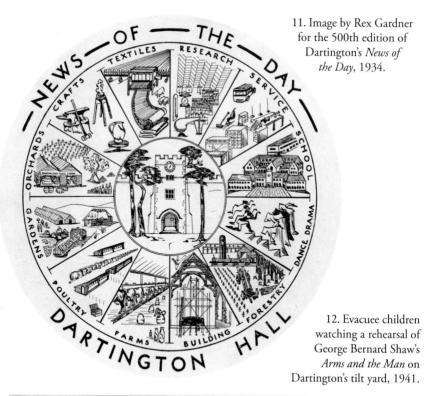

11. Image by Rex Gardner for the 500th edition of Dartington's *News of the Day*, 1934.

12. Evacuee children watching a rehearsal of George Bernard Shaw's *Arms and the Man* on Dartington's tilt yard, 1941.

13. Mushanokōji Saneatsu with other members of his literary coterie, 1909.

14. Harvest in Atarashiki Mura, 1919, with Mushanokōji in the centre.

15. New Villagers pausing for lunch, *c*. 1919 (Mushanokōji is on the left).

16. The New Villagers in 1919 (Mushanokōji wears a straw hat).

17. 'The New Village', *Asahi Graph*, 18 March 1925.

18. Mushanokōji painting in Atarashiki Mura, *c.* 1927.

pursuing a personal, spiritual quest could lead to peace and the spontaneous creation of a better world.

Gurdjieff felt that it was his responsibility to make a drastic push towards social transformation. He stressed that it would only be by converting as many people as possible to the Fourth Way that the 'complete disaster' of a prolonged war – or of new wars starting – could be avoided.[33] Gurdjieff believed that political approaches that 'treated man "in the mass"' would never achieve permanent peace. 'War cannot be stopped by ordinary means,' he told his followers – not by generals or ministers, emperors or parliaments, peace conferences or political theories.[34] For Gurdjieff, as for Mushanokōji Saneatsu, the only way to create the ideal, peaceful society was through an emphasis on the individual. By everyone focusing on their own 'separate, distinct growth' within the context of a supportive, like-minded group, social harmony would arise naturally.[35] If Gurdjieff could develop the perfect small-group model for individual development, then each of his followers could go out and 'win over as many as a hundred other men'; these men would, in turn, win more converts, until a new era of peace and fulfilment was secured for the world.[36]

*

Fourth Way evangelism became increasingly difficult in Russia during the First World War. By late 1916, the country's social order was disintegrating under the pressures of the conflict. Gregori Rasputin – a peasant spiritual teacher who had risen to be the Tsarina's close advisor, and whose mystic-cum-mountebank character bore a striking resemblance to Gurdjieff's own – was assassinated by a group of noblemen who resented his influence. Soon afterwards, a rash of strikes and riots spread across the country. Soldiers deserted the army, no longer willing to die in the service of officers they now considered class enemies. In February 1917, fearing for his life, the Tsar abdicated. Red flags were hung on the public buildings in St Petersburg and a long-drawn-out struggle began between the communist Red Army, the anti-communist White Army and numerous other political factions. Mass demonstrations, violent skirmishes and bodies in the streets became a feature of life. By spring, Gurdjieff had decided that he needed to find a safer place for his pupils, who were mostly members of the old ruling elite. This was no easy task.

For the next five years, Gurdjieff found himself shepherding an entourage of thirty or so disciples through a landscape devastated by conflict. They travelled by cart, railway, even by foot, and were never sure whether it would be safer to pretend loyalty to the Reds or the Whites. This was a character-forging period for Gurdjieff. The trials of the road forced him to set aside any lingering doubts about his vocation, and to inhabit fully the role he had chosen for himself as 'him who knows' – a devoted pacifist and spiritual redeemer for uncertain times.

To begin with, Gurdjieff tried settling in Essentuki, a spa town of mineral springs and luxury hotels at the foot of the Caucasian Mountains. Here the group was unexpectedly swelled by the arrival of twenty-eight of his relatives. They told him that most of the inhabitants of his home town, including his father, had been massacred by the Turks. The death of peaceable Yiannis Georgiades confirmed Gurdjieff in his view that the war, and nationalism in general, was a sign of a deeper human disorder. He decided that there could never be too many conscripts to his system of reform, and he invited his relatives to join his entourage. When his well-born disciples complained, he told them sharply that mixing with the lower classes was a good psychological shock. The setting aside of the class system would be a central component of the alternative life offered by the Institute for the Harmonious Development of Man.

By 1919, the violence of Russia's civil war threatened even the backwater of Essentuki. Gurdjieff and his group relocated to Tbilisi, the capital of Georgia, then the following year to Constantinople. They continued from there to Berlin. All these cities – reeling from the after-effects of the First World War – proved inhospitable to Gurdjieff's assorted band of followers. As he journeyed from one place to the next, he conceived the idea of establishing a permanent community as a training ground for the Fourth Way. Safe from the world of 'mad machines' – people lacking self-control and independence because they were out of balance – he and his followers would perfect a pattern of harmonious living. The community would attempt to redeem the world from future wars by setting an example of a proactively pacifist, balanced mode of existence. It could also serve as a refuge for the enlightened, Gurdjieff told his followers, in the event of another 'flood of evil engulfing the world'.[37]

The hardships of the road didn't mean that Gurdjieff let his pupils slacken in their regime of shocks. He imposed fasts, forced husbands and wives to live apart, ordered the women to give up their jewellery to pay for train tickets and food. His career as a teacher had always been laced with philandering, and his liaisons with his followers continued even on the move – justified as another source of beneficial upheaval. His disciples embraced this life of psychological challenges, which, one of them remembered, were 'so penetrating that everyone seemed to be stripped spiritually naked'.[38] In spite of this rough treatment, Gurdjieff's following only grew. The First World War had destroyed Europe's moral certainty, and this confident guru, offering 'to wake people up' to a new and peaceable society, attracted idealists in almost every major town through which he passed.

Not all of Gurdjieff's pupils fully appreciated his system. P. D. Ouspensky, who had been so taken by it when he first met Gurdjieff in the cafes of Moscow, remained convinced of the general outline of the Fourth Way. But he began to doubt whether some aspects – like Gurdjieff's endless shocks – were strictly necessary. By the time the group reached Constantinople, he was fed up. Rather than confronting Gurdjieff, however, he asked for his blessing to travel to England, where he had been invited to give talks on Fourth Way mysticism by Lady Rothermere, the wealthy wife of the owner of the *Daily Mail*. Gurdjieff, who had noticed Ouspensky's growing discontent, agreed, seeing the chance to get rid of a critic and gain a missionary for his spiritual system in one go.

It proved a highly successful move. A few months later, while Gurdjieff was still casting around in vain for a place to start his community, Ouspensky wrote with the news that the English wanted him to come to London. Gurdjieff arrived in 1922, leaving most of his disciples behind him to continue looking for a base in Germany. Ouspensky greeted him with enthusiastic accounts of how his lectures on the Fourth Way had been attended by London's foremost intellectuals – including T. S. Eliot, Aldous Huxley and Gerald Heard (future Dartington habitué and founder of Trabuco

College).[39] One day in the West Kensington Philosophical Hall, Clifford Sharp, the editor of the *New Statesman*, sat in the front row with A. R. Orage, editor of *The New Age*. The latter was so impressed by Ouspensky that he had brought along his favourite protégée, the New Zealand short-story writer Katherine Mansfield. While these famous names meant little to Gurdjieff, he grasped the salient point. The war had done for England what revolution had done for Russia: shaken people out of their complacency and set them longing for some new model for how to live. It was familiar territory, promising for furthering his goal of changing the world, so he began at once to organize lectures of his own.

Ouspensky delighted English moderns by packaging up the 'folk wisdom' of the Russian steppes in a clear, civilized lecturing style. But this was no match for the wild, anarchic mannerisms of Gurdjieff. Like Tagore, Gurdjieff seemed to be bringing the East's spiritual wisdom to the West in person, offering a tangible alternative to the mindset of materialistic competition that had led to the war. For many listeners, there was something irresistibly commanding in the way he sat in a salon or on a stage, entirely comfortable as he stared mutely at his audience, stroking his moustache with thumb and forefinger until the mood took him to speak. His discourse might be disjointed, meandering and contradictory, but this was obscured by the fact that it was in Russian – translated by his beautiful, aristocratic disciple Olga de Hartmann. The feeling that Gurdjieff was a prophet was solidified by his erratic, unmeasured behaviour: his heavy drinking and insulting brusqueness were taken by the reserved English as a sign of someone who saw beyond artificial social constraints and lived instead by a deeper wisdom.

A swathe of London's intelligentsia opened their purses and address books. Gurdjieff, heartened by this friendly reception, felt that here, at last, his message was being understood. He decided he would establish his utopian stronghold in a house in Hampstead – but the idea was short-lived. The Home Office, suspecting Gurdjieff of spreading Bolshevism, refused his entourage permission to stay on in England.[40] That autumn, Gurdjieff's English supporters, marshalled by Ouspensky, helped him to find a permanent home in France – a former Carmelite priory a few hours' drive from Paris. The building had once belonged to Madame de Maintenon, one of

Louis XIV's mistresses. Now Gurdjieff was to rent it from the widow of Fernand Labori, the lawyer of Alfred Dreyfus. He gave this grand property the name of the 'Harmonious Institute for the Development of Man'. He wanted it to be a prototype for Fourth Way life: a community of people following his system of self-development, rejecting the materialism and competition of the outside world and helping one another up the scale of spiritual consciousness. It would, Gurdjieff hoped, be a place so compelling in its example that it would inspire widespread conversion to the Fourth Way.

*

Ringing the bell beside the high iron gates of the Prieuré des Basses Loges and entering the courtyard of the elegant building of honey-coloured stone, Katherine Mansfield found herself in a community so bizarre that she felt as if she had washed up in *Gulliver's Travels*. It was October 1922, and Mansfield was thirty-four. She was in the late stages of tuberculosis, her emaciated body racked with pain. But it was existential discontent that had brought her to the institute. The death of her brother and so many friends in the brutal years of the First World War had convinced her that her solitary, intellectual existence of writing what she now thought of as 'little stories like birds bred in cages' wasn't enough. She began seeking out a more idealistic model of living, a place where she could pursue a life of the spirit, of the emotions and of community – an entirely new mode of existence.[41] At the Harmonious Institute for the Development of Man, she believed that she had found what she was looking for. 'Simply everything is different,' Mansfield wrote to her husband John Middleton Murry, who had stayed in London. 'Not only languages but food, ways, people, music, methods, hours – all.'[42]

Mansfield didn't meet Gurdjieff that first day; she was welcomed instead by the other communards. A disciple led her up the staircase to one of the luxurious suites of rooms on the second floor of the priory, known as 'the Ritz'. She admired its ornate ceilings, the gilt mirrors that hung on the walls, and the tall windows which looked onto a formal garden with fountains, long flower beds and an avenue of lime trees.[43] But she discovered that most inhabitants lived on the floor above hers, the 'Monks' Corridor', not seeming to mind the small, spartan bedrooms, each furnished with coarse blankets, a rickety chair, a scrap of carpet. She imagined that her literary reputation might be one reason she was lodged in luxury – Gurdjieff hoping she would draw more followers – but there was also a certain Alice-in-Wonderland arbitrariness to the allocation of rooms that seemed to fit this appealingly strange new world.

The next morning, a peal from the bell tower woke her at eight. She lay in bed and took stock of her situation, trying to ignore the iciness of the sheets against her legs. There were fireplaces in the rooms, and a central heating system, but several residents had already explained to her that Gurdjieff disapproved of their use – low temperatures were apparently a good way of shocking you into spiritual awareness. Mansfield had listened with interest to the descriptions of the shocks. She felt ready to try anything, live in any way that released her from bourgeois social conformity – from a world in which 'everything, and worse, everybody seemed a compromise and so flat, so dull, so mechanical'.[44] She wanted to learn how to cut through the artificial trappings of polite society to the true 'essence' of existence – 'to live by what is permanent in the soul' and to share her life with others who shared this desire for authenticity.[45] It was in this frame of mind that she had first heard Ouspensky speak about the Fourth Way in London. The lecture felt to her like a revelation, a sudden illumination of the type of enlightenment and idealistic companionship she craved. And so, eventually, she had done it. She had committed to joining the Institute for the Harmonious Development of Man, taking what she called her 'Leap into the Dark'.[46]

By the time that Mansfield had dressed and found the breakfast room, the priory's sixty-odd inhabitants had finished their toast and coffee and were being allotted work by Gurdjieff. Orage told her who everyone was. There was a nucleus of Eastern Europeans, including the de Hartmanns, and the artist Alexandre de Salzmann – a friend of Rainer Maria Rilke and Wassily Kandinsky – and his wife Jeanne, who had studied dance at the famous eurhythmics institute of Émile Jaques-Dalcroze in Hellerau. There were the disciples, like Orage himself, who had joined Gurdjieff from England. There was another group comprised of Gurdjieff's many relatives, who didn't appear so much interested in spiritual awakening as in their past. They read Russian newspapers, discussed Russian politics, and reminisced about the joys of black bread and borscht. A handful of children ran around the room, several of them, Orage said, Gurdjieff's own offspring with various of his followers.[47]

As people began to disperse to tackle their chores for the day, Orage told Mansfield that he had been ordered by Gurdjieff to continue digging the ditch that stretched across half the garden. She wondered at this well-respected middle-aged editor meekly submitting to an apparently pointless physical task. As if reading her thoughts, her friend explained that Gurdjieff had chosen this job especially for him; it was by undertaking the tasks most painful to him that he would awake to balanced self-awareness. 'I feel centuries old, years younger and infinitely stronger,' Orage assured Mansfield, 'and I do not despair of one day being real and really human.'[48] Envious of his clarity of purpose, Mansfield waited for her own task to be announced. It was an anticlimax to be told by Gurdjieff that because of her illness her only duty was to 'eat, walk in the garden, pick the flowers and rest *much*'.[49]

Wandering through the autumnal grounds, she found a group clearing the undergrowth from the woodland of fir, beech and oak – a Herculean task since the priory's land consisted of 250 overgrown acres. Others, dressed in ragged, paint-spattered trousers, were working on construction projects. On one side of the lime avenue, a 'study house' capable of seating an audience of 300 was being cobbled together from iron girders taken from an old French air force hangar. On the other side, a group was digging out a Turkish bath so that Gurdjieff could introduce the community to one of the great pleasures of his youth. Mansfield was impressed by how, at the institute, philosophy took second place to activity. 'Practice is first,' she reported to her husband. 'You simply have to wake up instead of talking about it.'[50] She admired the labourers' cooperation, and the single-minded determination with which they went about their tasks. But this dedication didn't seem to satisfy Gurdjieff, who flitted between the projects, appearing silently behind a group of workers and urging them on to 'super-efforts', shouting at them in Russian and the words of English he was quickly acquiring: 'Scurry! Queeker! Queeker!'[51] He told Mansfield that it was essential that the priory open to public visits in the new year: this was the next step in converting the world to the Fourth Way.[52]

Mansfield soon realized that, at the institute, hard physical labour was not just the means of creating a model community. It was a purpose in itself: to waken people's physical centres and to teach them composure and stoicism. It also provided an opportunity for Gurdjieff's ongoing campaign to dismantle people's routine behaviour and beliefs: he would deliberately disrupt his followers' work, or set them tasks that flaunted common sense. One morning Mansfield watched him order Orage to fill in the ditch he had spent the last week digging. Another day he drove cows over a freshly planted flower bed. And he instructed several Englishwomen to learn foreign words as they gardened: every ten minutes, they had to stop digging to pull out lists of phrases they kept tucked under their watch straps. Mansfield admired her fellow communards' absorption in this strange way of being, describing them in a letter to her husband as 'living people who are strange and quick and not ashamed to be themselves'.[53] She felt instinctively that she belonged to this community of seekers: all resisting the stultifying return to normality that so many people had succumbed to after the war; all trying desperately to live in a more balanced, more self-knowing way – and by doing so, to find a better path for the world. 'They are my own people at last,' she told Murry.

As her physical condition deteriorated, Mansfield began to spend afternoons in the outbuildings and the priory itself. She watched six women tend a motley collection of farm animals, charmed by what she thought of as the 'mystical pigs' and the 'cosmic rabbits and hens'.[54] These were Gurdjieff's attempt to make his community self-sufficient – although the institute would never come anywhere near to being able to feed itself, even less so than the other practical utopias of the period. In the large kitchen, Mansfield sat observing Gurdjieff's wife Madame Ostrowska presiding over the cooking. The chopping, banging saucepans and joking of the cook's assistants filled her with the pleasant sense that she had transcended the isolated intellectualism of her past. She wrote to her Russian-born literary friend S. S. Koteliansky, thinking his origins would help him to sympathize with her joy in the Slavic bustle, that here they were all learning how to 'really live'.[55] When her lungs were at their worst, forcing her to breathe in quick, painful gasps, she withdrew on Gurdjieff's orders to a wooden platform in the cow byre, breathing

in the cold air and the bovine odour – a Russian remedy for tuberculosis.

At six o'clock in the evening, the priory bell rang for the second
time and manual labour gave way to sociability. Mansfield liked to
sit with the de Hartmanns in their cramped room on the Monks'
Corridor, discussing methods of spiritual advancement; she mended
the British psychologist Dr James Young's trousers while he built
up her fire; she listened to stories about Gurdjieff's past told by the
two young women he had asked to tend her because of her fragile
health – Adele Kafian, a Lithuanian, and Olgivanna, an aristocratic
dancer from Montenegro.[56] The theme running through all these
conversations was people's dissatisfaction with 'the old ways and
means of achievement', Kafian remembered, and their desire to find
a new shape for their lives.[57] To her surprise, Mansfield found a
particular pleasure in the company of the female communards. 'I
remember I used to think – if there was one thing I could not bear
in a community it would be the women,' she wrote to her husband.
'But now the women are nearer and far dearer than the men.'[58] She
also delighted in feeling part of a place where the envious national-
isms of the external world had so demonstrably been replaced by
another philosophy – an internationally inclusive quest for harmony.

The inhabitants of the institute met for supper in one of two
dining rooms. The first was gloomy, furnished with a rough table
and benches, and was preferred by Gurdjieff's relatives. The so-called
'English' dining room, where everyone else ate, was gilt-mirrored
and wood-panelled – a room where Madame de Maintenon had
once entertained Louis XIV.[59] Food at the institute was highly unpredictable: sometimes a 'Gogol feast' was served, as Mansfield
described it, lavish with butter and cream and food from every
corner of the world; sometimes home-grown vegetables and meat,
boiled together in their juices to promote nutrition; on a few occa-
sions a total fast.[60] Gurdjieff explained that variety was what was
necessary to wake people up – although, like the lack of heating, it
also had something to do with the volatile state of the community's
finances.

On Saturday, suppers usually ended with the 'toast to the idiots'.
In this unique Fourth Way ritual Gurdjieff classified everyone around
the table as a species of idiot, and ordered a toast to be drunk to

each species.[61] There were 'ordinary idiots' and 'hopeless idiots', 'compassionate idiots' and 'enlightened idiots', 'doubting idiots', 'swaggering idiots' and 'patented idiots'.[62] The notion that all of mankind was bound together in common idiocy – along with the effects of the assorted calvados, slivovitz, vodka and Armagnac they drank – united the community as much as, if not more than, all of Gurdjieff's preaching or lecturing about the fellowship of mankind. Like the shocks, the toast was another way of paring back the artificial layers of civilization, emphasizing that all people were equal in their ignorance. It was only when they admitted this freely, Gurdjieff told his followers, that they would start to learn to control their own lives – to 'act rather than be acted upon'.[63]

After supper everyone congregated in the salon. Mansfield, sitting close to the fire, watched as Gurdjieff conducted his pupils through the exercises that he said were vital to developing harmonious balance.[64] Some evenings Gurdjieff led everyone through a series of mental gymnastics: communicating in Morse code, calculating sequences of sums, memorizing opera titles.[65] On other evenings there was the 'Stop!' exercise: while dancing around vigorously, pupils would be ordered by Gurdjieff to freeze in position – long-held pauses designed to be painful, and thereby to 'raise consciousness'. Orage, coming to sit, panting, beside Mansfield after one such session, said that for him it symbolized everything the Fourth Way was about. 'The institute is just a "Stop!" exercise for all one's former habits.'[66]

The exercise Mansfield liked best was the one that closed the evening: sacred dancing. With the help of Thomas de Hartmann, Gurdjieff had composed music for tambourines, drums and the priory's prized Bechstein piano, featuring strains from Caucasian and Central Asian folk music, from Russian Orthodox liturgical music and countless other sources. Disciples danced according to 'the movements' – sequences choreographed by Gurdjieff, inspired, he explained, by 'the sacred gymnastics of the esoteric schools, the religious ceremonies of the antique Orient, and the ritual movement of monks and dervishes'.[67] Mansfield particularly loved the 'Initiation of a Priestess' dance, in which a young woman is shown renouncing the world and being blessed by the chief priestess. This represented 'the whole life of woman – but everything!', Mansfield wrote ecstatically to her husband – a performance that 'gave me more of a woman's life than any book or poem'.[68] Gurdjieff, she wrote, had shown her that art need not be a solitary, drily intellectual pursuit, but something richly infused with spirituality and a part of communal life.

Mansfield was touched when Gurdjieff organized an English-style Christmas feast for her and the other disciples from London (Russian Christmas was celebrated a fortnight later): there was wine, whisky, gin, cognac and an immense Christmas tree; a sheep, a pig and two turkeys were slaughtered.[69] Shortly after the festivities, her husband John Middleton Murry arrived, finally persuaded by her ecstatic descriptions of the institute to overcome his fear of tuberculosis. But on 9 January 1924, after watching the 'Initiation of a Priestess' one last time, Mansfield suffered a haemorrhage while going upstairs. She died almost instantly.

In Mansfield's last letters from the priory, she described her experience there as the 'very great wonderful adventure of my life'.[70] She had escaped from an outside world that felt like 'a dream' populated by 'sleepers'.[71] She had discovered a new kind of existence, one where people seemed fully awake. Gurdjieff, with his charismatic presence, manual tasks, toasts and shocks, was, for Mansfield, 'the embodiment' of this new existence – 'but at a remote distance', since she spoke with him rarely.[72] What really set life at the institute apart from the outside world, she thought, was its regime of physical labour, creativity and spirituality – and, above all, its dedicated inhabitants, idealists like herself, who were united and supportive of one another in their search for something deeper and more vital in human existence.

*

Gurdjieff seemed an invulnerable, superhuman figure to most of his followers, but in the early years of the institute his private feeling was that he had entered 'one of the maddest periods of [his] life'.[73] He was faced with the challenge of running and financing a community of nearly a hundred people in a foreign country. His difficulties were increased by his own hubris: his vaulting ambition to expand the community exponentially, to draw in disciples who, once trained, would go out into the world and continue to spread the Fourth Way.

This evangelism was driven partly by personal vanity, but also by the sincere belief that his spiritual philosophy held the key to world peace – much more so than the League of Nations, the disarmament conferences and the various other political initiatives to promote international cooperation that were flourishing in the 1920s. These, Gurdjieff thought, were merely extensions of the world of 'mad machines'. Yet instead of his institute becoming a place that was actively reforming the world, he found himself struggling simply to keep it going, afflicted by money troubles, by the mockery of onlookers, and by the refusal of the scientific establishment to support him.

Gurdjieff's disciple P. D. Ouspensky, who had remained in England, played a vital fundraising role in the institute's early days. He marshalled a group of wealthy British patrons who agreed to pay most of the priory's rent. But through the 1920s, Ouspensky began to have doubts about the validity of the Fourth Way as it was made manifest in Gurdjieff's community. A deeply cerebral man himself, he couldn't understand the point of the endless manual labour; nor did he think it right that Gurdjieff was treated by disciples with such reverence. His relationship with Gurdjieff began to cool, and funds from Britain no longer crossed the Channel in such abundance. In 1924, Ouspensky cut ties with Gurdjieff completely (although his independent-minded wife Madame Ouspensky remained living at the institute, a constant reminder to Gurdjieff of his former pupil's betrayal).

How, Gurdjieff wondered, was he to pay for the priory now? He had given up on the goal of self-sufficiency, which had never been central to his hopes for the community. Half his disciples were indigent, and though the other half were better off, they were far from capable of meeting the costs of renting and restoring the huge building, equipping it with everything from linen to livestock, and feeding a hundred people daily. Added to these expenses was Gurdjieff's determination to purchase the priory outright, in order to create a permanent stronghold for his philosophy.

Rising as always to a challenge, the guru launched an array of businesses in Paris. The capital was in full modernist bloom: Ernest Hemingway wrote, Gertrude Stein entertained, Man Ray photographed, Jean Cocteau staged plays. Gurdjieff arrived on the fringes of this scene, offering his services as a hypnotist for rich drug addicts and alcoholics. He set up two restaurants in Montmartre with Russian émigrés, and began speculating in Middle Eastern oil shares.[74] His boldness and personal magnetism fitted him well for such dealings and, notwithstanding his inability to speak much French, several of the enterprises became reasonably successful. But the income was irregular, and whatever came into the priory was quickly spent.

Gurdjieff bought a car to ease the exhausting commute between Fontainebleau and Paris. He had never driven before, but after a few days grinding jerkily around the priory grounds, he set off victoriously in the Citroën through the front gates. It was the beginning of a love affair with motoring so passionate that it even crept into the language of his philosophy: he began to compare his pupils to 'spoiled automobiles', and his community to 'a repair shop for broken-down motor-cars'.[75] He remained a terrible driver all the same, ploughing erratically down the *route nationale* as if his were the only vehicle on the road. His passengers derived little comfort from his assurance that it was possible to escape from the mechanical laws of accident by developing your inner will.

Despite Gurdjieff's new business ventures, the institute was again soon on the verge of financial ruin. Katherine Mansfield had put the priory on the cultural map, but she hadn't won Gurdjieff the additional support he had hoped for. Instead, rumours began to circulate in London of the priory's Dickensian lifestyle of hard labour and short rations.[76] D. H. Lawrence (who, with his wife Frieda, had briefly tried out communitarian living with Mansfield and Murry in a draughty cottage in Cornwall) condemned the institute as a 'rotten, false, self-conscious place of people playing a sickly stunt', after a brief visit.[77] Gurdjieff tried to diversify his base by winning backing in Paris, but he found that the French preferred rationalism or Christianity to the Fourth Way. The foreigners in the capital city seemed more interested in bohemian living and art than in spiritual progress. Few new members were joining the community.

Gurdjieff opened the study house to visitors on Saturdays, hoping both to raise funds and to turn the tide of public opinion. As the warm summer evenings faded into night, the priory entrance gates admitted a stream of journalists, special correspondents and literary voyeurs, local dignitaries, bohemian artists, tourists and seekers after spiritual redemption.[78] They swarmed across the grounds, past well-tended flower beds and glow-worms dancing at the edge of the woods, craning to see Gurdjieff's followers as if they were on safari. If they were lucky, they glimpsed the eccentric Mrs Finch, mother of a famous mountaineer, who liked to tie blue ribbons to the tail of her favourite cow before walking it around the garden.[79] Inside the study house, visitors found long benches waiting for them below windows painted in imitation of stained glass. They watched, fascinated, as Gurdjieff took his pupils, clad all in white, through the memory and 'Stop!' exercises, and the sacred dances.

But the donations and mass conversion that Gurdjieff had hoped for did not follow. While some visitors were genuinely interested in the institute's unique principles, others viewed it as an elaborate absurdist joke. The American novelist Sinclair Lewis called it 'a cross between a cabaret and a harem' – and 'a hell of a place to live'.[80] Despite his wish to convert the world, Gurdjieff refused to modify his system of shocks to make the community more palatable to visitors. Instead, he singled visitors out for doses of Fourth Way treatment. One of his favourite tactics was to offer a sheep's eyeball to a guest at dinner, with no indication as to whether this was an honour, a spiritual test or a joke.[81] Another was brusquely to demand money at inopportune moments. He also liked to take strait-laced male guests into the Turkish baths. Lying back in the steam, naked but for the towel wrapped around his head, he joked about his fellow bathers' bodies and sexual prowess, or held forth with mock gravitas about how the 'little mister' could lead the 'big mister' astray.[82]

Much of this fell flat. Without an acceptance of Gurdjieff's theory of shocks, his tactics were obnoxious, and worked against his aim to win people over. But it was his philosophical system that was the biggest stumbling block. Before he had set up the priory, the woolly vagueness of his ideas had been an asset: listeners of many hues could align their own ideas with the Fourth Way, and it was possible for them to believe that Gurdjieff knew more than he was telling – that all his ideas *did* fit together in a logical system, which they would understand once they attained enlightenment. Now that the Fourth Way was embodied in the daily life of the priory, however, its faults and inconsistencies became remarkably clear – at least to the outsiders looking in.

When opening the community to the public failed to inspire a wide uptake of the Fourth Way, Gurdjieff decided to court the scientific establishment directly. Since his boyhood in Kars he had loved science (without quite applying its methodical, rational principles), and he was certain there was a scientific basis for the Fourth Way. He told visitors that the system amalgamated the 'mystical spirit of the East' and the 'scientific spirit of the West'.[83] Fortunately for Gurdjieff, the interwar years, with their apocalyptic fears and outré hopes, were a period when the newly emerging disciplines of psychology, psychoanalysis and psychiatry were often combined with philosophy and spiritualism.[84] From D. H. Lawrence to Carl Jung to the Theosophical leader Madame Blavatsky, it was common for those seeking new ideas about humankind's inner life to bring scientific and spiritual concepts together. Yet from the point of view of the eminent British psychiatrist Lionel Penrose, who agreed to visit the institute for a weekend, Gurdjieff's hopes of scientific validation were in vain. Penrose complained that all that Gurdjieff was offering his students was a 'birth fantasy' in the guise of becoming a harmonious soul; and that if his system did manage to rid people of neuroses, it was only by dint of replacing those neuroses with a narcissistic identification with Gurdjieff himself.[85]

Gurdjieff had better luck with Maurice Nicoll and James Young, respected British psychologists who had served in the First World War, and who had a deep interest in spiritualism. The two men had studied with Jung in Switzerland, but were not satisfied that his system offered an effective cure for neurosis.[86] Hoping Gurdjieff's would do better, they sold their shared Harley Street practice to join the priory and find out. Gurdjieff showed his pleasure at their arrival by setting them the most arduous tasks he could think of – a way of showcasing his system of shocks. Nicoll, who had brought with him his wife and newborn daughter, was appointed kitchen boy. For several months he rose before dawn to light the boilers, then washed everyone's plates three times a day.[87] Despite – or because of – this torment, he was won over. After his time at the institute, Nicoll would go on to teach the Fourth Way in Britain. He was exactly the kind of scientific disciple Gurdjieff had hoped for: intelligent and with an established professional reputation, but also fully persuaded by the Fourth Way. James Young, on the other hand, left the priory after only six months, convinced that there was no science behind the Fourth Way at all.[88] Still, it is remarkable that Gurdjieff's system, bizarre as it was, had seemed promising enough to two leading doctors that they uprooted their lives to try it out.

Courting scientists did not solve Gurdjieff's money troubles or help him win many new converts, and so he was driven to try yet another strategy. On 13 December 1923, a notice appeared in a Paris theatrical paper: 'Professor Gurdjieff may be unknown in Paris, but he is famous throughout the world. The first performance by his institute, which will be given tonight in the Théâtre des Champs-Élysées, is to present his "movements".'[89] The theatre was decked out as an oriental palace with Turkish carpets, cushions and goatskins. Gurdjieff's pupils greeted the audience wearing oriental costumes and carrying trays of perfumed wine.[90] But as he watched the audience gather, Gurdjieff's mask of cryptic wisdom concealed acute anxiety. He had announced to his followers that 'if within three months' he didn't have 'at least one "cool" million francs' he would 'go up the chimney [. . .] forever'.[91] Everything depended on this new money-making venture.

The performance began: Gurdjieff strode up and down the stage, directing his disciples in an amped-up version of the exercises they practised in the study house. The audience was delighted at the show's originality, although worried by the degree of control Gurdjieff seemed to exert over his followers. Despite the interest of those who attended, ticket sales barely covered the cost of putting on the performance.[92] No mass of converts flocked to the institute. It was clear to Gurdjieff that if things continued in the same vein, bankruptcy would follow. It was not the Fourth Way that needed to change, Gurdjieff told himself. No, the problem lay in the people who had been coming to see the priory and his performances: sophisticated Parisian modernists, cynical journalists, conventional scientists. They were too unbalanced, too wrapped in machine-like somnolence to be candidates for conversion. He must, he thought, seek out people more suitable for Fourth Way enlightenment – open-minded people who were not bound by tradition. He would go to America.

*

The young idealists of Manhattan knew and loved the Sunwise Turn. It was one of the first bookshops owned by women in the United States, and a magnet for progressive thinkers.[93] Intellectuals, artists and political activists lounged in the modern, orange armchairs by the open fire, browsing the books piled in heaps on the tables and returning to a subject close to their hearts: contemporary ethics. We live in one of the freest, safest countries in the world, they lamented, but all people care about is getting and spending – the very ideals that precipitated the First World War. Theirs was a generation, as F. Scott Fitzgerald put it in his newly published *This Side of Paradise*, that had grown up 'to find all Gods dead, all wars fought, all faiths in man shaken'.[94]

For one of the regulars at the Sunwise Turn, the playwright Eugene O'Neill, the only meaningful response was existential despair. Others advocated plunging headlong into hedonism, or joining new cultural movements like Dadaism – where nonsense art was a protest against the irrationality of war. But there were others still who longed to address the shortcomings of the time more constructively. They found inspiration by looking to Europe – citing its expanding social democracies, or the psychoanalytical theories of Freud and Jung.[95] The announcement that A. R. Orage, editor of *The New Age* and a leading English radical thinker, was crossing the Atlantic to speak at the bookshop on New Year's Day 1924 filled the group with anticipation.

Gurdjieff had learned from experience that the best approach to launching the Fourth Way was to send a herald before him to whip up expectation, and Orage was the perfect choice. Perched among the batik fabrics and Cézanne prints that the Sunwise Turn sold as a sideline, he enthralled his audience with descriptions of a guru steeped in the mysticism of the East, and of the community he had created after years of spiritual questing. The poet Margaret Anderson found him 'the most persuasive man I have ever met'.[96] Jessie Dwight, one of the owners of the bookshop, immediately offered her services as a secretary – and later married him. By the time Gurdjieff steamed into New York a month later with thirty-five pupils in tow, Orage had a group of the city's idealists lining the harbour to greet him.

Gurdjieff's aim, as he put it with characteristic bluntness, was to sniff out funds and followers from this 'dollar-growing country' like a 'thorough-bred hunting-dog'.[97] 'We live in calm, monotonous days and peaceful nights, we stultify,' he began his lectures, pausing a moment to wait for his Russian to be translated. As he talked, his eyes would scan the audience for the diamond necklace that bespoke a possible donor, for the intense gaze of a likely convert, or – best of all – for someone possessing both at once. His voice rose in a gradual crescendo as he ripped apart the tenets of modern society, his delivery so confident that his listeners felt sure they had stumbled on a truth-teller.[98] As the talk approached its conclusion, Gurdjieff moved from diagnosis to solution and brought in the Fourth Way, with its offer of rebalancing and awakening. While he was describing the institute where the devoted gathered to achieve enlightenment, he gestured discreetly to Orage, indicating those among the crowd he thought would be susceptible to a more intimate discussion after the lecture.

His tactics worked. New York in the Roaring Twenties had an insatiable appetite for the novel and exotic. Within a short time, attending one of Gurdjieff's performances had become a badge of honour among artists, intellectuals and anyone else in search of new values or a good story. Those who heard him speak included the writers Rebecca West, Zona Gale and John O'Hara, the actress Gloria Swanson, and the occultist and explorer (and reputed cannibal) William Seabrook. The venues Orage booked for Gurdjieff grew bigger: after the Sunwise Turn came theatres where Gurdjieff's followers could give demonstrations of their spiritual exercises, and finally there was a talk at Carnegie Hall, where Rabindranath Tagore had spoken just a few years before. Sensational reports of Gurdjieff's community circulated in the newspapers. One *American Weekly* headline read: '"Dr" Gurdjieff and his Magical Secret Life – How to Be a Superman or Superwoman by Feeding Pigs, Dancing Weird Dances All Night and Other Fantastic Antics'.[99]

While some of this interest was voyeuristic, there was much genuine yearning for spiritual enlightenment. At the Neighborhood Playhouse in Greenwich Village, the performance led by Gurdjieff – the 'monk in a tuxedo', one watcher called him – was so compelling that it won over three influential cultural groups to the Fourth Way in a single night.[100] The first centred on Margaret Anderson and Jane Heap. Romantic and literary partners, these redoubtable women edited the journal *The Little Review*. They were famed for showcasing pioneering writers like W. B. Yeats and Ezra Pound, and for serializing James Joyce's *Ulysses* (acquiring a legal conviction for circulating obscenity in the process). The second group included the intellectual Waldo Frank, the Harlem Renaissance novelist Jean Toomer and the critic Gorham Munson.[101] Third, there was a circle of intellectuals whose chief spokesman was Herbert Croly, editor of *The New Republic*, the journal set up by Dorothy Elmhirst, co-founder of Dartington Hall. While listening to Gurdjieff, these writers and artists began to feel that they must abandon the aridity of a purely intellectual life and take a leap into an esoteric existence of harmonious balance, becoming pioneers in forging a saner world. Gurdjieff returned the compliment of their enthusiasm by pronouncing the Americans a race more intelligent, energetic and generous than any other.[102]

Not all of America fell at Gurdjieff's feet. As winter shaded into spring and he toured Boston, Philadelphia and Chicago with his disciples, he was sometimes greeted with scorn and laughter – or with a sheer lack of interest (the most depressing reaction of all). Yet Gurdjieff had achieved what he set out to do – raising money and sowing the Fourth Way in America – and when he finished his tour in June 1924, it was with his head held high. He could pay off the priory's debts. The three groups he had won over at the Neighborhood Playhouse continued to send contributions across the Atlantic for years, and, in a number of cases, crossed over themselves to visit or join the priory. Some of those who heard Gurdjieff speak started Fourth Way groups, fuelling Gurdjieff's hope that each person he converted would go on to win a hundred converts of their own, contributing to the transformation of the world. Amid the fervour for finding alternative ways of living that was such a central feature of the 1920s, Gurdjieff's methods and his community in France appeared to many like a true utopian vision.

In spite of all his evangelizing, Gurdjieff was wary of the ardour that his ideas had inspired internationally. The Fourth Way by this time had adherents not only in America, France and Britain, but in many of the cities Gurdjieff had stopped in on his flight from Russia. Mabel Dodge Luhan, wealthy literary patron and leading light of the artistic colony of Taos, New Mexico, had even offered him a ranch and $15,000 to set up a new institute in the desert.[103] But Gurdjieff refused her offer. His was a controlling personality, and he decided that, rather than encouraging the opening of new communities, he would focus on the one place where he was absolutely in charge. He returned to France, leaving Orage in America with instructions to ensure that the Fourth Way groups that were starting up there followed the system correctly.

*

Less than a month after Gurdjieff returned to France, the institute met its greatest challenge yet. As the guru was driving back from Paris to Fontainebleau after a well-lubricated lunch, he crashed his Citroën into a tree. His unconscious body, thrown free of the wreckage, was discovered by a gendarme on a bicycle. Since little could be done for him at the hospital, he was taken back to the priory, where he lay in a coma for five days. To his followers it was as if their world teetered on the brink of collapse. 'Without him,' Thomas de Hartmann said, 'the forces of life would stop.'[104] Gurdjieff's disciples silenced the bell in the belfry. His wife and mother lived at his bedside. His pupils kneeled in prayer at the sickroom door, or resorted to superstitious rituals – Fritz Peters, an eleven-year-old boy tasked with tending the chateau's two huge lawns, mowed them obsessively each day, as if it were the only thing keeping Gurdjieff alive.[105] It was a sign of how completely Gurdjieff's community depended on the force of his character.

Gradually Gurdjieff recovered. He began to hobble about the grounds, followed by Peters, who carried an armchair in which he could rest. As if to reassure himself that his influence was still intact, Gurdjieff ordered his followers to embark on a new set of labours. A road was to be built, entire acres of woodland cleared. In a gesture of revenge – after all, it was a tree that had almost killed him – Gurdjieff had his armchair placed in front of a bonfire where the felled trees were burned, and sat for hours enjoying the flames, enveloped in his black coat and astrakhan hat in spite of the summer heat.[106]

Since his long-standing disciples were by now used to his idiosyncrasies, they took this behaviour – distinctly lacking in harmonious balance – in their stride. According to one American visitor, Jean Toomer, who arrived just after the accident, 'extra zest, extra power, extra will' sprang up among them as soon as Gurdjieff was out of bed.[107] But the crash had also sown doubts. How could it be, people whispered to each other in the safety of the vegetable garden, that a man of Gurdjieff's spiritual stature could be subject to the accidents that befall ordinary men? Hadn't he taught them that they could escape from the laws of chance by developing their will? Some decided that it was sacrilegious to scrutinize the meaning of events too closely. Others reached the comforting conclusion that Gurdjieff had crashed on purpose, sacrificing himself in a Christlike gesture to create a grand 'shock' that would test their loyalty.[108] But none of them could forget what the accident had taught them: the man who held their community together was mortal.

Gurdjieff himself, usually so quick with words, offered no explanation. He, too, had been deeply shaken by the affair. He was now almost sixty, and he feared that, had he died, the Fourth Way and the institute that embodied it would have perished with him. That summer he was continually reminded of the fragility of things: his wife was diagnosed with cancer and his mother with liver disease; and in spite of the inflow of American dollars, the account books of the priory remained perilously in the red. In late August, he called everyone together in the study house. 'I don't want to continue as before,' he told them, 'and my new principle is – everything for myself. From today the institute will be nothing.'[109]

There was shock, consternation, and uncertainty. What did Gurdjieff mean? his pupils asked each other. They knew not to question him directly: he always played his cards close to his chest where practical strategy was concerned. Was he giving up on his teaching? Closing down the community? Put off by the continuing uncertainty, a number of less committed pupils left the institute for good. Long-standing followers, many of them with nowhere else to go, looked on anxiously as Gurdjieff delegated control of his Paris businesses to partners and appointed an Englishwoman, Ethel Merston, as the priory's 'director'.

Gradually the future became clearer. Gurdjieff wasn't giving up on teaching the Fourth Way or on his institute. What he had meant by his dramatic announcement was that he was going to write a book. It wasn't an unusual plan for the founder of a utopia, but Gurdjieff was never one to go about things straightforwardly if a dramatic alternative presented itself. After terrifying his disciples with the prospect of the community closing its gates, he abruptly passed all responsibility for its daily routine over to Merston and a few other loyal followers. As the priory's life went on around him, he struggled hour after hour to set down on paper his elaborate but foggy ideas on mysticism, philosophy and balance. He was determined that his book – his utopia translated into literary form – should be nothing less than the Bible, the Koran, the Torah of the twentieth century.

*

While Gurdjieff wrote his way through the second half of the 1920s, his community continued to fascinate idealists on the other side of the Atlantic. More and more Americans turned up at the priory, among them the critic Gorham Munson, the poet Waldo Frank and a quartet of romantically entangled lesbians – Margaret Anderson, Jane Heap, the writer Solita Solano and the actress and singer Georgette Leblanc (formerly the lover of Mushanokōji Saneatsu's hero, the Belgian playwright Maurice Maeterlinck). They had expected to sit at the feet of the charismatic teacher they had met in New York, and to take part in the lifestyle described in such alluring detail by Orage. Instead, they found that the community was being run mainly by Gurdjieff's pupils, who lacked his talent for explaining the purpose of its regime of domestic chores and outdoor labour. The evenings had changed, too: in place of the exotic spiritual exercises, music and dance, there were long readings from Gurdjieff's near-incomprehensible work in progress.[110] In spite of charging his American visitors a hundred dollars a week to visit, Gurdjieff largely ignored them, now convinced that a book would win more converts than teaching ever could.

A few Americans, including Solita Solano, left quickly. But many others still found themselves drawn in by the unusual life at the priory. The community, enriched by dollars, had become more surreal than ever. Gurdjieff spent all new funds rapidly and quixotically, on grand feasts and bizarre acquisitions like his fleet of red bicycles, which left the grounds filled for days with the sound of crashes and laughter as the inhabitants learned to ride.[111] Even more alluring for the Americans than this daily circus was the sense that every member of the community was straining to achieve personal enlightenment – or even the enlightenment of humankind as a whole. Whether digging, eating, or listening to Gurdjieff read, they were earnest and single-minded in their concentration.

In some ways Gurdjieff's withdrawal from teaching helped the Fourth Way rather than hindered it, since it made it easy for incomers to project their own hopes and dreams onto the community. Jean Toomer, who wanted to find a way to tear down the colour barrier, was struck by how spiritual seekers of every background were welcomed at the priory. Jane Heap, having closed down *The Little Review* to free herself to pursue enlightenment, thought the Fourth Way could be used to reform the 'world-mind', ultimately leading to the production of a higher form of culture.[112] Gorham Munson saw Gurdjieff as someone who stood apart from the mainstream of Western thought and who, in a time of acute ideological crisis, was one of the few people to offer a real intellectual alternative.[113] Visitors were able to embrace the parts of his philosophy that resonated with them, and to ignore the rest. This multivalence kept the community relevant and attractive to idealists looking for radical ways to confront social problems. But it also led to the gradual breakdown of any feeling of unity among the institute's inhabitants. With no active leader, no manifesto of ideals like that of Atarashiki Mura, the sense of the institute as a practical utopia – a group of people advancing collectively towards a better way of living – began to disintegrate. It started to seem just an ill-assorted collection of people who happened to be in the same place, each one independently pursuing spiritual fulfilment.

Meanwhile, Gurdjieff had decided that his book would have to be a trilogy. One volume wasn't sufficient for all he wanted to accomplish – although even that first book was proving hard to write. The task of articulating his ideas coherently did not come naturally to him, but he was by now well-practised at rationalizing his difficulties. It was, he told his disciples, because he was reaching for higher truths than anyone before him that his writing demanded such 'super-efforts'. Since he liked to be surrounded by admirers at all times, he also informed them that higher truths were best arrived at when he was distracted by company (forcing him to concentrate harder). This theory manifested itself in a unique literary approach: he would scribble on a bench in the priory grounds while surrounded by labouring work groups; invite pupils on jaunts to all-night cafes in Montmartre, instructing them to talk at him continuously while he wrote; or select a group to accompany him on a road trip in the Fiat that had replaced his damaged Citroën.[114] Driving at breakneck speed to the Monte Carlo casinos, or to Switzerland to picnic in the snow, Gurdjieff would suddenly screech to a halt, jump out and sit down at the roadside, noting a promising idea that had just come to him, while his passengers grew colder and colder.[115] Several pupils took to hiding behind bushes when they saw Gurdjieff approaching in his driving cap and gloves.

In 1926, Gurdjieff's mother died from liver disease; a few months later, his thirty-seven-year-old wife died of cancer. Fearing that his turn would be next, Gurdjieff turned to his writing with renewed determination. By the autumn of 1928 he succeeded in finishing a draft of the first volume of the trilogy that he named *All and Everything* – a characteristic indication of what he hoped he would achieve. The book was made up of a series of stories that a Gurdjieffian figure called Beelzebub tells his grandson on an interstellar space-ship. It aimed to lay out the structure of the universe, the fallen state of man, and the path to redemption. But its opening line is a good indication of its shortcomings: 'It was in the year 223 after the creation of the World, by objective time-calculation, or, as it would be said here on the "Earth", in the year 1921 after the birth of Christ'.[116] Its obscure style, dislocated syntax and opaque allegories meant that it was all but unreadable.

A few of Gurdjieff's pupils, including Orage, who was still leading the Fourth Way movement in America, gently drew the author's attention to his book's deficiencies. They offered the excuse that the problem probably lay in the translation: Gurdjieff, claiming that no single language gave him access to spiritual truth, had written in Armenian, Russian and a smattering of other languages, which then had to be deciphered and translated by his pupils as he went along.[117] In reply to his critics, Gurdjieff insisted that he had in fact intended the book to conceal as much as to reveal – that people must search for the truth themselves, reading the book at least three times for its full value. It was not just a matter of 'burying the bone', he told his disciples with pride. 'I bury whole dog.'[118] Nonetheless, he allowed his literary followers – Orage, Margaret Anderson, Jean Toomer and others – to help polish the book. The editing process was so lengthy that it was only published in 1950, twenty-two years later.[119] *All and Everything* never achieved the wide readership that Gurdjieff had hoped for. Yet the vagueness of his writing, like the woolliness of the philosophy that underpinned his community, had the advantage of allowing people to interpret his system how they wished. His trilogy would have a surprisingly strong influence on spiritual thought in the second half of the twentieth century.[120]

*

The glory days of the Harmonious Institute for the Development of Man ended in 1929. After the Wall Street Crash, the American dollars and visitors Gurdjieff had come to rely on disappeared. At the same time, the growth of totalitarian regimes across Europe gave rise to a widespread sense that immediate, practical paths to securing world peace were needed – not esoteric spirituality, however pacifistic its intent. But the factor that most undermined the institute was Gurdjieff himself. With age, his magnetism declined, his charm and mystique giving way to an unappealing insecurity. Plagued by the sense that the passing years were eating away at his powers, that he had failed to secure his spiritual system in either utopian or literary form, he continually and obsessively tested his pupils' loyalty – and whatever their response, he was never re-assured. He became difficult and disruptive, making ever more peremptory demands on his followers so that they could not focus on their spiritual training. When Orage visited the priory with his new wife, he was so enraged by Gurdjieff's efforts to separate him from her that he broke with Gurdjieff entirely.

The loss of this vital disciple was followed by others. Seasoned pupils like Madame Ouspensky and the de Hartmanns began leaving the priory, no longer able to stand Gurdjieff's antics. Gurdjieff tried to control the situation by telling anyone who would listen that he had planned this general dispersal, since he now required solitude to finish his trilogy. But the absence of a chorus of adoring followers meant that these words rang hollow even to him. Apart from anything else, Gurdjieff and the handful who struggled on with him were in dire need of money. Ouspensky was no longer sending anything from London; Orage's contributions from the States had all but dried up; the rich Americans had left the institute; and the businesses in Paris were no longer thriving. Practically the only person contributing to the priory's budget was the ancient Moscow lawyer Rachmilievitch, whose meagre offerings came from peddling bric-a-brac door to door in Fontainebleau.[121]

Gurdjieff's efforts to overcome these financial difficulties bore none of the aplomb of earlier years. He visited America several times, but only succeeded in alienating the Fourth Way groups there with his brusque demands for cash. Even dedicated disciples like Jean Toomer could not ignore the fact that Gurdjieff was using his charisma 'merely in order to obtain money, money, and more money'.[122] Back in France, when the American Pulitzer Prize-winning author Thornton Wilder turned up to view the priory, Gurdjieff pulled him close and sniffed him. 'Yes,' he said, 'I smell him. I think he have money.'[123] The international Fourth Way movement began to switch its allegiance from the teacher and the community he had built in France, and onto his teaching. The original aims of the institute – pacifism, spiritual seeking, a lifestyle that focused on turning its adherents into 'genuine, natural men' – lived on independently from Gurdjieff himself. It would have been convenient for the Fourth Way's disciples if Gurdjieff had died at this point – then they could safely have put him on a pedestal. But as it was, he remained stubbornly alive, going to seed with maximum publicity, unable to relinquish his lifelong quest for influence and adulation.

The priory's mortgagees foreclosed in 1932, after the community failed to pay its coal merchant's bill. The building and its contents – including its seventy dented bicycles – were repossessed.[124] The last visitors to the Institute for the Harmonious Development of Man, among them the American writer Kathryn Hulme, found a house haunted by silenced music, spectral dancers and the phantom laughter of the community's children.[125] The paint was peeling from the walls and the Turkish carpets in the study house had been nibbled by mice. In the gardens and woods, the paths were overgrown and nearly impassable. Hulme found Gurdjieff wandering up and down the avenue of limes, seemingly too exhausted to contemplate what to do next. After a lifetime of being venerated, he had no more familiars left to shore up his belief in himself as 'him who knows'. The chaotic drafts of his trilogy were scattered for editing on both sides of the Atlantic. His latest book, *The Herald of the Coming Good*, which he had insisted on publishing against everyone's advice, had provoked Ouspensky to the tart observation that the author must have contracted syphilis and gone insane.[126] Gurdjieff looked, Hulme thought as she left him at the priory gates, like 'the loneliest man in the world'.[127]

Gurdjieff's existence after the collapse of his community was more circumscribed, but it was also more tranquil. For a decade he had borne the responsibility of leading a large group of followers, and of funding a property he could ill afford. Freed from these burdens, he moved to a small Paris apartment where he earned a living treating mental and physical ailments. In 1936, aged seventy, he started another small Fourth Way teaching group composed only of women – most of them American, literary and lesbian. It was a surprising departure, since he had always held that women were less capable of enlightenment, and that homosexuality was a form of psychopathy.[128] The group's name, 'the Rope', was chosen to indicate that its members were harnessed together to make a dangerous mountain climb in Gurdjieff's wake, but his methods were gentler than in earlier days.[129] He still set exercises and shocks (including taking one woman to a brothel); but he also cooked meals for the group, gave them affectionate nicknames based on their 'inner animals', and treated them with a patience that would have astonished former pupils.[130]

During the Second World War the Rope was disbanded, but Gurdjieff remained in German-occupied Paris, stocking his larder on the black market, dabbling in currency trading, growing the paunch of the ageing bon viveur. He continued to teach during and after the war, still promulgating the Fourth Way, still asserting that personal enlightenment and international peace could come only from spiritual balance. On 29 October 1949 he died, and was buried in the same graveyard as Katherine Mansfield, close to the Prieuré des Basses Loges.

Gurdjieff's practical utopia in Fontainebleau did not, of course, lead to the worldwide conversion to the Fourth Way that he had desired. But it did inspire an impressive constellation of Fourth Way organizations – even if these organizations were often at odds with one another. Orage established several groups in New York. In Wisconsin, Jean Toomer set up a short-lived residential community for single men and women called Portage Potential. Elsewhere in the same state, Olgivanna – who had taken care of Katherine Mansfield at the priory – and her husband, the pioneering architect Frank Lloyd Wright, founded an architectural school called the Taliesin Fellowship that was inspired by Gurdjieff's teaching. Back in France, one of Gurdjieff's early followers, Jeanne de Salzmann, formed a group in Sèvres, whose members included the surrealist René Daumal – the first Frenchman to show an interest in the Fourth Way. And in Britain, no fewer than three of Gurdjieff's pupils – P. D. Ouspensky, J. G. Bennett and Maurice Nicoll – set up residential communities (Lyne Place, Coombe Springs and Great Amwell, respectively), all of which promised to teach the 'definitive' version of the Fourth Way.[131] In an effort to gain complete control of Gurdjieff's legacy, Ouspensky also founded the 'Historico-Psychological Society' in London, an organization with a complex set of rules that aimed to render the Fourth Way's 'secrets' obscure to the undeserving. The accusations of heresy, schism and apostasy between these various groups continue even now.[132]

This fractious and fractured legacy was not altogether surprising. Long-term stability is not to be expected of a community of spiritual seekers held together largely by the force of one man's personality and vision. Gurdjieff, while he lived, had refused to endorse other Fourth Way teachers and initiatives, fearing they would reduce his own power. His cryptic writings gave no clear theology or structure for the Fourth Way once he had died. Such a discordant legacy might have pleased a guru who had no desire to be displaced by others in the memory of his followers, and whose central message was that shocks and friction promote enlightenment.

It was perhaps only in those questing first decades of the twentieth century that the Institute for the Harmonious Development of Man could have seemed, for a few years at least, like a real attempt at utopia. The idealists who travelled to the forests outside Paris from America, Britain and various European cities – the psychologists, artists and writers, the businessmen and aristocrats – genuinely believed that this community, uniting modern science from the West with ancient Eastern spirituality, offered a plausible vision for the way people should live. For the institute's inhabitants, it seemed an antidote to the moral malaise and uncertainty of direction in the wake of the First World War. 'One can and does believe that one will escape from living in circles,' Katherine Mansfield wrote to her husband in her last weeks. She was, she felt, on the verge of learning how to 'live a CONSCIOUS life'.[133] From a modern perspective, it is difficult not to read elements of Gurdjieff's pattern for living as more psychologically disturbing than truly idealistic. 'This place,' Mansfield wrote, 'has taught me so far how unreal I am. It has taken from me one thing after another (the things never were mine) until at this present moment all I know really really is that I am not annihilated and that I hope.'[134] Yet, to those who joined the Institute for the Harmonious Development of Man, its ideals of pacifism, internationalism and companionable spiritual seeking seemed to offer a path forward for a world that had lost its way amid competition, conflict and the race for gain.

FIVE

SEEKING THE KINGDOM OF GOD
IN RURAL GERMANY

Eberhard and Emmy Arnold's Bruderhof

The Bruderhof's birthplace was improbably sedate and bourgeois: a newly built house in the Berlin suburbs with six rooms and a tranquil view over a park. This was the home of a middle-aged couple, Eberhard and Emmy Arnold, ostensibly happy with their lot in life. But after Germany's defeat in the First World War, nobody – not even sober private citizens like the Arnolds – could escape the question of what the nation should do next. Two million able-bodied German men had been killed out of the thirteen million mobilized.[1] Almost no family emerged untouched. Thousands of crippled, embittered and deeply traumatized veterans were coming back to find the old economic and political system crumbling. Paramilitary and communist groups were on the rise. Night after night across Berlin, people gathered in cafes, beer halls and behind the blinds of darkened shops to discuss what shape the future would take.

An agitated crowd, sometimes numbering eighty or a hundred, squeezed into the Arnolds' drawing room twice a week. Evangelical Christians shared sofas with anarchists, army officers rubbed shoulders with artists and journalists. The conversation was tense, the air filled with cigarette smoke. It was the old regime led by the Kaiser that was to blame for the current crisis, one young man asserted: its hierarchy, its individualism, its obsession with material gain. These

values had to be abolished if the nation was ever to be restored to
its former glory. Other voices rose in a clamour, objecting that it
was all very well to criticize the past, but the alternatives were just
as dreadful: the workers' councils advocating a violent communist
revolution like the one in Russia; the extreme right gathering
strength in Bavaria; even the democratic Weimar government then
in power, which was so chaotic, and seemed to have no appetite for
meaningful social reform. The owner of the drawing room stood
up. When he began to speak, his tone certain and measured, the
packed room fell silent. Here was the clarity of vision that they
sought.

Eberhard Arnold was tall and thin, his gaze probing and earnest.
With his dark suit and small, round spectacles, he appeared just
what he was – a moderately successful preacher of evangelical
Protestantism. The path to the redemption of Germany, and of
humankind at large, he told his listeners, lay in resurrecting the first
church: a community dedicated to work, worship and brotherly
love. His conviction came from a text that everyone in the room
knew. He brandished the Bible, called it a manual for the way they
should be living. As he elaborated confidently on his vision of a
peaceful, Christian world, the future seemed to metamorphose from
a place of confusion and fear to one of straightforward promise. The
men and women crowded into the drawing room wanted to follow
him there.

*

Eberhard Arnold was one of hundreds of ideologues who promoted
religious or spiritual panaceas in the post-war chaos. His efforts to
revive the Christian way of life echoed a global spate of religious
reform initiatives, ranging from the Muslim Brotherhood, founded
in Egypt to restore an Islamic state ruled by sharia law, to the World
Council of Churches, which was established to promote international
Christian unity in parallel to the League of Nations' promotion of
political unity.[2] Only a few of these projects crossed over into the
territory of practical utopianism, aiming to offer a working prototype for a complete new way of life. One such was the group of
Zionists in Palestine who reinvigorated the kibbutz movement, a
settlement programme that combined socialism with the ambition

19. G. I. Gurdjieff, 1931.

20. Katherine Mansfield, *c.* 1921.

21. Inside the study house of the Institute for the
Harmonious Development of Man, 1923.

22. Gurdjieff's followers making costumes, *c.* 1921–35.

23. A performance of Gurdjieff's movements, *c.* 1921–35.

24. Prieuré des Basses Loges, 2019.

25. Sannerz, 1921. Emmy and Eberhard
Arnold are front left and Else von
Hollander is seated second from the right.

26. Emmy and Eberhard
Arnold in 1922.

27. The Arnold family in the Sannerz community.

28. Communal event at the Rhön Bruderhof, 1932.

29. Expanding the Rhön Bruderhof in defiance of Hitler, 1933.

30. Folk dancing at the Alm Bruderhof, Liechtenstein, 1930s.

31. Gerald Heard (*right*) and Leonard Elmhirst, 1925.

32. Heard and Christopher Isherwood with Swami Prabhavananda.

33. (*opposite page top*) Heard and Felix Greene at Trabuco College during construction, 1942.

34. (*opposite page bottom*) Aldous Huxley at Trabuco College during construction, 1942.

35. Ramakrishna Monastery – previously Trabuco College –
in 1960, with Heard's Oratory to the right.

36. (*Left to right*) Christopher Isherwood, Heard, architect Richard Neutra,
Julian Huxley, chemist Linus Pauling and Aldous Huxley, 1960.

to create a Jewish state. On a far smaller scale were the very different spiritual approaches of the Institute for the Harmonious Development of Man in France and the Bruderhof in Germany.

Gurdjieff's community was defined by its esoteric mixture of religious sources, exotic connections, dubious finances, whimsical spending, and above all its flamboyant leader. The Bruderhof contrasted with the institute in every way – except for the fact that it too was triggered by the spiritual crisis that followed the war. Eberhard's blueprint for a better society was the first church in Jerusalem as it is described in the Acts of the Apostles: where members were of 'one heart and mind, and shared all things in common'.[3] He drew on a mainstream religion with an accepted text and set of ideas, but he was nonetheless radical in his vision for how people should live. The result of Eberhard's interpretation of the Bible was a practical utopia in which participants shared possessions, work, daily life and housing, all in an attempt to express God's order of peace, justice, unity and love. Members of the Bruderhof embraced many of the same ideals as other utopians of the period: egalitarianism; the desire to join spirituality with practical work; and the hope of promoting international peace. They aspired to influence people beyond the bounds of their community with their demonstration of how to live in the spirit of Christ.

When Eberhard founded the Bruderhof in 1920, it was far from evident that it would continue to flourish into the next century. It was one of a multitude of German experiments in living sparked off by the country's defeat in the First World War, all seeking social salvation in new communities based around unorthodox ideas. Most of these collapsed quickly under the weight of participants' conflicting and overblown expectations. The Bruderhof, though, managed to survive these early tensions, only to find itself threatened by the rise of National Socialism. Through the 1930s, the Nazis went to greater and greater lengths to eradicate this 'dissident' group, which insisted on preaching pacifism and universal brotherhood even as the country began mobilization for another war. The Bruderhof's clearly articulated principles, combined with a strong organizational structure and emphasis on expressing devotion through hard work, helped the community emerge from the turbulence of the mid-twentieth century as a thriving international movement.

Of the many practical utopias set up in the interwar period, it is the Bruderhof whose original vision and method has best endured.[4] There are currently over 2,900 people still living in the pattern forged by Eberhard and Emmy Arnold and their fellow communards.[5] They are based in twenty-three settlements in places as far apart as North America, South Korea and Austria, but they are united by a single leader, and by a mode of existence whose basis has not altered for a century. They live according to their understanding of the early Christian Church, and believe that in their daily life they are demonstrating the reality of God's coming kingdom. People are still drawn to the community today for the same reason that they were drawn to it in the wake of the First World War: it shows that an alternative social model is not just the stuff of dreams and theories, and demonstrates that a radically different social pattern can actually be lived.

*

Eberhard Arnold was born in 1883 and raised in a devout Lutheran household, where discussions about religion played a central role. 'You are intellectually dead,' his father Carl Franklin Arnold, a professor of theology at Breslau University, would rebuke his five children at the dinner table if their conversation wandered onto less existentially significant subjects.[6] Like many of the other utopians of the era, Eberhard was stubbornly independent from an early age. He responded to his father's high-handed treatment by acting out. He skipped school to watch the horse racing, or to spend hours gazing at the voluptuous statue of Venus that stood in the local museum.[7] His misbehaviour was compounded in his schoolmasters' eyes by the fact that his classmates tended to follow his example. While Eberhard didn't have the flamboyant panache of a young Gurdjieff, his peers still found his quiet self-confidence magnetic.

Eberhard's rebellious period was brief. At sixteen he went to stay with a militantly evangelical relative, Ernst Ferdinand Klein, and his admiration for the man sparked off an intense spiritual search. In a short space of time he had read the New Testament and Thomas à Kempis's fifteenth-century spiritual handbook, *The Imitation of Christ*. The experience transformed him. He was convinced that he was an instrument of God's will, that the 'Great Commission' in the Bible

– where Christ urges his Apostles to spread his message – applied particularly to him. His mission in life became the dissemination of the teachings of Jesus.

By his early twenties, Eberhard was fast gaining a reputation as a preacher and writer. He was studying theology and making waves in the thriving network of Protestant evangelicalism that stretched beyond Germany to Switzerland, the Netherlands and Britain.[8] This network – held together by lecture tours, pamphlets and journals, associations and reams of correspondence – was one of the numerous international webs facilitated by the technological developments of the nineteenth century. A century before, a committed preacher would usually only have been able to touch a small, local circle. But Eberhard could spread his ideas quickly and widely, and could draw on inspiration from thinkers around the world. He was a compelling speaker and writer. He grasped instinctively how to rouse people's emotions with his steadfast faith in the Bible, how to challenge their intellects with his sophisticated grasp of theology, and how to nimbly relate the motifs of the Bible to the hopes and fears of the present.

One afternoon in 1907, a twenty-two-year-old nurse, Emmy von Hollander, went to a Bible study meeting led by Eberhard in the city of Halle.[9] The daughter of a prominent family of academics, she was intellectually curious and deeply spiritual. Since her early teens she had been preoccupied with discovering how to live what she called 'a true Christian life'.[10] Emmy admired Eberhard's six-foot frame, his pince-nez and dapper suit. But she was even more impressed by his eloquence on matters of faith.[11] Arnold asked to walk her home. She accepted. Soon they were engaged, and they seemed destined for a relatively conventional life together. Arnold would finish his theology degree and become a pastor in the state-backed Lutheran Church, while Emmy would keep house and raise their children.

Within a short time this prospect of an ordinary life crumbled. Some members of a prayer group Emmy and Eberhard attended began to question the validity of infant baptism – a central Lutheran practice – and the idea of a state-run church. Emmy and Eberhard became convinced that baptism should only be valid when candidates were old enough to make a free, conscious decision to undergo it, and that the church should function independently of the state, as a community of committed disciples.[12] They found support in the Bible for both of these principles. Eberhard was the first to move from theory to practice, breaking with the state Church in 1908 and having himself re-baptised as a believing adult. Emmy – welcoming Eberhard's emphasis on action – was inspired to do the same, and the pair's move caused uproar. Their families called it social suicide, and in a way it was. The couple had been embedded in Lutheran circles, welcome guests at the religious revival meetings and lectures that were held in the houses of the leading doctors and professors of Halle and other nearby towns. Now they found themselves ostracized. Eberhard was shut out permanently from a career in the Lutheran Church.[13] The two of them would have to seek out a Christian path of their own.

Eberhard switched his course of study from theology to philosophy, as his unorthodox religious beliefs would have guaranteed him failure in his former course. He wrote his dissertation on Friedrich Nietzsche, sharing all his thinking and research with Emmy.[14] The German philosopher, who had died only nine years before, famously asserted 'God is dead' – part of his argument that humanity had reached a post-Christian phase, a phase defined by the power of individual will. Eberhard completely rejected this notion, but he did embrace Nietzsche's criticism of the modern Church as an institution fatally embroiled in power politics and greed. This taint of worldliness was, in part, why he and Emmy had abandoned the Lutheran Church. Like Nietzsche, Eberhard began to believe that the early Christian modes of religion – in particular the simple, communal way of life of Jesus's Apostles – were far purer than those of the contemporary Church. Eberhard and Emmy's discussions about how the first Christians lived, and what they believed, became the underpinning of a dream to recreate that simpler, more godly way of living.[15]

*

Faith drove the First World War. It is easy to forget this in today's more secularized society, but Protestant Germans and Protestant Britons – to name two chief combatants – both identified their national cause with God's, a patriotism strengthened by the fact that in each country the head of state was the head of the established Church.[16] Little attention was paid by religious warmongers to the improbability of a Protestant God backing both sides at once. Instead, clerics and preachers across Europe described the struggle as an opportunity for spiritual renewal.[17] They glibly elided nationalism and religion, trumpeting from their pulpits the message that theirs was the country waging a just and pious war, supported by God, while the enemy was the impious aggressor. During the first months of the conflict, Germany's churches were full, with congregants' apocalyptic sense heightened both by the rhetoric of the clerics and the knowledge that 1917, the four-hundredth anniversary of the state religion of Lutheranism, was fast approaching.[18]

When war broke out, the Arnolds were just as inclined as their countrymen to conflate the military ambitions of the German nation with its Christian destiny. Eberhard joined the army, serving a stint as a driver in the Service Corps in eastern Germany, but his weak lungs meant that he was invalided out after a few months.[19] To assuage his sense of failure about not contributing to the national cause, he began revising a book of religious reflections he had been working on since before the war. The conflict, he wrote, was 'a crucial battle for freedom of conscience'.[20] Once won, it would bring about the triumph of German spirituality over the egotism and materialism of Britain and her allies. *The War: A Call to Inwardness* received little critical notice when it was published, not least because it appeared in the bookshops alongside a slew of similar titles.[21] But Eberhard was not disheartened, and he continued writing nationalist articles in the religious press. Even the death of his older brother Hermann from wounds sustained on the Eastern Front did not cause his patriotism to falter. He hoped that victory in the war would bring Germany closer to becoming a truly Christian state.

In 1915, Arnold was appointed co-editor of the Student Christian Movement's monthly journal, *Die Furche* ('The Furrow'), and the literary director of its newly founded publishing house. The SCM was a nationwide evangelical youth organization with links to Christian student movements abroad. Financially, the job was a great advance on Arnold's pre-war situation, during which he depended on a portfolio of writing and lecturing that barely brought in enough money to support Emmy and their children. The change allowed the Arnold family to decamp to Berlin, where they joined in the capital's war fever, listening to stirring speeches in the squares and cheering at the sight of any man in uniform. Little attention was being paid at this point to the human cost of the war. 'We are German Christians and God will give victory to our cause,' Emmy – an acute observer of her times – remembered people saying at religious meetings. 'God will punish England.'[22]

Eberhard's work included organizing the printing and dispatching of religious poetry collections and sermons to the men at the front, and he took satisfaction from the thought that in his new position he could still contribute to the war effort. The life he and Emmy led showed every outward sign of a well-regulated, middle-class existence: Eberhard set off for the office early each morning, dressed in a neatly pressed suit, necktie, hat and coat, while Emmy stayed at home in the suburbs to look after the children. On the surface, this was a far remove from social radicalism and idealistic action. But in the Arnolds' minds they were soldiers of God, fighting, as Eberhard put it, against 'satanic and anti-Christian powers', like early Christians amid the apocalyptic plagues and martyrdoms of the Book of Revelation.[23]

*

By 1917, everything had changed. The decisive military triumph Germany had dreamed of no longer seemed possible. Caught in the stranglehold of the British naval blockade, the country's supplies were dwindling fast. 'People ate turnips morning, noon, and evening,' Eberhard remembered.[24] Some were near to starvation; even middle-class children like the Arnolds' were chronically malnourished. Eberhard saw a cab horse fall in the street, a mob rushing in to cut pieces off its body while it was still alive, lugging the bloody hunks home to eat.[25] The Arnolds were no longer able to be so blindly enthusiastic about the war; it was impossible to ignore the suffering of those struggling to survive at home, and the horrifying stories told by the wounded and shell-shocked soldiers Eberhard visited in Berlin's military hospitals. 'How does all this fit in with the love of Jesus Christ?' the couple asked one another in the evenings. 'How can a Christian kill his brothers?'[26] Was it fair that the poorest were bearing the brunt of the war, while those who initiated and promoted it – the Kaiser, the government, the elite, the Church – were insulated from its worst effects by their wealth and power?

Like thinkers all over the Western world and beyond, the horror of the war led the Arnolds to question the mindset that drove it: the nationalism and militarism; the prioritization of power, territorial gain and profit over the welfare of ordinary people. Quietly at first, and then with increasing passion, they spoke out. The current regime, Eberhard said, was 'falling apart, disintegrating, rotting and expiring'.[27] Germany had been corroded by its own selfishness and greed, which obstructed men's loving relations to one another and to God. Eberhard and Emmy came to the conclusion that Christians should not take part in war, and Eberhard did not hide this opinion at work. His criticisms of *Die Furche*'s nationalism brought him into conflict with his colleagues. In his lectures and articles for the Student Christian Movement, he argued that what was needed was 'an upheaval, the complete reversal and re-evaluation of all conditions and standards'.[28] At the start of the war, he would have been branded a traitor for this sort of statement, and perhaps imprisoned, but times had changed. In the last months of 1918, the desire for a negotiated peace was widespread.

By October of that year, it was clear that Germany was going to lose the war. A group of sailors stationed at Kiel refused to obey orders to fight a last, futile battle against the British navy. Their protest sparked a nationwide revolt against Kaiser Wilhelm II – a revolt fuelled by the ideals of socialism and communism, and a general hatred of the war. Since Germany had been drained of soldiers, the dissidents found it easy to seize control of the main towns. They raised the red banner of revolution over public buildings in place of the black, white and red tricolour of the German empire. The Kaiser was forced to abdicate, fleeing to the Netherlands, where he would remain for the next twenty years, until his death. In November, representatives of Germany's new, democratic regime signed a peace treaty with the Allies. The streets of Berlin filled with returning soldiers. Emmy remembered them as 'silent, bearded, and gray' with 'great sadness and mourning, disillusionment, emptiness and fear' written on their faces.[29] Neither they nor anyone else in Germany were sure how to proceed with their lives.

With the signing of the Versailles Treaty in June 1919, peace returned to Europe – but life in Germany continued to be marked by turmoil. The Weimar Republic that replaced the Kaiser's imperial rule started with a losing hand. The Versailles Treaty demanded Germany make heavy financial reparations, deprived the country of its colonies, and imposed a 'guilt clause' by which it had to accept full responsibility for the war. Burdened with these crippling terms, and despised by many of its citizens for accepting them, the Weimar government could scarcely hold the economy together, let alone create the new framework of social meaning that people craved in the wake of defeat. A great questioning began. 'It cannot go on like this,' Emmy recalled people saying. 'What, after all, is the meaning of life?'³⁰ It was an era in which parents had no confidence in tradition, no time-tested value system to pass on to their children. People needed a new social path, and so Germany became a breeding ground for revolutionary world views: pacifism, anarchism, communism and fascism all began to gain supporters.

During this period of dramatic upheaval, Eberhard came to be seen as something of a prophet. He had voiced doubts about war, nationalism and the social hierarchy earlier than most, and he seemed one of the few with an optimistic belief that there *was* a way forward. The lectures Eberhard gave about the life of Christian brotherhood were now being attended by crowds of over a thousand, filling out the public halls. His articles in *Die Furche* inspired passionate debate. Eberhard accepted his new-found fame with quiet satisfaction. He had little interest in personal glory. His sole ambition, as he put it, was to encourage people to 'set their hearts on God'.³¹

The atmosphere of cataclysm, of cults, crusades and causes that brought Eberhard to the fore did the same, in a more dramatic fashion, for another man with a vision for a new society. The Austrian-born Adolf Hitler, who had been gassed while serving in the German army, believed that the peace settlement imposed on Germany by the Allies was an unjust humiliation that must be avenged. The nation had to be raised again to greatness. Like Eberhard, Hitler was interested in the work of Nietzsche, particularly the philosopher's idea that humankind would be redeemed by a superior race – the *Übermensch* or 'superman'. But Eberhard interpreted this portion of Nietzsche's thought in an entirely different way. Where Hitler understood the *Übermensch* to mean the biologically superior Aryan-Germanic master race, Eberhard identified the *Übermensch* as being embodied in Jesus Christ and, by extension, in those who followed his teachings. In these frenzied post-war years, the same stimuli were feeding into starkly different visions of what a remodelled society should look like.

The Arnolds were now convinced of the need for total social transformation. Since 1917 they had been evolving their inchoate ideas into a vision for change. When people began to gather in their drawing room in 1919 to discuss how Germans should live in the wake of apocalypse, Eberhard – always the spokesman for the couple – had an answer ready. Since the world was 'full of murderous intent and mammonistic injustice', he told the men and women crowded into the room, the solution was to embrace universal brotherhood, living in a 'spirit of love and justice' and bringing about the victory of the reign of God.[32] To do so required following the Bible literally. This would mean a return to the way of life described in the Acts of the Apostles: a church-community that shared all property and lived all life in common and in the spirit of Jesus.[33]

Eberhard's audience, inspired by his confident, persuasively articulated vision of Christian socialism, asked him how it would be possible, practically speaking, for them to start such a church-community. Here they met with disappointment. Eberhard had no clear conception of how to go about enacting the vision he had grown so adept at describing. This is not to say he and Emmy hadn't tried. The Arnolds' early experiments in reform, which focused on their own household, were touchingly absurd: Eberhard volunteered to clean everyone's shoes, a rare act for a male, middle-class head of household; he and Emmy moved their servants into the best rooms in the house; and made those servants thoroughly uncomfortable by inviting them to eat at the family table in the evenings (the invitation had to become an instruction when they demurred).[34]

One afternoon, Eberhard came home from a weekend-long evangelical conference dressed in an entirely new costume: he had swapped his sombre suit for knee breeches, an open-necked tunic and sandals.[35] It seemed like another passing fancy, the ingredients of the next comic interlude. Emmy and their children, now numbering five, greeted the outfit with protests and laughter.[36] But

Eberhard explained to them earnestly (he was rarely anything other than earnest) that he had, at last, found the path forward to achieving practical social reform.

*

Eberhard's costume was more than just an outfit. It was the uniform of the youth movement – a wave of organizations run by young men and women who came together to talk, sing, dance, hike and camp in the countryside.[37] The movement had begun in Germany before the war, and had been growing exponentially ever since. It had numerous groups and factions, like the *Wandervögel* ('Birds of Passage'), the Free German Youth and the *Neuwerk* ('New Work') Christian Socialist Movement. These organizations shared no coherent manifesto. Some veered towards the right wing of politics, some to the left; some were religious and some secular. But in their jumble of ideas, certain principles surfaced again and again.

The men and women of the youth movement were all turning away from the values of the old regime, a regime they blamed for the slaughter of the First World War. Like the hippies half a century later, they rejected industrialization, capitalism and the big cities that went with them; they rejected paternalism, class divisions and social convention. What they embraced instead was the romance of nature, the pre-modern, the pre-industrial. They wore colourful 'folk' clothes, swam and sunbathed in the nude, and favoured communal cooperation and self-realization over private material gain. Again like the hippies, the German youth movement was essentially middle-class. A large part of their rebellion consisted of rejecting bourgeois 'softness' and adopting a spartan, no-frills exist-ence – whether in the form of long hikes, alcohol-free folk singing around the campfire, setting up agricultural communes, or holding conferences to discuss how to live. In less than a decade, many of these same groups would be practising goose-stepping and giving the Nazi salute, but in the years immediately following 1918 their beliefs and activities were still largely free from militant nationalism.

Eberhard and Emmy Arnold, now in their late thirties, hardly qualified as 'youths', but they were drawn to the movement anyway, turning up at rallies and retreats held around the country. The move-ment's translation of their ideals into a practical lifestyle impressed

Eberhard. When he had the chance, he spoke to fellow members about his and Emmy's vision for the future. He knew that many of those involved were not Christian: Catholics and Protestants played a role, but so did pagans, Zionists, anarchists and naturists. He hoped nonetheless that he could persuade these idealistic young people to follow Jesus, and that the youth movement could become a vehicle for Christian socialist revolution.

In forest clearings or on mountain plateaus, youth movement meetings usually opened with a round of folk dancing. A group of a hundred or so would settle among rucksacks, violins and guitars to discuss how to change the world. 'Outward formality and social conventions had been cast off,' Emmy would remember later. 'A spirit of joy and comradeship was alive among us.'[38] Eberhard was particularly interested in the discussions about collective settlements: the peasant land communes being set up in post-revolutionary Russia; the kibbutzim in Palestine; and, nearer to home, the ideals of the recently murdered German anarchist Gustav Landauer, who thought that young people should flee the corrupting influence of the cities to begin new communities in the countryside.

Up to this point, the Arnolds' dreams of Christian revolution had been vague and disembodied. But in the face of these young men and women's appetite for practical action, their ideas rapidly changed. After one conference in Schlüchtern, forty miles north-east of Frankfurt, in the spring of 1920, the Arnolds went to visit a 'life reform' settlement – the Habertshof – set up by members of the youth movement a year earlier. There they found a community of young people embracing a simple way of living: farming on a hillside, dressing in peasant clothes, and sharing their vegetarian food with all comers. Emmy and Eberhard began to believe that it was truly possible to live in a different way, to give their Christian ideals a concrete form. In the months since the war, the Arnolds had talked endlessly about leaving their constrained life in the suburbs. They had dreamed of buying a gypsy caravan and touring the countryside with a group of friends, preaching and helping wherever they could.[39] But now their ideas crystallized into a life of farming and cooperation like the one they saw at the Habertshof.

After their visit, Eberhard, Emmy and a few others walked the two hours to Sannerz, a picturesque village enfolded in hilly farmland and forests of beech and pine in central Germany. They inspected an empty house – a capacious red-brick villa with a large garden – which they hoped might serve as a base for a settlement of their own. On the way, the group discussed how their community would model the early Church in practice. By pursuing a selfless existence of Christian cooperation, they would demonstrate how to end capitalism, individualism and materialism – the competitive ideologies that they blamed for war. Their settlement would show their fellow Germans that a life of Christian brotherhood was possible in the here and now. Its participants might be few at first, but their number would grow. Their example would inspire other settlements, and once their ideas had swept through Germany there would be a 'volcanic eruption' of idealism across the globe, presaging the arrival of the kingdom of God on earth.[40]

*

When the Bruderhof began at Sannerz in the summer of 1920, Christian communal ideals had already been inspiring practical utopia-builders for several hundred years. In eighteenth-century England, a group following Mother Ann Lee prepared for Christ's return to earth by pooling their resources and living together celibately (partly as a path to Christian perfection, and partly because sex might undermine communal solidarity). The Shakers, as this group became known, sailed for America in 1774, starting a settlement in New York State.[41] In the next century, also in New York State, the American preacher John Humphrey Noyes enacted his own vision of 'Bible Communism' by founding the Oneida Community. Noyes' idea of bringing God's kingdom to earth included the practice of 'complex marriage', or polyamory (on the basis that such sharing would strengthen communal unity). The Arnolds' settlement at Sannerz was less idiosyncratic in its sexual politics: as in the world outside, monogamous marital relations were the order of the day. But in other respects they had much in common. As in Lee's and Noyes' communities, the Bruderhof members planned to share all possessions; to treat each other with pious generosity; and – since God had given humankind the earth to cultivate – to support themselves by tilling the soil.[42]

To start with, the brotherhood consisted only of Eberhard, Emmy and the five Arnold children, Emmy's sister Else von Hollander, and Suse Hungar, a former member of the Salvation Army. Since the group was so small, they could not afford to rent the fifteen-room house they had admired. They settled instead for a nearby barn that had been used for storing saddlery and apples. But a few weeks after they were installed and had begun their communal life of farming and spiritual dedication, more people began knocking on the door. Within months, that trickle turned into a flood, and the community was able to take over the house as well. News of the Bruderhof had spread by word of mouth, through Christian, pacifist and youth organizations, through the articles Eberhard was writing for various religious journals, and through the lectures he continued to deliver in cities across Germany. The people drawn to the community were those who wanted to live based on principles that ran counter to the individualistic and materialistic mainstream, to join a group that tried to turn the Christian utopia hinted at in the Bible into a real place.

In 1921 alone, 2,500 visitors stayed at the house. Some remained only for a few days, others for several months. A portion committed to the community for life. The majority of visitors were young, in their twenties or even their teens, their interest fuelled as much by a generalized desire to make the world anew as by Christian conviction. Among them were the bohemian participants of the youth movement, with their signature long hair, colourful clothes and backpacks; the clean-living members of various Christian organizations; and even a few older academics and theologians – including the famed philosopher Martin Buber – who, in these days after the war, were no longer contented with a life of the mind.[43] The Bruderhof hosted writers and artists; First World War veterans who were haunting the countryside, unable to settle back into their pre-war lives; expectant single mothers who had heard about a refuge where no one was turned away; and a sprinkling of the misfits and eccentrics that are drawn to utopian endeavours in any age. One dialogue between two new arrivals, overheard by a third, sums up the atmosphere of those early days:

'Where are you from?'

'Prison. And you?'

'The madhouse.'[44]

German arrivals were supplemented by visitors from abroad. People came from England, the Netherlands, the United States, France and Switzerland, either out of simple curiosity or a determination to spend their lives in this model Christian community; others – like an international group of young Zionists who would go on to start a kibbutz in Palestine – wanted to learn about the practicalities of communal living. Throughout their history, the Bruderhof would look fondly on the kibbutzniks as fellow religious idealists – 'a partner,' as one Bruderhof member put it, 'in achieving an ideal of brotherhood and social justice'.[45] The arrival of so many international visitors, particularly those from 'enemy' nations, filled the Arnolds with hope. The community was, Emmy said proudly, taking steps towards 'a new world – a new age in a new spirit of reconciliation'.[46]

For the Arnolds, forging international links was an essential part of building a utopia: unless their community had a wider resonance, they thought, it would not result in a real Christian revolution. Through the 1920s and 30s Eberhard would exchange hundreds of letters with foreign evangelical and pacifist organizations, and travel to the Netherlands, Britain and the United States to broadcast the Bruderhof vision. The Arnolds would send their eldest son Hardy to university first in Zürich and then in Birmingham, to build further connections. Their efforts would win the Bruderhof a reputation out of all proportion to its size. From the Quakers in London to the Werkhof, a Christian socialist settlement in Switzerland, fellow religious idealists looked to the Bruderhof as a demonstration of how the pacifist, socialist tenets of Christianity could be turned into a complete way of life. As a rare, lived example of idealism, the influence of the Arnolds' community was remarkable.

Nearly all the Bruderhof's permanent members were Christian, but many of the men and women who came to stay in Sannerz were not. Non-religious idealists were drawn to the community as a lived example of radical socialism. The communards completely rejected private property and private life; in staunch contrast to the predominating interest in individual gain, Bruderhof members sought only the possessions and money necessary for survival – and all these goods were owned by the community as a whole. 'How could we, who wanted to share the suffering of the masses in those post-war years, keep anything for ourselves?' Emmy remembered later. 'That is why we shared everything in common, giving away all we had to those who wanted to serve the same spirit of love with us.'[47] Although marriage and family were held to be vitally important in the Bruderhof, these institutions did not interrupt the communal nature of all aspects of daily life: members lived, worked, worshipped and relaxed together and rarely indulged in private time. The Arnolds told non-believing visitors that they were welcome to stay – as long as their 'hearts beat for the cause of justice and peace for all nations, for the brotherhood of all social classes, and for the welfare of all people in all parts of the world'.[48] The Bruderhof, they said, was not about 'any dogma, any stringing together of religious words', but about 'a love and unity that extends into the outermost aspects of life and action and work'.[49]

The Bruderhof's popularity with visitors notwithstanding, daily life was far from smooth. The community grew to fifty permanent residents within two years, but they struggled to forge themselves into anything resembling a harmonious religious community. To begin with, the Arnolds were reluctant to direct their fellow communards, believing that the Bruderhof's members were equal before God, and that their only true leader was Christ. When it became clear that some earthly leadership would also be necessary if the community was to survive, Eberhard became the 'word leader', the community's spokesman, and Emmy the housemother, in charge of domestic arrangements. Both of them, as a visiting English Quaker would later observe, continued to behave like 'ordinary individuals among all the rest', taking on leadership roles only because it was generally agreed that they had 'the gift to understand, put into words, and accomplish the things to which the Spirit of God is leading the whole community'.[50]

The Arnolds were unused to practical leadership. They found themselves overwhelmed by mundane problems – where to house forty or fifty guests, what to feed them, how to make sure everyone did a share of the housework and farming.[51] As with so many utopian communities, the most pressing problem was money. The Arnolds had managed to pay the first year's rent by selling off their life insurance and collecting donations from a circle of supporters, including a handsome contribution from the shipping magnate Kurt Woermann.[52] Anyone who decided to join the Bruderhof permanently gave over all their possessions to the communal treasury. But these weren't sustainable sources of income – particularly when, in the spirit of Christian fellowship, all of the many visitors to the Bruderhof were fed and housed free of charge.

Eberhard and Emmy tried to expand the community's farming activities beyond the grounds of their house, hoping that this would bring in some income, or at least make the Bruderhof more self-sufficient. They had admired the wholesome, earthy practicality of the back-to-the-land lifestyle when they had visited the Habertshof, and they viewed farming as a particularly virtuous form of labour since there was so much of it in the Bible. The Bruderhof members bought four cows, several goats, pigs and chickens. They rented land. But they were too inexperienced to realize that they were being offered the scrawniest animals and the stoniest, least fertile fields by local sellers.[53] Although they became more skilled with time, their agricultural activities were never profitable. Their amateur approach is encapsulated in the image of Eberhard attempting to tend the community manure heap 'correctly' – with a pitchfork in one hand and an advice book in the other.[54]

Fortunately, Eberhard had been running a small publishing house since before he had founded the Bruderhof. It printed books and a journal for *Neuwerk*, the youth movement group that combined Christian mission with radical socialism. Now Eberhard transferred this operation to Sannerz, hurriedly drilling the communards in the basic principles of publishing. He saw this business not only as an income stream for the community, but as an opportunity: once the Bruderhof had the equipment, it could release its own publications as well as working for others. Among the early books the community published was a collection of letters by Mushanokōji Saneatsu's hero Leo Tolstoy – another demonstration of how the idealists of the interwar period, far-flung though they were, drew on similar sources of inspiration. From the 1920s right up to the present day, publishing has performed double duty for the Bruderhof – bringing in funds and broadcasting its ideals to the world.

Spirituality remained the driving force of the community and, for a long time, daily life was haphazard. People drifted in and out of the villa at will. Often there were so many visitors that straw pallets had to be laid out in the barns at night.[55] Residents did more or less what they felt like. Some devoted their waking hours to work, helping with the printing, tilling the fields, or cleaning out the cow stalls, pigsties and chicken coop. Others did no work at all, or brought to their tasks such an independent spirit that their efforts were worse than useless – like the cook who wandered off to paint, leaving stews to burn, or the young aesthete who blithely arranged to give the community's 'unsightly' manure heap away to local peasants free of charge, ignorant of its value as fertilizer.[56]

The growing number of children added to the chaos. Marriage and childbearing were encouraged in the Bruderhof. Alongside the children born into the community, the Arnolds took in a large number of war orphans and children from broken homes. A school was set up for them, but the Arnolds – in the same spirit as Tagore at Santiniketan-Sriniketan and the Elmhirsts at Dartington Hall – wanted the children integrated with the wider community rather than confined to an institution.[57] They would, Emmy and Eberhard thought, best learn to be responsible Christian citizens through practical experience: as Eberhard put it, 'Children must grow up in a broad context of life.'[58] The result was that the Bruderhof children spent much of their time running around the farm and neighbouring countryside – a blissful experience for them, if less so for the locals.

Still, the Bruderhof members got on surprisingly easily with the Sannerz villagers. Where Gurdjieff's Eastern ideas and his multi-national entourage aroused deep suspicion among Fontainebleau's inhabitants, the Arnolds' community – mostly German, pious and earnestly determined to do good works at every opportunity – seemed to their neighbours peculiar but not at all threatening. The Bruderhof members bartered goods and took part in village activities from making jam to maypole dancing. Since several other youth movement communities had been set up in the region (in addition to the Habertshof there was a group run by a schoolteacher called Georg Flemmig), they would meet fellow idealists in the surrounding countryside to hike together and exchange strategies for communal living. Sannerz turned out to be a well-chosen place for a practical utopia: it was not an insular community, but part of the world, publicly demonstrating the virtues of the good life of Christian socialism.

With so many participants coming and going, and no routine in place, the only fixed point in the Bruderhof day was its community meetings. As with the weekly meetings at Dartington, these were supposed to be an egalitarian forum where all voices could be heard. While Eberhard was the nominal spokesman, he and all the other 'brothers' and 'sisters' – as the communards called each other – were understood to be equal in their efforts to live out God's design. But Eberhard was older than most, naturally charismatic and used to lecturing. He often dominated, reiterating his ideals at length during the meetings in the hope that this would hold the Bruderhof together. On some days the session started at seven in the evening and went on well beyond midnight, while Eberhard preached on communal cooperation and overcoming selfishness. 'Community life', he told his listeners, was 'like martyrdom by fire: it means the daily sacrifice of all our strength and all our rights'. The Bruderhof should be like a hearth fire, in which 'the individual logs burn away so that, united, its glowing flames send out warmth and light again and again into the land'.[59]

Eberhard's rhetorical skill was such that even non-Christian visitors were moved by his words. For some of the most pious members, the experience of being part of the Sannerz community went further. Inspired by their lives of devotion, they experienced a remarkable phenomenon: periods of religious joy so intense that it amounted to ecstasy. Georg Barth, who came to Sannerz via a Christian youth organization, said, 'So strongly did I feel the nearness of the kingdom of God that I could physically taste it and smell it.'[60] The sudden sense of being mentally transported, of being filled with both the spirit of God and utter certainty that the Bruderhof were living in the right way, could strike people at any time: while picking up stones from the fields, weeding the beans, or preserving vegetables. Residents even talked of the rooms of the community's buildings being 'filled with the atmosphere of the kingdom of God', as if their utopia existed on a divine plane, separate from the very air of the world around it.[61] This experience of transcendence seems to be peculiar to religious utopians – perhaps because it is so closely bound up in the exhilarating notion that God's kingdom is near at hand.[62]

Eberhard was as much affected by this ecstasy as the other communards. He crawled into bed beside Emmy at the end of a long day late in 1921, shoulders aching from crouching for hours over a desk as he edited yet another lengthy religious tract. At the back of his mind there was the ever-present worry about the community's fragile finances. He was ruffled from a near-argument he had had that afternoon, trying to persuade a recovering alcoholic that the Bruderhof was 'not a welfare or salvation institution' but a group seeking to live and work together according to the Bible.[63] And yet, as he blew out his candle after reading a few verses of the Bible, he felt elation. Now, he whispered to Emmy, for the first time in his life, he was engaged in 'something living'.[64] 'There was a wind that blew through our rooms. In every pore, through every wall, the lively spiritual movements penetrated.'[65] Emmy was more reserved about her feelings than her husband, but forty years later she wrote that, 'for those of us who experienced this beginning, the "first love"' of living in the spirit of Christ was 'unforgettable'.[66]

In 1922, two years into its existence, the Bruderhof was hit by a crisis that brought its initial honeymoon period to an abrupt close. Eberhard and his family travelled to the Netherlands for a fortnight in the summer to spread the word of their community among foreign evangelical groups. They were warmly received by friends running a pacifist settlement in Bilthoven. But while they were away, inflation in Germany began to spin out of control. This was a moment that burned certain images into the country's collective memory: the housewife wheeling banknotes to the grocer to buy a loaf of bread; the man whose coffee tripled in price as he drank it; children building towers with stacks of marks held together by elastic bands. Several of the Sannerz publishing house's investors suddenly withdrew their funds, and the business – along with the community that relied on it – faced collapse. The Arnolds received panicky messages from the Bruderhof, but Eberhard refused to return early from the Netherlands. God, he responded in letters, would resolve the situation.

Eberhard was proved right, in a sense. A well-wisher who had attended one of his talks in the Netherlands made a timely contribution that staved off financial meltdown. But at the first meeting on the Arnold family's return home it became clear that his community was deeply divided. Many participants, however steadfast their faith, thought it naive, complacent and irresponsible of the Arnolds to expect God to take care of their finances. Eberhard doggedly held that genuine faith in God's salvation must encompass all areas of life, even economics – and that anyone who thought otherwise had been seduced, as he put it, by 'the dark demonic force of Mammon'.[67] It was the same kind of tension – economics versus high idealism – that troubled so many of the practical utopias of the age.

Thirty people left the Bruderhof soon after this meeting, most of them going on to found a new settlement that would collapse within a few years. This represented the majority of the community's permanent membership. Since all property was owned in common, when the Bruderhof's possessions were divided the departing communards took with them the publishing contracts for the *Neuwerk* journal and most of the bestselling books. Of the seven adults who remained to carry on the community, four were from the Arnold family circle: Eberhard and Emmy, along with Emmy's sisters Else and Monika von Hollander. It seemed that the community was going the same way as so many of the other youth movement initiatives of the post-war years. Almost every week a new settlement was begun somewhere in rural Germany, only for the experiment to be torn apart shortly afterwards by ideological differences and the pressures of cooperative living. Participants turned to new communities or to other modes of social reform, leaving behind them nothing but half-dug vegetable patches. The Arnolds, though, were determined that the Bruderhof would be different.

*

Emmy and Eberhard did their best to learn from the breakdown of the community in 1922. Factionalism, they decided, had been one of the chief causes of the rupture. Instead of things being worked out reasonably and openly, cliques had formed, and members made attacks on one another that only entrenched divisions and undermined the atmosphere of brotherly love. They introduced what they called 'The First Law of Sannerz', a rule to end gossip once and for all: criticism was still allowed – but if you wanted to indulge in it, you had to admonish someone to their face. Eberhard summarized the rule, which was based on Jesus's teaching in the Gospel of Matthew, as 'There is no law but the law of love.'[68]

Over the next five years the Bruderhof members reshaped their community in other ways too, hoping always to make it more united and resilient. Previously, they had avoided rules and laws, seeing them as artificial and spiritually constraining – tools that were used too eagerly by the established Church. But the lack of rules, they began to think, may also have contributed to the disorganization that had plagued Sannerz. They gradually established a more formal system of laws, rituals and routines – which also helped organize the community as it began to grow larger again. When people joined the Bruderhof, they now had to serve a year as a novice. If they survived this with their enthusiasm intact, they would be baptized and give up all their worldly possessions, formally joining the community of goods. The Bruderhof moved to making all decisions unanimously at a daily 'brotherhood meeting'; casual visitors and novices weren't allowed to participate. The Arnolds saw these new processes as a way of encouraging individuals to surrender themselves to the collective, promoting total unity. Such unity, they hoped, would make the Bruderhof stronger and help to turn it into a 'perfect vessel' for containing the Holy Spirit.[69]

While the Bruderhof members were reconfiguring life at Sannerz, Germany itself was changing. The hyperinflation of 1922 and 1923 had ended when the Weimar government issued a new currency. But the country was plagued by high prices, food scarcity and wide-spread unemployment through the later 1920s. Citizens grew less and less trusting that their government would ever be able to solve these problems. Their desperation fuelled extreme left- and right-wing groups, conspiracies and madcap investment schemes. Faced with continual turbulence and uncertainty, many people longed even more ardently than they had in the immediate aftermath of the war for a new direction – or a redeemer, a person with an answer to their country's social, economic and moral ills.

The majority were less hopeful than they had been in the earlier part of the decade about the potential of small, experimental settlements. Communitarian living, several visitors told the Arnolds, was irresponsibly escapist. It was not a cure for society's ills. What the nation needed was radical, state-led social transformation. The prevalence of this point of view was part of the reason that membership of the National Socialist Party increased eightfold in the late 1920s. In the towns close to Sannerz, Bruderhof members began running into young people wearing the tan shirt, black shorts and red armband of the Nazi youth organizations. These National Socialist supporters spent their weekends on military drill, their evenings listening to lectures on racial purity.

The Bruderhof continued to appeal to people in search of a spiritual route to social renewal. By 1927, the Bruderhof had reached forty-five permanent members, nearing its size before the breakdown of 1922. The villa and barns were crowded, so the group bought a larger property in the Rhön mountains, thirty miles to the north-east of Sannerz. The seventy-five-acre farm was perched on a weather-swept hillside, its buildings dilapidated, its soil stony and thin, and the local population of poor peasants were renowned for their roughness and inhospitality. But the Bruderhof could not afford any other location; as it was, the first instalment of the purchase had to be covered by a gift from Prince Günther von Schönburg-Waldenburg, a philanthropic aristocrat who was just one of the wide networks of supporters that Eberhard had created. The Arnolds cared little about the harsh nature of the landscape. What mattered to them was the property's size, and whether it would allow their community to expand.

In this new, isolated stronghold, Bruderhof life finally settled into a regular pattern. The daily routine was simple, spartan and repetitive, dominated by long hours of work: hoeing, planting and harvesting; turning out bowls and candlesticks in a small craft workshop; printing off runs of books and pamphlets in a newly established publishing house. Visitors were shocked by the intensity of the labour that stretched from dawn to dusk. 'Seldom can a Bible quotation be applied so literally,' commented one. 'Up there they "ate their bread in the sweat of their brows".'[70] For the communards, this hard work was part of their religious devotion.[71]

All areas of life were subsumed to the communal spiritual experience. Local hikes, attempts to win over the hostile locals by putting on plays, picnics beneath a spreading beech tree on a hill above the farm – all these, as Emmy wrote, aimed for 'the true inner liberation of the individual from himself, for a true peace and a just society'.[72] Mealtimes were marked by devotional singing – a useful distraction, given that the food consisted largely of potatoes and sauerkraut, and not enough of either. Lacking fat and protein, the hard-labouring inhabitants were permanently hungry. A motto they frequently repeated ran: 'Ten have been invited and twenty will come. Add water to the soup and welcome them all.'[73] They were hungry, but at least they were hungry in the name of virtue.

In spite of the hardships of life at the Rhön, the Bruderhof grew as the Arnolds had hoped. Its example continued to draw international interest, its reputation spread by the circulars that were sent out regularly to well-wishers, both as a form of evangelism and to raise funds. The community's new publishing house was funded by a donation from a Dutch Quaker and his wealthy English wife, who was a member of the Cadbury chocolate family. In Eberhard's view, such gifts were of benefit to the donors as well as the community, giving them a chance at a 'really good deed'.[74] Members continued to join from abroad: several young couples arrived from Switzerland and Sweden, bringing with them welcome additional funds. By 1930 the Bruderhof had seventy permanent members, but this gives little sense of how crowded life was in the community on a daily basis. In the course of the summer of 1932 alone, 2,500 guests came to stay.[75]

The Rhön community began to seem to the Arnolds like the 'good place' they had always dreamed of. They hoped that its way of life would continue indefinitely, the utopia on a hill a witness to God's love, perfecting itself and guiding society at large towards conversion. Eberhard had a vision, as he told his wife, of 'all manner of people coming – men of industry, professional people, workers, teachers, washerwomen and the very poorest', and said that it was their job to prepare for them by constructing new buildings.[76] Eventually, he said, the Bruderhof would expand to encompass all seven of the farms that surrounded it. Emmy's response was to quote a popular folk song at him. 'I cannot keep up with your long, high leaps!'[77] But she, too, was determined to see this vision come true.

*

The Bruderhof grew rapidly, but its business enterprises steadily failed to cover the running costs. Every few weeks a policeman would toil up the steep path to the farm to confiscate a few possessions, or even a cow, in lieu of unpaid debts.[78] The communards decided that outside support was urgently needed to shore up their finances. They tried sending begging letters to their European network of friends, asking for support and for funds. In reply to these appeals they received only silence or apologies; no one had money to spare. And so the Bruderhof members thought of a new, more ambitious tactic, one that would safeguard the community spiritually as well as financially if it worked.

An afternoon in 1929 found Eberhard sitting at his desk in his chilly study in the Rhön community. In front of him was a 355-page manuscript, a sixteenth-century theological treatise on the Hutterites, which some of the communards had copied out from the public archives. Beside the treatise was a book: *Der Anabaptismus in Tirol* ('Anabaptism in the Tyrol') by Johann Loserth. Both texts were open. Eberhard, Emmy and the other Bruderhof members had long been interested in the Hutterites' spiritual writings, their history and their mode of living.[79] The plan now was to try to build a financial and spiritual alliance with the Hutterites – a richer and more securely established community whose religious ideals were nearly the same as those of the Bruderhof. The only trouble was that the Hutterite settlements were all on the other side of the Atlantic. Eberhard had been tasked with writing a letter powerful enough to win over these unknown communards.

He picked up his pen. He started by setting out his hope that the Hutterites would 'take our Bruderhof as a most humble daughter colony like an adopted child and set us up and equip us'.[80] Then he went on to try to persuade Elias Walter, one of the most prominent elders of the community, that the Hutterites and the Bruderhof were a match literally made in heaven – since both of them, as Eberhard put it, rejected 'all private property and all private life, all evil occupations for earning a livelihood, all work for self, all self will, and sin'.[81]

In his letter, Eberhard stressed that the Hutterites, too, had started out in Germany – during the Reformation of the sixteenth century. He emphasized the group's extraordinary similarity to his own community: like the members of the Bruderhof, Jacob Hutter, a Tyrolean hat-maker and preacher, had turned away from society to create a community modelled on the early Church as it was described in the Bible. Many in Germany had assumed that the group had died out. Then Eberhard received a letter from a professor at a college in Kansas, telling him, in the course of their lengthy theological correspondence, that the Hutterites were now the largest group of religious communitarians in North America, where they had migrated following persecution.[82] Surely the arrival of this news in the Bruderhof community had been a sign from God.

Eberhard's letter received a response. The Hutterites agreed that he could come and make his case for unification in person. But this was no easy task. The Hutterites functioned as a decentralized organization. To ensure the incorporation of the Bruderhof, Eberhard would have to visit all thirty-three of the community's colonies, which were scattered across rural Canada and the north-west of the United States. Emmy was reluctant to part from her husband, but she supported the idea of strengthening the Bruderhof by allying it with a group that had already managed four centuries of radical, faith-based community-living.[83] It seemed uncertain, without outside support, how the community they had devoted their lives to building could continue.

In May 1930, Eberhard Arnold left the Rhön and set foot for the first time on an ocean liner. He was forty-seven years old, and was leaving behind his prospective son-in-law, the twenty-three-year-old Hans Zumpe, standing in as community leader. Emmy, two decades older and effectively the co-founder of the community, might have been a more obvious choice. But in both the Arnolds' interpretation of the Bible, all 'pioneering and conflict' was to be left to the men, so she was not an option.[84] While few of the utopians of the age were notably progressive when it came to women, the Bruderhof members were among the most reactionary. Women were mainly assigned the roles of cooking, cleaning, doing laundry and raising the children.[85] They were, nonetheless, seen as just as valuable as the men in maintaining the vitality of the community – even if that value rarely extended into spiritual leadership.

Eberhard did not come back for over a year. When he stood up at the brotherhood meeting on his return, he looked much older. His clothes were worn, his face bore new lines, he had almost lost sight in one eye from the inflammation of an old injury. It was clear to all in the room that the journey had been an exhausting one. But his expression was quietly satisfied as he announced that the Hutterite colonies had agreed to unite with the Bruderhof. He himself had been ordained a Hutterite minister. Their future was secure, he told his followers: at nearly 5,000 strong, and with an established status, economic stability, and an 'almost perfect communal life', the Hutterites would provide the security that their community lacked.[86] In private, Eberhard told Emmy that he was doubly pleased with this unification, because it would protect their community in the case of their deaths. 'I would not find it too hard to give both eyes and more for the sake of ensuring the inner and outer life of our Bruderhof for the next fifty to a hundred years,' he said.[87] Even with the routines and rules they had established since moving to the Rhön, the Arnolds were not yet sure the Bruderhof would be strong enough to survive without them.

In the weeks following Eberhard's announcement, details of the terms of unification with the Hutterites began to emerge. Already before his return, he had sent kerchiefs from the Hutterites for the women at the Rhön Bruderhof – directing them that 'through this unity of dress you may make it known that you love and belong to the brothers and sisters'.[88] He had brought home trunks of clothing as a further gift from the Hutterites and, at a meeting, he told the community that they were now to put aside the colourful folk outfits they had worn since they attended their first youth movement rallies. There was to be a new dress code: sombre colours, unadorned trousers and shirts for the men, and for the women, ankle-length, long-sleeved dresses, aprons, and a kerchief over their hair. Was this a joke? some of the members of the Bruderhof asked Eberhard incredulously. They would look like they belonged in the sixteenth century.[89] Others, though, were enthusiastic about the new costume. The Hutterites had made it a condition of the unification that the Bruderhof should adopt their customs – and the Hutterite interpretation of living out the Gospel on a day-to-day basis was only a little more austere than the Bruderhof's own.

Eberhard introduced more changes in the year after his return. Once the new, conservative dress code had been absorbed, he told his brothers and sisters that they would need to rearrange their way of life further still. The Hutterites aimed to promote individual obedience to the community through hierarchy and strict discipline. From now on the Bruderhof would be adopting this method – which included an exclusion system by which a 'sinner' could be shut out first from community meetings, then from social activities, and

finally from the community entirely.[90] Eberhard would be titled a
'Servant of the Word' – the Hutterite term for a community leader.
He would be supported by a council of 'Witness Brothers', including
his son-in-law Hans Zumpe, who would have more influence in the
affairs of the community than the other members.

Eberhard introduced these changes gradually, but he had to work
hard to convince everyone that they were necessary. Even Emmy, who
was at first enthusiastic about the idea of unification, confessed to him
that she was 'disappointed at the overall results of his strenuous
efforts'.[91] The Hutterite communities 'had given precious little' – they
might be far richer than the Bruderhof, but it turned out that they
expected each colony to run its own finances.[92] And she was reluctant
for the Bruderhof to adopt 'laws and regulations that were not born
out of our own living experience'.[93] The nature of the 'good life' they
were leading seemed, arbitrarily, to have changed shape. Eberhard
urged her and the other communards that all these rules were surely
valid if they helped rid the Bruderhof of their sinful, individualistic
selves, and guided them to unity. 'The Church-community is a living
building,' he exhorted. 'The people in it are the living stones. These
living stones have nothing perfect in themselves: they must be hewn
and trimmed to fit better and better into the building.'[94]

Most people, including Emmy, were eventually persuaded by
Eberhard's certainty. The Bruderhof would remain part of the
Hutterite community until 1955, and then renew the connection
between 1974 and 1995, before breaking it off permanently over
disagreements about leadership, decision-making and discipline.[95]
After the union with the Hutterites, life in the Bruderhof remained
largely autonomous and independent. Participants' daily routine,
beliefs and ideals continued much as before. Yet the new, conservative clothing, which emphasized the already patriarchal power
structure, and the shunning of those whose behaviour did not
conform to the community's standard, have attracted sporadic criticism to the present day.[96]

*

On New Year's Eve 1932, just before midnight, Eberhard Arnold
gave a talk at a members' meeting that was astonishingly prophetic.
The Bruderhof was, he said, at 'an hour of the greatest crisis'. Close

at hand was Hitler, his philosophy 'merely love to those nearest, and hatred against those further away'.[97] Abroad, Mussolini was 'wielding the weapons of militarism and mass-suggestion'; there was unrest in Japan and China; and, 'in spite of all peace treaties, the new and perhaps last world war is being prepared'. This coming war, Eberhard warned, would be 'more barbaric than the last', since it would be waged 'not only against men and military bases, but just as much against women and children far from the front'.[98] At this juncture, he urged, 'nothing is more necessary, nothing more urgent than that a place is maintained where love triumphs'.[99] The Bruderhof members, wandering outside to see the starry night sky of the new year of 1933, sombrely reflected that their community had acquired additional significance. What they were doing was not just a response to the chaos sown by the First World War. They were building an alternative to a Europe that seemed on the verge of tearing itself apart again.

Later that year, Hitler was appointed Chancellor. The National Socialists began to tighten their grip on Germany. They were unwilling to countenance the continued existence of any community they saw as opposed to their own ideals – whether Jewish, Romany or Bruderhof. Nazi officials appeared at the Rhön, confiscating all the books with red covers in the Bruderhof library as evidence of its 'communist' leanings. In the following months, Nazi delegations continued to turn up at the remote, windswept farm, trying to terrify its inhabitants into supporting the Third Reich – or failing that, to persecute them until they disbanded. Their visits alternated with raids by the SS, the Gestapo and the local police. Officials banned the sale of Bruderhof publications and craft products, ramped up the taxes on the farm, and announced that the community was out of bounds to visitors. The secret police examined the community's mail. The Bruderhof was under siege: condemned to near-total isolation, its lines of communication and sources of income all but cut off.

The community followed the Bible's parable of turning the other cheek. They received their official visitors politely, and even offered them coffee and cake – luxuries which they rarely allowed themselves. This politeness did not signify capitulation. 'It was no question to us what spirit Hitler served,' Emmy wrote, 'and we refused to have anything to do with it.'[100] They refused to accept Nazi teachers in their school, which led the government to close it down. They refused to surrender their men for military service. They refused to give the *Heil Hitler!* salute, or to utter the mandatory oath of allegiance to the Third Reich. Their printing press continued turning out pamphlets about God's love for all his children – including foreigners and Jews. Amid this oppression, in the autumn of 1933 Eberhard slipped on a patch of wet grass and broke his leg. From his bed, he explained to the raiding Nazis that the Bruderhof was an 'embassy' from the kingdom of God: it could only be subject to the diktats of the ruling regime if those diktats didn't contravene Christian principles. The Bruderhof could not swear oaths to the state, or serve as soldiers, he said, since the kingdom of God was opposed to power politics and militarism. 'We represent a different order,' he told his hostile listeners, 'that of the church as it was in Jerusalem.'[101]

While the communards framed their resistance to the Nazis in reasonable tones, they seemed at times to be deliberately thumbing their noses at them. Disregarding their perennial shortage of funds, they launched a series of ambitious building projects, almost as if to emphasize to those watching that the Bruderhof intended to keep expanding, whatever opposition it faced. Some part of them seemed almost to welcome the prospect of repression, reprisals and persecution, since these would bear out their long-standing expectation of a clash between the forces of God and Satan. They would go into the coming battle with their heads held high. As Emmy wrote, it was impossible to take half measures in opposing the Nazi regime: 'It had to be all or nothing.'[102]

Eberhard sent a manifesto directly to Hitler, urging him to embrace universal love.[103] He was preoccupied during every waking moment with fears of a final seizure of the community at Rhön, and even began to dream about having a heart-to-heart with the Führer. He knew exactly what he would say: 'My dear Adolf Hitler, this can't go on much longer [. . .] in every instance killing is against love.'[104] The tone of all the Bruderhof's communications with the Third Reich, actual and imaginary, was exquisitely, painfully earnest. 'If we reach a man's heart,' Eberhard reassured his followers, 'we will find there the hidden spark from God, even if he is the greatest criminal.'[105] In the face of all indications to the contrary – the public book burnings, the smashing of Jewish-owned shops, the peremptory shooting of communists and other 'enemies of the state' – the Bruderhof community maintained that it was possible for a blacklisted minority group to reason with, even to convert, Hitler.

But the mood in the Rhön darkened as the Nazi regime tightened its grip across Germany. The Arnolds decided that only those in the community who were fully committed to the Bruderhof beliefs should risk dying for them. Once Eberhard's leg began to mend, and he was up and hobbling about with it in plaster, he called his fellow community members together. They now numbered 140. Their ranks had surged as Hitler's power grew, with people joining the community less as a commitment to the Bruderhof's particular utopian vision than as a way of rejecting the society the Nazis were creating. Eberhard told his fellow members that they must either be baptized into full Bruderhof membership or leave. The 'brotherhood circle', he warned them, would soon have to be forged into an army of peaceful resistance.[106] In a demonstration of the extreme loyalty inspired by the ideals, resolution and unity of the community, nearly every member opted to remain.

Notwithstanding his to-the-death rhetoric, Eberhard began searching for an escape route – a way to save his community by finding it a suitable new base. He suggested to the Hutterites that the Bruderhof cross the Atlantic to join them, but they were unable to grasp his desperation, and would not help raise the financial guarantee that would have been necessary for emigration on such a large scale. He tried Switzerland, but the government refused to host men who wouldn't serve in the army. Then he contacted his wide network of acquaintances in the Netherlands and Britain, but they seemed oblivious to political developments in Germany, and could not understand the urgency of his letters. Finally, Emmy and Eberhard – his leg still healing – visited the tiny principality of Liechtenstein. Here they discovered a mountainside hotel standing empty out of season. The owner agreed to allow them to rent it. It would be a second home to the Bruderhof, at least temporarily. All the children were smuggled out of Germany into Liechtenstein, along with a few adults. They restarted the school there, and put

down the groundwork for a new community, which they called the
Alm Bruderhof.

In March 1935, Hitler introduced compulsory military service in
Germany, and the Bruderhof men who were of military age were
forced to flee as well. They travelled by different routes to the Alm:
some by rail, some by bicycle, and some on foot, all eventually
making it safely across the border. On the Arnolds' suggestion, a
few women and older men – those beyond the age of being called
up – stayed on at the Rhön. Emmy and Eberhard saw their presence
as a vital way of keeping the torch of Christian brotherhood burning
even as fascism cast Germany ever deeper into shadow. But the
remaining members struggled to keep the community going. Why
plant crops if they might not be around to harvest them? Why print
books if their publications were banned from the shops? The idea
that all work – even futile work – was a way of serving God did
not seem enough.

Things were hardly better in Liechtenstein, where the hotel,
although picturesquely alpine, was 4,500 feet above sea level and
permanently freezing. Farming was impossible – snow lay thick on
the mountains much of the year – and the printing equipment was
still at the Rhön, so there was little to occupy communards apart
from worrying about the future. The anxious Bruderhof members
agreed that it didn't seem likely that Liechtenstein would be able
to withstand an incursion of Nazi troops. The country had a minute
army. And a large portion of its citizens sympathized with Germany.

The Arnolds travelled backwards and forwards between the Alm
and the Rhön. They spent most time at the latter, because – as
Emmy wrote – 'we felt we belonged with those who had stayed
where the danger was greatest'.[107] Determined to stave off his fellow
communards' despair, Eberhard ignored the pain from his injured
leg, even after it became infected. His efforts to make the best of
things momentarily heartened his listeners. 'Let us not be a small
generation met by great things,' he told them, face alight. 'Let us
become worthy of a great time and a great calling.'[108] But late in
1935 his leg worsened. It was too late to save it, he was told. It
would need to be amputated. Eberhard agreed.

In December, aged fifty-two, Eberhard Arnold died on the operating table. The Bruderhof members were shocked and shaken when

they heard the news. Eberhard was still so young, so energetic. Could this really be part of God's plan? Emmy was devastated. 'How could it be,' she asked, 'that, just in this critical hour, Eberhard, my husband and friend, counsellor, and spiritual guide, had left us forever?'[109] Hans Zumpe, Eberhard's son-in-law, was installed as the new leader of the community, but it was difficult to keep the Bruderhof going without Eberhard's charisma, optimism and determination. The community's members remained split between the Rhön and Alm settlements, uncertain of what next step they should take to oppose Hitler and defend their ideals. Ultimately, action was forced on them.

The morning of 14 April 1937 dawned misty and wet. The inhabitants of the Rhön were working on a circular stone wall to mark the ground where Eberhard had been buried when fifty police, SS and Gestapo officers emerged from the woods. Wielding revolvers, the officials herded the terrified brothers and sisters into their dining hall. A Gestapo commissar read out a notice dissolving the community because of its 'violent communistic attacks'.[110] The communards were told that they must either join the army, return to their 'proper' homes or immediately leave the country – in which case they could take with them only what they could carry.

While the Bruderhof brothers and sisters were detained in their hall, officials carried armfuls of books and papers out of the library and study and loaded them into their cars. Then three members of the community's executive committee, Hans Meier, Hans Boller and Karl Keiderling, were taken away by the Gestapo. The rest of the communards were convinced that this was the last they would see of their comrades – that they were fated to go to a concentration camp. They would probably have been right, had it not been for two American Hutterites who were just then visiting the Rhön. At this point, the Nazis were still unwilling to create an international incident. After six weeks of lobbying by the Hutterites, the captives were released.

Three days after their official dissolution, the entire Bruderhof community fled from Germany, travelling by various covert routes to Britain. Those members who were in Liechtenstein, including Emmy, remained where they were for another year, before joining the others. The Arnolds' eldest son Hardy had made a great number of contacts in Britain during his time as a university student. Eberhard himself had visited to lecture, building links with the Quakers, with university and pacifist groups, and with various social reformers – including Muriel Lester, a Christian socialist and philanthropist who was also a friend of Dorothy Elmhirst and Rabindranath Tagore.[111] Since Britain was politically liberal, had a strong pacifist movement, and was separated from Hitler by the sea, there seemed to the members of the Bruderhof no better place to rebuild their community. But as they gathered their energies to move, the communards found themselves struggling. This was the fourth time they had begun a new community, and each transition felt more exhausting than the last. Many were close to despair at the loss of Eberhard. They wondered whether they had the fortitude to go on.

*

The Bruderhof's British supporters found the community a new home: a large but run-down farmhouse in the Cotswolds.[112] Here the brothers and sisters meticulously replicated the living pattern of the Rhön. They continued to farm, publish and follow the austere dress and discipline introduced after the amalgamation with the Hutterites. Emmy remained central to the community. She dedicated herself to gathering, sorting and disseminating her husband's extensive writing – his books, articles, letters and lecture notes – which the Bruderhof members referred to when in doubt about decisions. Her children all committed themselves to life in the Bruderhof – one, Heini, would become the community's leader in the 1960s and 70s.

The Bruderhof remained outward-looking. The turmoil of international politics had, as Emmy remembered, inspired in its members 'a renewed urgency' to spread their pacifist ideals and to 'call others to join us'.[113] The communards paid visits to other like-minded projects, including a trip to Devon where they looked around Dartington Hall. They launched an English-language journal, the *Plough*, with the motto 'Towards the Coming Order'. Its aim was to unite the Bruderhof members' activities with those of others promoting communal living and pacifism in Britain (there was also a German version of the journal – *Der Pflug*).[114] The journal's contributors included leading figures in the Arts and Crafts movement, like the writer Laurence Housman and the sculptor Eric Gill

– who had founded his own Christian-cum-arts community, at Ditchling in Sussex in 1913.[115] Another contributor was John Middleton Murry, Katherine Mansfield's widower, who had experienced a spiritual conversion soon after her death.

As with the aftermath of the First World War, in the tumultuous run-up to the Second thousands of people were again looking for social alternatives to militant nationalism. Many of them saw salvation in the Bruderhof's pacifist, communalist Christian socialism. A group of refugee German Jews arrived at the Cotswold Bruderhof, staying for some months to learn about communal living before heading off to kibbutz life in Palestine. The first half of 1939 saw over a thousand visitors to the Cotswold community: British and foreign; socialists, pacifists, communists, vegetarians, and seekers from various spiritual groups.[116] Most were impressed, although one visitor, W. H. Garbett, found the community 'dirty, untidy and inartistic' (he much preferred Dartington Hall, which he went on to visit afterwards).[117] By the time the Second World War broke out, the Bruderhof had permanent members who were German, British, Swiss, Swedish, Dutch and Czech. It had become a refuge from the fascist dystopias of Europe.

During the Second World War, the Bruderhof were forced to emigrate again. The British government was beginning to intern the Germans within its borders as enemy aliens. Now 350-strong, pacifist and conspicuously international, it wasn't easy for the Bruderhof to find a new host nation. Canada and the United States refused its application for asylum, in spite of the Bruderhof's continuing links with the Hutterites. Only Paraguay opened its doors. The country had long had a liberal policy towards immigrants, having welcomed, among others, Mennonites, White Russians, Australian socialists, and Friedrich Nietzsche's sister Elisabeth, who went there in the 1880s to set up the anti-Semitic Nueva Germania to enact her ideas about the superiority of the Aryan-Germanic race.[118] The 20,000-acre Primavera Bruderhof in Paraguay became the centre of Bruderhof operations for the next two decades.[119] In the 1960s, the headquarters of the community was moved to the United States, which remains its centre to the present day. It was in the Woodcrest Bruderhof in New York State that Emmy Arnold, by now a revered elder of the community, died in 1980, aged ninety-five.

The Bruderhof has survived, largely intact in its ideals and lifestyle, for over a century. Today it carries on its evangelical mission to reform the world along peaceful, loving lines; its members volunteer at prisons and hospitals, and work to help humanitarian aid organizations. All its settlements welcome visitors and continue, quietly, trying to persuade outsiders of the rightness of Bruderhof ideals. A digital signboard on the narrow country lane that runs beside the Darvell Bruderhof in Sussex blazes out a new verse of the Bible each day for the instruction of passers-by.

Several factors that distinguished the community from others set up in the same era have contributed to its long-term vitality. Its blueprint was codified in the Bible — in the early Church in Jerusalem whose members strove to be of 'one heart and mind, and shared all things in common'.[120] Leaders of secular communities, or of those based on unorthodox spirituality, had to grope their way towards finding a physical shape for their visionary ideals. Their decisions were vulnerable to the criticism of participants, to the effects of the changing zeitgeist, and to the leaders themselves changing their minds. This was not so for the Bruderhof members, who felt that their communal ideals were 'not based on human nature but on the eternal God'.[121] It is largely due to this faith-based conviction that, throughout history, it has often been religious utopias that last the longest.[122] The Bruderhof was also sustained by its absolute belief in universal brotherhood, which was outstanding even among a post-war wave of internationally oriented utopias — the only kingdom its members were affiliated to was that of God, as Eberhard had told the Nazi officials. This meant that the community was able, with relative ease, to change locations, allowing members to settle wherever they were safest and most in tune with the zeitgeist.

Amid Germany's disorientation after losing the First World War and the desire for a more certain direction during the Depression of the 1930s, many radical social visions emerged. The story of the Bruderhof is a reminder that there were other approaches to the chaotic conditions than Nazism — that even in the face of persecution, financial struggle and bitter hardship, some still raised their voices in favour of pacifism, internationalism and universal love.

SIX

CALIFORNIA DREAMING

Gerald Heard's Trabuco College

Bloomsbury, London; a winter's evening in 1929.[1] The literary critic
Raymond Mortimer fidgeted around the dining room of his flat in
Gordon Place, recently redesigned by Duncan Grant and Vanessa
Bell. An experienced host, he was uncharacteristically nervous about
introducing two of his most brilliant friends, Gerald Heard and
Aldous Huxley, at dinner. The bell announced the arrival of Heard
– winningly eloquent, a man reputed to read 2,000 books a year
and to be able to reference their contents at will. As soon as Heard
came into the room, he launched into a monologue that tacked
between the latest gossip of the Bloomsbury set and ideas for the
article he was composing for *Time & Tide* on human evolution. When
the bell rang again, Mortimer tensed.

Aldous Huxley entered. His long billowing overcoat and lean
face, pinched from the cold, were in marked contrast to Heard's
sleek appearance. In his introductions, Mortimer was sure to mention
that both men were habitués of the Elmhirsts' community at
Dartington Hall. It turned out they had several times just missed
running into one another there. As they exchanged memories of
the unruly children on the estate, the experiments with factory
chickens and the plays staged in the old tilt yard, Mortimer watched
them with an acute sense of their differences. Where Heard was a
collector of ideas and ideals, taking pleasure in weaving them

together into dreams of a better world, Huxley's talent was for dissecting and rejecting. The well-known thirty-five-year-old novelist seemed the ultimate anti-utopian, the spokesman for a disenchanted post-war generation who refused to believe in anything.

They sat down to eat. Mortimer watched his guests nervously. Heard continued to talk, his melodious voice rising high with enthusiasm. Huxley, tall, cadaverously thin, was silently balling up pieces of bread, shooting the occasional sharp glance at Heard through his thick-lensed glasses. Mortimer half expected the dinner to end in a dispute, with one of the two men walking out. Huxley was notorious for his ability to undermine those he took against with a few well-chosen words. But by the time the main course was over, Mortimer noticed that Huxley was no longer just listening. He had begun speaking, and so quickly and enthusiastically that it was hard even for as prodigious a talker as Heard to get a word in. Long after midnight, the two men sat hunched in conversation, oblivious to their host.

After a decade of mercilessly poking fun at all moral and transcendental values, Huxley confessed to Heard that he had started to feel the emptiness of his cynicism.[2] He found himself wanting to discover a 'new religion', a faith that would give to society and to himself the higher meaning he felt had been lost.[3] In Heard – five years older and with an ability to infuse everything from psychoanalysis to palaeontology with idealism – Huxley had discovered someone who might be able to guide him on that path. Their discussion ranged freely from utopian socialism to spiritualism, theosophy to back-to-the-landism, pacifism, fascism, vegetarianism and surrealism. It was the kind of eclectic exchange characteristic of the interwar years, when the urgent search for a better framework for living fuelled an unusual intellectual fluidity. The technocratic era that followed the Second World War would sort such ideas and -isms rigorously into specialist areas, but in these years people were willing to try any formula, to combine any number of disciplines in their quest to find a new way forward for society.[4]

On the back of the acquaintance they struck up that evening, Huxley and Heard began collaborating on the development of a new religion, what Heard called a system of 'unity, sanity, self-forgetfulness and communion'.[5] They intended to scour the social sciences, spiritualism and religious traditions from around the world for ideas and methods, and to meld the best of these together. Their religion would offer a guide to a way of living that was both devotional and practical, creating a complete new social model. It would replace Christianity, which Heard and Huxley felt was not a faith fit for modern times, since it did not incorporate science and had failed to prevent the First World War. It would provide an antidote to the individualism and materialism that they believed had long been stunting humankind's progress, and which had triggered the outbreak of the war.

Over the next ten years, Heard and Huxley's quest for a new religion would evolve from abstract conversations to active involvement with utopian projects like Dartington Hall and pacifist organizations like the Peace Pledge Union. But nothing they tried seemed satisfactory. Finally, in the late 1930s, Heard decided that to perfect his spiritual system he needed a physical stronghold for it: a community of his own, where he could collaborate daily with like-minded idealists. His plan was astonishingly hands-on for such a theoretical man, but in this turbulent period even those who would naturally have remained armchair philosophers were pushed to practical action. In 1942, with Huxley's encouragement, Heard founded Trabuco College in a dusty canyon not far from Los Angeles, under the blue skies of southern California.

The other practical utopias in this book were all begun in the immediate aftermath of the First World War. Their founders hoped and believed that their communities would inspire a spontaneous change in behaviour, a transformation of the social pattern which would make a second world war impossible. Trabuco College, however, was started during the war these other communities wanted to prevent. From the vantage point of the 1940s, it was difficult for Heard to believe that the great mass of people could be trusted to follow the example set by a small community. Instead, he intended Trabuco College to produce a caste of visionaries who would guide the world – men and women who were endowed with superior talents in spiritual and social leadership. This 'International Police Force', as Heard sometimes termed them, would live together communally during the war, honing their expertise in how best to live.[6] Afterwards, they would emerge to guide, coax and marshal the rest of humanity into a more peaceful, spiritually enlightened mode of existence.

*

Gerald Heard was born in London in 1889 to Anglo-Irish parents.[7] Like many raised in devout Christian households during the nineteenth century, from a young age he was filled with the sense that his aim in life should be to serve others. Driven by this ambition, his early trajectory was similar to that of Leonard Elmhirst. Both decided to follow in their fathers' footsteps and become vicars; both were preparing to take holy orders and were studying theology at Cambridge when the First World War broke out (they had the same tutor, the pacifist Goldsworthy Lowes Dickinson, who coined the term 'league of nations', and undoubtedly shaped their internationalist thinking). Both Heard and Elmhirst were horrified by the war, in which each lost close family members – in Heard's case, his older brother, who died on the North African front in 1915. They both suffered mental breakdowns during which they lost their faith in Christianity, in large part because the Church had supported the war. By the end of the conflict, it no longer seemed to either of them that it was possible to improve the world by becoming a vicar. As the English reformer Beatrice Webb observed of their generation as a whole, they transferred 'the emotion of self-sacrificing service from God to man'.[8]

Heard's route into utopia-building was less direct than Leonard Elmhirst's. Well into middle age he was still seeking, rather than committing to any one particular solution to society's problems. As an author, broadcaster, peace campaigner and spiritual guru, he was drawn to the gleam of new concepts and projects. He always worried that in committing himself to any one set of ideas he might miss out on others and, crucially, on how all ideas were connected. It took the shock of the outbreak of the Second World War to convince him that he at last needed to move from the universal to the particular: from collecting theories together to living by and promulgating a single system.

The path that led Heard to create Trabuco College began in the early 1920s, when he began working for the founder of the Irish

cooperative movement, Sir Horace Plunkett.[9] This reformer had
spent his life promoting Irish independence, working to free his
country from its British colonizers by strengthening it from the ground
up, encouraging cooperation in agricultural communities under the
slogan 'Better farming, better business, better living'. He wanted to
remake Irish society, and, like many of the idealists of the period, his
instinct was to start with reforming the village. His community-based
strategies influenced many of the utopians of the early twentieth
century, inspiring Rabindranath Tagore's reform work in the Indian
countryside, as well as President Theodore Roosevelt's efforts to
address rural problems in America between 1901 and 1909.[10]

As Plunkett's personal secretary, Heard encouraged farmers to
share machinery, to exchange information on new agricultural techniques, and to organize livestock and produce sales together, but he
found himself only moderately interested in this work. His cast of
mind was more abstract than practical. What he was enthused by
was Plunkett's view that the community group, working cooperatively, was the vital unit for forging social progress. This idea planted
the seed that would, nearly two decades later, grow into Trabuco
College. Heard's work in Ireland was cut short when republican
terrorists burned down Plunkett's house in 1923; they were angry
that this celebrated reformer was deflecting energy away from the
imperative of securing Ireland's political independence. Local cooperation, they thought, was nothing more than a distraction.

Plunkett and Heard sought refuge in England, where Heard found
himself drawn into a group of raffish writers and artists that included
Raymond Mortimer, Duncan Grant, Christopher Isherwood and
W. H. Auden. Heard did less and less work for Plunkett as he
discovered a new outlet for his desire to serve society: explaining
new ideas, particularly scientific ones, to the general public.
Lecturing to a crowded hall, sitting on a panel or reporting for the
BBC as its first science journalist suited his insatiable curiosity, quick
tongue and gregariousness far better than seeing to Plunkett's correspondence. It was in these years that Heard began work on the
first of the thirty-eight books he would produce in his lifetime: a
rich mix of publications that would cover spirituality, popular science
and psychological evolution, and include detective novels, science
fiction and even a solitary study – one of the first ever written – on

the existence of flying saucers.'' He was, he kept telling his friends, promoting democracy in the way that best suited him: by bringing enlightenment to the masses.

Heard's audience admired him for his expansiveness of thought, optimism, bold speculations, and ability to explain obscure scientific discoveries – but not for the rigour of his logic. His arguments, when written down, tended to become swamped in an excess of ideas, ideas that he piled one on top of the other without clear segue. One critic went so far as to accuse Heard of adopting the tactics of the cuttlefish, 'which emits its ink not to enlighten but to confuse its pursuers'.'' Though clarity was not his strong point, what Heard did have was passionate idealism, a formidable power of synthesis, and an ability to persuade those around him of the vital importance of whatever idea currently had him in its grip.

Through the 1920s, Heard channelled his feelings of social responsibility into supporting progressive education and agricultural cooperatives, and paying visits to prisons. But much of his life was oriented towards the pursuit of pleasure. With his lover Christopher Wood – pianist, film critic and wayward heir to a jam-factory fortune – he lived in a luxurious flat in the West End that overlooked Selfridges. A familiar figure at salons, dinners and country-house parties, he made friends with some of the era's leading thinkers and writers, including Virginia Woolf, E. M. Forster and Harold Nicholson. Heard's sociability did not prevent him from continuing to wrestle with the question of how to prevent a second great war. This was, it seemed to him, his life's vocation. Between parties he was reading constantly, ploughing through history books, scientific journals and novels. Whatever he read about – from the evolutionary significance of people's clothing to Gandhi's non-cooperation movement in India to recent advances in psychical research – he strove to relate it to the ultimate question of international harmony. It was Heard's urgent search for a better world, as much as his erudition, that won him admirers, even among the educated and opinionated polymaths of Bloomsbury. The novelist Naomi Mitchinson thought he was struggling towards some insight 'which was at the back of all our minds, of extreme importance but so far unexpressed. In fact he was our prophet.''

*

Heard's thinking coalesced into an idiosyncratic book, published in 1929 – one that approached Gurdjieffian proportions in its opaque abstractions. *The Ascent of Humanity: An Essay on the Evolution of Civilization from Group Consciousness Through Individuality to Super-Consciousness* wove various ideas from history, anthropology, biology and sociology together to offer a new method for advancing social harmony.[14] Human consciousness, Heard believed, had evolved over millennia. To begin with, tribal man had no sense of himself as a separate individual, but shared a common, harmonious 'co-consciousness'. Gradually, this social unit had atrophied, until humankind reached its present state – a state where people strove against one another, driven by materialism and self-obsession. This was what had led to the First World War. Heard believed that humankind needed to work out a new evolutionary step, both psychologically and spiritually, to lift itself beyond individualism. The individuals of the world would be 'fused' back together – as he put it – into a shared, spiritual 'superconsciousness', an organism infused with divinity (although not presided over by any particular god). Materialism, social competition and international conflict would be replaced by mutual love and concern.

The question that remained, at the end of the book, was how, practically speaking, the much-needed act of 'fusing' could be accomplished. Heard's initial hope was that by publishing *The Ascent of Humanity*, and giving accompanying lectures, he would convince the world – particularly the British cultural elite – of his ideas, and a practical method for constructing the superconsciousness would spontaneously arise. His theory, fantastical as it now sounds, appealed to many of his contemporaries. But the spontaneous fusing of a superconsciousness failed to materialize. Heard gradually came to the conclusion that he would have to work out the practicalities himself. Hoping for inspiration from others similarly preoccupied with transcendence, he tried attending the meetings of Gurdjieff's disciple P. D. Ouspensky. He took part in so many of these meetings that Ouspensky decided he was a possible convert, inviting him to stay in the grand Palladian mansion where he lived with his most devoted pupils.[15] Heard, however, concluded that the Fourth Way could not offer a solution to 'fusing' either – it seemed more concerned with strengthening the individual consciousness than assimilating it into the consciousness of the rest of humankind.

But the Fourth Way did help convince Heard that theory – writing and lecturing – might not be enough to accomplish all that he wanted. Change would only be achieved if people actively embraced a new approach to life. After much thought and conversation, he began to turn the evolutionary theories he had set down in *The Ascent of Humanity* into a system of living. He called this the 'third morality', to suggest a move beyond what he saw as the preceding two 'moralities': anthropomorphism, in which the universe was seen as an expression of individual people; and mechanomorphism, which conceived of the universe as functioning like a machine.[16] Both of these, he believed, had been proven false by advances in human knowledge. The 'third morality' was intended as a new paradigm for society, promoting spiritual enlightenment through connection with the superconsciousness. Man's evolution from individualist to unit in the superconsciousness would be achieved, in part, by spending long hours each day meditating and researching spiritual techniques. But the linchpin of Heard's system was borrowed from his old mentor Sir Horace Plunkett: the small-group format. Those taking up the third morality were to join together to form local 'generating cells', whose meetings would be the foundation for their efforts to transcend their individuality.

The next step was to form the first generating cell. If Heard could create a successful test unit, he was sure other cells would sprout up all across the world, and the fusing of the superconsciousness would finally happen. A global network of spiritual and psychological interconnection would emerge out of the network of local groups. Heard turned to Horace Plunkett for help in beginning his practical undertaking. Plunkett introduced him to the founders of Dartington Hall, whom he had been advising on agricultural cooperation, and Heard persuaded the Elmhirsts to let him set up a generating cell on their estate. Between 1932 and 1935, Heard took the train regularly from London to Devon to lead the group, working with Dorothy and others at Dartington to 'fuse with the superconsciousness'. 'You challenge us, you will not let us sleep,' Leonard Elmhirst wrote to Heard, thanking him for bringing new energy to the community.[17]

Disappointingly for such an exotic-sounding process, what 'fusing' meant in reality was a group of people sitting around in a room talking. Sometimes the generating cell's meetings were confessionals, where participants tearfully admitted their troubles as a way of overcoming their individuality, outlining their squabbles, their petty jealousies and preoccupation with personal gain.[18] Other sessions were dominated by Heard, who guided members through different unifying theories and techniques, taken from religion, psychology, music and any other source he found inspiring. Between meetings, participants wrote to Heard, letters that stretched to many pages and vibrated with emotion as each member of the cell spoke of their struggles to integrate the third morality into their lives. 'The moment that one realises that one's own thread is woven into the general tapestry,' Heard reassured them, 'then one begins to see the eternal life.'[19] He was delighted by the group's progress, and he felt, for the first time, that he was achieving something of practical benefit to the world, rather than indulging in disembodied theorizing. With characteristic grandiosity, he told his London friends that his generating cell was achieving 'psychic metamorphosis', a social advance that would prove to be far more remarkable than all the technological inventions of the nineteenth century put together.[20]

*

When the Elmhirsts began their process of economic rationalization at Dartington Hall during the Depression, it seemed to Heard nothing short of a tragedy. According to his carefully evolved theories, the perfect world was one in which economic imperatives simply didn't exist. There was no doubt in his mind that Dartington was sliding back down the evolutionary scale. 'You must pay your own way, that is the one regulation,' he complained to a member of his generating cell, Margaret Isherwood. The community was becoming 'conventional, national and orthodox'.[21] It had been infected by materialism, the kind of second-order motivation he thought could only lead to social division and conflict. But even as Heard's disillusionment with Dartington grew, he kept on hoping that his generating cell was going to make a breakthrough in connecting with the superconsciousness.

Meanwhile, the threat of war gathered. Authoritarian and

aggressively nationalistic rulers were tightening their hold, testing the League of Nations' peacekeeping skills by invading and occupying nearby countries. In the canteen of Dartington Hall and in Bloomsbury's sitting rooms, Heard listened to labourers, artists and intellectuals agonizing over whether it would be wiser for Britain to concentrate its efforts on preventing war, or whether the government ought to be girding itself for the inevitable fight. Heard was among those who continued to maintain that war must be avoided at all costs. On the basis of his knowledge of recent scientific advances, he was sure a second world war would be far more destructive than the first. It was now possible to obliterate a city in a matter of hours, he told anyone who would listen. War could wipe out European civilization entirely.[22]

In 1936, gripped by fear, Heard decided that his small-scale experiment at Dartington was not yielding results quickly enough. He disbanded the generating cell and began to work more directly for world harmony by entering the ranks of the Peace Pledge Union. This pacifist organization had been set up by the popular Anglican priest H. R. L. Sheppard in 1934, and by the time Heard joined it had over 100,000 members – several of whom would move to the Bruderhof when the community migrated from Germany to England. The Peace Pledge Union's members marched, petitioned and lobbied Parliament. They wrote pamphlets, organized lectures and meetings, and toured Britain in a van with a film projector – all to convince people that, as Sheppard wrote, 'war of every kind or for every cause' was 'a crime against humanity' which should no longer be permitted 'by civilized people'.[23] Heard and Huxley participated in these activities, with Huxley speaking at a meeting in the Albert Hall that was so well attended that the overflowing crowd had to be accommodated in Kensington Town Hall. At every possible moment, they emphasized that the pacifist movement must go beyond preventing the next war: it needed to reform society along more harmonious lines, constructing a 'radically new way of life' based on a new set of ideals, or even a new religion.[24]

With Huxley's help, Heard tried to adapt his third-morality methods to the Peace Pledge Union cause. The two friends suggested 'pacifist mind exercises', and petitioned the organization to help them set up hundreds of generating cells worldwide, a web which, they assured their fellow pacifists, would be the surest way of securing global harmony.[25] People needed 'a cell, or team, club or group' to renew their direct sense of connection with humankind, Heard insisted.[26] Unsurprisingly, this idea didn't appeal. The group was preoccupied with the concrete reality of rearmament in Germany and Oswald Mosley's black-shirted fascists terrorizing the streets of London. Heard and Huxley were greatly disappointed. Their disenchantment with the peace movement was sealed when members began defecting to support the campaign for rearmament, having decided that war might be a terrible thing, but that a world controlled by fascists would be infinitely worse.

In the 1920s, Huxley's writing had been characterized by light-hearted cynicism – what he later called his 'philosophy of meaninglessness'.[27] But by the 1930s, his essays and novels had become freighted with agony at the world's social and political problems – problems ranging from people's propensity to embrace fascism to overpopulation and the evils of free-market capitalism. It was in this state of mind that he wrote *Brave New World*, his famed dystopia about a society where science is used to curb citizens' individuality and freedom.[28] Huxley was close to succumbing to depression – contemporary society was, he wrote, 'unviable', and doomed to 'self-frustration and suicide' – but Heard's continuing belief in the possibility of change buoyed him up.[29] All of humanity's problems would be solved, Heard kept saying, once people began to live in a more spiritual fashion. Everything, Huxley decided, 'finally resolves itself into a religious problem'.[30]

Even with this hope in mind, it was difficult for Heard and Huxley to come up with a plan of action. But after much debate, they concluded that they had exhausted the routes for achieving spiritual transformation in Britain: they needed to find a safe haven where they could work on their new religion until calmer times returned. America, they decided, would be the best refuge. They would undertake what Heard termed 'a second Mayflower voyage' – 'an alternative', as he told his friends, that was 'far more attractive than staying on in an insane Europe'.[31] The United States had been pursuing a policy of isolation from world affairs all through the 1930s, and it seemed to Heard and Huxley it was unlikely to be touched by war. It would be a place where they could concentrate undisturbed on remodelling human behaviour – on the 'creation of small-scale societies of chosen individuals', as Huxley put it, 'outside and on the margin' of the mainstream.[32]

In 1937, Heard and Huxley boarded a transatlantic liner. Their leave-taking was sombre. Heard warned anyone who would listen that 'old Europe is finished', and that they, too, ought to head west.[33] Heard and Huxley did have a few travelling companions: Huxley's wife Maria and their son Matthew, and Heard's former lover Chris Wood. (Heard had taken a vow of celibacy in the mid-1930s, hoping to sublimate his sex drive to spiritual ends.)[34] Raymond Mortimer, the man who had first brought Huxley and Heard together in Bloomsbury, thoroughly disapproved of their 'fleeing' a Britain under threat of war. He warned Maria before the ship left that she would need to be on her guard against her husband and his friend abandoning her to live on top of a pillar in the American desert, fasting and praying for peace like the Christian stylites of ancient times.[35]

*

Heard and Huxley were drawn to America because of its long history of utopian experimentation. The Pilgrim Fathers, the first permanent European settlers in the country in the early seventeenth century, were Christians fleeing persecution, hoping to create a godly way of life on earth. These pious idealists were followed by thousands of other groups driven by the desire to create new, purer modes of living – though they notably failed to take into account the indigenous way of living that they were disrupting. From the *Mayflower* to the Mormons, America's social freedoms, its wide-open spaces, the peculiar value that the national culture placed on independent endeavour, all lent themselves to the concept that it was possible, at any time, to build a better society from scratch in the United States.

The America that Huxley and Heard travelled to in the 1930s was dominated by the Depression: by loss of confidence in the banks; dust-bowl conditions in Texas and Oklahoma; factories closing and soup kitchens opening; thousands of families migrating West in search of work. But Huxley and Heard were heartened by how this hardship had not impeded social dreaming. In fact, it seemed to have fuelled it. The biggest response to the economic crisis had been

President F. D. Roosevelt's New Deal – a series of national recovery programmes so ambitious in scope that it amounted to a plan for the restructuring of the country. At the other end of the scale were the hundreds of independent projects intended to strengthen the all-round vibrancy of particular local communities or to reform society at large. These initiatives included a self-help colony for struggling war veterans in Texas, a series of Catholic houses for people 'living in accordance with the justice and charity of Jesus Christ', and an elaborate plan for a 'moneyless government' that would control all of America's resources and provide for the needs of its citizens for free.[36]

The experiment that Heard knew most about was Arthurdale in West Virginia, which he had discussed with Dorothy Elmhirst during his stays at Dartington Hall. Arthurdale had been set up in 1933 by the First Lady, Eleanor Roosevelt, to help unemployed miners. Her aim was to show that there was an alternative to people relying on jobs that were vulnerable to market forces. Families selected for her 'Little Village' would engage in subsistence homesteading instead. Their community would be self-governing, and it would run cooperative businesses including a gas station and a furniture workshop. Eleanor Roosevelt had partly been inspired to start Arthurdale by her own discussions with Dorothy Elmhirst. The two women had worked closely together on social schemes while Dorothy lived in New York, and had talked over the idea of Arthurdale by letter and in person, when the Elmhirsts visited the United States, dining with the Roosevelts at the White House.[37]

But none of America's many utopian enterprises seemed to Heard to offer the solution the world needed. As with Dartington, he felt that the majority focused too much on the 'superficial' question of economics. Beyond his continuing advocacy of the third morality and of generating cells, he still was not sure exactly what practical form his own ideal society would take. For a short period after their arrival in the States, he and Huxley spent time in yet another community. At the invitation of D. H. Lawrence's widow Frieda, they went to stay in Taos, New Mexico, where Mabel Dodge Luhan, G. I. Gurdjieff's would-be patron, had started a settlement in a twenty-room adobe house where she championed creative and spiritual values.[38]

Taos's atmosphere was congenial to Heard. The warmth of the long, New Mexican afternoons, discussions with Luhan about the conviviality of the 'primitive' indigenous cultures of the state, and her idea that they could act as a panacea for 'modern' humanity's individualism.[39] But there were too many bohemian artists around. Their passions – painting the scrubland and adobe houses in the daytime, drinking and talking in the evenings – seemed to him a distraction from the greater quest for spiritual enlightenment and world peace. Soon he and Huxley left to travel across America, promoting their brand of pacifism on a lecture tour. But each week, more of Spain fell to Franco. In the spring of 1938 Hitler occupied Austria. Refugees from the Third Reich began to trickle, then flood into America. Both Huxley and Heard felt that their preaching about peace had become futile. Huxley, who had a family to support, turned to screenwriting in Hollywood, blotting out his fears by immersing himself in the sepia unreality of films and picnics with Greta Garbo and Charlie Chaplin.

Heard moved into an annex at the back of Chris Wood's luxurious house in Laurel Canyon in the Hollywood Hills, a few miles from the Huxleys. He fell into depression, giving up on lecturing and all forms of socializing. 'I am increasingly realising that I can do nothing for peace or any form of goodness until I am far better myself,' he wrote to H. R. L. Sheppard late in 1937.[40] While Wood spent his days at the beach, perfecting his suntan, Heard fixated obsessively on the need to rid himself of his ego and achieve fusion with the superconsciousness – trying to turn his third-morality theory into lived reality on an individual scale. Six hours a day were spent meditating. He lived on a diet of raisins, raw carrots and cups of tea.[41] When the novelist Christopher Isherwood visited him, he found the rakish raconteur he had known in London dressed in worn-out clothes, creeping around with an air of uncertainty, obsessing over the international news. He seemed, Isherwood thought, like Wood's 'poor relation'.[42]

After a few months of crisis, Heard began to regain confidence in himself. He invited guests over so that he could tell them about the ascetic techniques for achieving self-transcendence that he had come up with in his isolation. His American acquaintances were intrigued, which inspired Heard to start writing again, and to lecture at venues ranging from Hindu temples to Baptist halls. Like many gurus and idealists of the interwar years, Heard was increasingly focused on how melding Western and Eastern traditions could generate international harmony. Many young Americans were seeking a new philosophical framework amid the uncertainty of the Depression, and Heard began to attract a considerable following among them. Admirers across the country deluged him with mail, turning up at his door at odd hours to talk to him.

While Heard was winning followers, he was also discovering gurus of his own. California's openness and wealth had attracted colourful spiritualists from India. Heard took up with two of these: Jiddu Krishnamurti, who had been groomed as a child by the Theosophists to be their new 'World Teacher', before rebelling in adulthood and setting himself up in America as an independent religious guide; and Swami Prabhavananda, a Hindu monk renowned for his wide smile and fondness for smoking, and for the Vedanta temple he ran on a hill overlooking Hollywood.[43] Both these men emphasized the common moral and mystical threads that unite human experience, regardless of sect or nationality. Their teaching confirmed Heard's own idea that humankind shared a fundamental unity, and he incorporated some of their techniques into the toolkit he was developing for promoting fusion with the superconsciousness. Heard often brought Aldous Huxley to listen to them talk.

The outbreak of the Second World War in September 1939 – the war Heard had so long been expecting and fearing – jerked him out of a lifetime of gathering ideas about spiritual enlightenment. Now, he decided, was his moment, the time when he must start a community of his own: a stronghold for perfecting and promoting a model of life guided by the third morality.

*

Most of the utopians of the interwar years advocated egalitarianism and democracy – in theory if not in practice. The Elmhirsts wanted Dartington Hall to be a stronghold of self-government and fulfilment for all; in Mushanokōji Saneatsu's and Eberhard Arnold's communities in Japan and Germany, participants shared property and had an equal vote on governance. Even Gurdjieff, at the Institute for the Harmonious Development of Man, believed that everyone shared the capacity to find the '*real* I', if only they applied themselves to the Fourth Way. At the time these communities were founded, Gerald Heard, too, had believed in equality and democracy. His lectures, broadcasting and writing in Britain were driven by the idea that all people were open to enlightenment. He described his work at Dartington as 'psychological communism' or 'democratic confessionalism', and the members of his generating cell were (theoretically at least) all on an equal footing, helping one another to achieve spiritual wisdom.[44] But the outbreak of the Second World War changed Heard's ideas. Seeing the masses follow their leaders into war – a war everyone he had ever spoken to wanted to avoid – he came to the conclusion that, for better or worse, this was a world run by the elite. Most people were unequipped to handle individual freedom; they fled from it, straight into the comforting grips of 'devotional figures', as he called them, who wielded authoritarian control.[45]

When visitors came to call at Heard's studio in Hollywood, he started talking to them of a new kind of group project: not a generating cell for democracy, but a community that would act as an incubator for the social and spiritual leaders of tomorrow. Sitting in the lotus position, sipping a cup of herbal tea, Heard told guests that to face down charismatic nationalists like Hitler and Mussolini, the world needed alternative guides: enlightened men and women who would convince the masses to transcend social divisions and fuse with the superconsciousness. Not everyone, Heard warned his listeners, had the potential to become such a leader – only a privileged group was endowed with higher spiritual insight. He took to calling these elites 'neo-brahmins', a term he borrowed from the Hindu Brahmin caste, seen as the protectors of sacred learning across the generations. The idea that one group of people was inherently better than any other carried with it a worrying tinge of eugenics. The notions that biology predetermined people's paths in life, and that population should be quantitatively and qualitatively controlled, interested a number of idealists of this period, including Heard and Huxley – although many began to distance themselves from such ideas, as the Nazi programme of 'racial hygiene', starting in 1933, demonstrated the devastating consequences they could have when practically applied.[46]

Leaping from theory to action, Heard started canvassing his acquaintances, asking whether they would like to join his training community. Only potential neo-brahmins would be permitted, he told them, but it seemed that the chief requirement for being a neo-brahmin was an active interest in Heard's ideas. His close friends and the most avid followers of his lectures and books were excited by the project. It was Huxley, though, that Heard was keenest to convince. And Huxley was enthusiastic – he went so far as to help Heard write a prospectus for his community. 'Humanity is failing,' it began. 'We are starving – many of us physically, all of us spiritually – in the midst of plenty. Our shame and our failure are being blatantly advertised, every minute of every day, by the crash of explosives and the flare of burning towns.'[47]

Huxley's support for Heard's plan only went so far, however. He was by now living outside Los Angeles, in a farmhouse in the Mojave Desert set among the remains of a failed socialist utopia called Llano del Rio.[48] This location, dotted with ruins, constantly reminded him of the fragility of social experiments. When Heard pushed him to commit himself to joining his neo-brahmin community, Huxley admitted to his friend that he thought it would be more socially profitable for him to continue with his private life of thinking and writing. Heard was disappointed, but Huxley's decision was probably for the best: the two men had qualities that sparked just the wrong sort of creativity for practical achievement. When they were together they spurred each other into coming up with ever more fantastical ideas; a few hours of frenzied conversation that usually amounted to nothing concrete – a shaken head, the decision that the time wasn't quite right for action. Grace Hubble, the wife of astronomer Edwin Hubble and a friend of Heard and Huxley in America, likened them to 'two small boys working over a conjuror's box', looking for 'the secret words, the open sesame that rolls back the door'.[49] For Heard's community to have any chance of coming into existence, he needed to surround himself with people who balanced his idealism with pragmatism and practical application. He needed a sidekick such as Leonard Elmhirst had been for Rabindranath Tagore at Santiniketan-Sriniketan.

Heard found this kind of help in the person of Felix Greene, a young English journalist whom he had first met at Dartington Hall back in the early 1930s, when Greene had been working at the BBC.[50] After he had established himself as a pioneering correspondent – chiefly by interviewing the unemployed in northern England and southern Wales – the broadcasting corporation sent him out to run their radio network in North America. When the Second World War broke out, Greene abruptly resigned. He was a pacifist, and the war, which he felt the BBC supported, induced in him a sort of existential meltdown. He was grasping for a way to pull himself together. It was while he was attending a meditation seminar organized by the Quakers near Los Angeles that Greene ran into Heard, who was lecturing. Greene was deeply impressed by what the older man had to say. 'In no man have I ever seen more of God, more gentleness, more selflessness, more humility, more audacity in following his principles wherever they lead him,' Greene wrote reverently in his diary.[51] Heard saw in Greene a neo-brahmin, and told him about his plan to create a new community. Greene instantly pledged himself to helping make it a reality.

Heard's idea of what his community would look like had until now been vague and abstract. Greene, naturally and enthusiastically efficient, gave it tangible form. He organized the purchase of a plot of land on a 392-acre orange ranch in Trabuco Canyon, fifty miles from Los Angeles, making use of a legacy that Horace Plunkett had left to Heard in his will, a small amount of money that Heard had from his own family, and donations from various supporters of the project. Greene hired a Californian architect, Garrett Van Pelt, and by the autumn of 1941 he was buying up building materials – just in time, as it turned out. In December, the Japanese bombed Pearl Harbor and brought America into the war. Large-scale purchases for construction became all but impossible overnight. But south of Los Angeles, in Trabuco Canyon, the construction of the community was already in full swing. Greene camped on the grounds in a wooden hut, and during the day he set to work with a few labourers, razing the small farmhouse on the property, constructing new buildings, laying drains, and designing a garden. 'It seemed to me that a new cult, Heardism, was being born,' wrote Christopher Isherwood after visiting the building site, 'with Felix, a sunburnt and smiling Eminence, holding the real power behind the throne.'[52]

While Greene sweated over architectural plans amid the dust and debris of building, Heard – providing the spiritual leadership to go with Greene's administrative leadership – sought out neo-brahmins to populate the community. He touted his scheme for humankind's redemption around Los Angeles parties, composed letter after letter explaining its importance to his more distant acquaintances, and sent copies of his and Huxley's prospectus to people as far away as the Elmhirsts in England. Heard informed everyone that at Trabuco College participants would lead a self-sufficient communal life. They would grow their own food, live cooperatively, and learn how to combine the insight of ancient religions such as Buddhism, Hinduism and Christianity with modern psychological theories. Together, Trabuco's inhabitants would transcend their individualism and merge with the greater reality. Unlike the other utopians of the time, Heard did not make any promises about his community influencing the outside world – at least not immediately. Rather, he said, the neo-brahmins would shelter at Trabuco for the duration of the war, like the monks in remote monasteries in the Dark Ages after the fall of Rome, developing an ideal way of living.[53] They would only emerge once the chaos was over, ready to lead whatever was left of society into a harmonious new way of living.

Heard had set himself a difficult task. There was a war on, and he was trying to convince people to throw off their responsibilities, their duty to family and nation, in order to live in a half-built structure in rural California and follow a strict regime of study, prayer and ascetic living. And for what? The hope of cultivating their connection with a 'superconsciousness'. Pure escapism, came the replies. Surely, people said, if Heard wanted to do real social good, he should go back and face the bombs with his fellow countrymen in Britain. The more charitable suggested that he at the very least engage with real-world reform, rather than the spiritual transformation he seemed to be obsessed by. Heard responded to these criticisms with his characteristic rhetorical facility, arguing that to help the world without reforming the individual would be like a surgeon 'operating with septic instruments' – infection would be the result.[54]

His efforts at persuasion were not entirely in vain. By the time the construction of Trabuco College was completed in 1942, twenty-five men and women – most of them in their twenties and early thirties – were ready to start living as neo-brahmins. They were a miscellaneous bunch of conscientious objectors, out-of-work actors and artists, students and recovering alcoholics. Not quite the high caste of visionaries that Heard had hoped for. But here finally, he thought, at the age of fifty-three, he had the chance to put his ideas into action. If it was possible, he would turn these people into enlightened leaders.

*

Trabuco College did not grow up piecemeal like the huts of Atarashiki Mura or the eclectic buildings at Dartington Hall and Santiniketan-Sriniketan. Heard's vision for utopia was translated fluently into stone, all in one stroke. Greene built a structure that resembled a small Italianate monastery, with a view out over the wooded hills to the distant Pacific Ocean. Simple cells for thirty inhabitants opened onto a central courtyard. There was a library stocked with books on all the major religions and many minor ones, a refectory, storeroom and large kitchen. A bell, nearly two feet in diameter, hung in an elaborate tower and was used to mark out the community's daily routine. As befitted southern California, the whole building was clad in whitewashed adobe, with red tiles on the roof – a style well-suited to the constant, baking sunshine.

The surrounding garden was ablaze with oleanders, orange trees and scarlet zinnias, and amid its beauty stood the centrepiece of Heard's spiritual strategy: a round, domed, windowless meditation building called the Oratory. Heard intended Trabuco College to model a complete lifestyle rather than just a spiritual training, so the extensive agricultural acres around these structures were also essential, offering the opportunity for the community to be self-sufficient and to engage in the manual labour that Heard deemed a vital part of the balanced development of a neo-brahmin.

Life at Trabuco College followed a strict daily timetable – what Heard called 'twenty-four hours a day practice'.[55] It had the all-consuming asceticism of the prayer-and-work routine of a Benedictine monastery, but it differed from a monastery in that it was led by a living guru, a man of flesh and blood and considerable charisma. Each day there were three bouts of meditation in the Oratory and three frugal, vegetarian meals in the refectory (the austere diet was supposed to help promote self-transcendence). Afternoons were dedicated to manual labour – hours of working in the fields, orchard and garden, or maintaining the buildings and paths. This was seen as the low point in the regime by most members of the community, who, like Mushanokōji Saneatsu's New Villagers, had envisaged their utopia as a training ground for the mind rather than for the body.

Heard insisted that his followers keep working. It was not that he expected the agriculture to bring in money – Trabuco College was paid for by a combination of the funds he had inherited and the small amount donated by its residents and supporters. He liked the idea of self-sufficiency as a philosophical end, symbolizing his community's separateness from the rest of the world. California was so fertile, he reasoned, how hard could it be to grow a decent crop? But none of his followers – not even the eminently practical Felix Greene – knew the first thing about farming, and Heard's inability to inspire a work ethic, and lack of interest in leading the manual work by example, meant that hardly anything was produced in the first year. The ambition to achieve self-sufficiency was quietly dropped, although the outdoor labour continued. The day ended early at Trabuco College. When darkness fell, most people withdrew to their cells, leaving Heard on his own in the library, studying religious books by a kerosene lamp, since there was no electricity.

When Christopher Isherwood visited, he found Heard very much changed from his time as an 'exaggeratedly clean-shaven, barbered and tailored' intellectual in London. His friend, he observed, now looked 'disconcertingly, almost theatrically Christlike', with his little pointed red beard and his 'dramatically shabby' outfit of painter's smock, washed-out jeans and sneakers.[56] When the bell rang at 5.30 a.m., Heard led Isherwood and his neo-brahmins into the Oratory, a strange, shadowy space Isherwood thought smelled 'very peculiar – a blend of glue, carpets and mice'.[57] After an hour of meditation, everyone gathered in the kitchen to eat oatmeal and drink coffee. Heard perched above them all on a high stool, and read for a period from a religious text, stopping to expound on the life of one of the Christian mystics.[58]

Isherwood was one of many visitors to Trabuco College. In theory, the community was supposed to be cloistered from the outside world. Radios, newspapers and visitors were frowned on as distractions from the quest for spiritual perfection. Heard told his neo-brahmins that they would only be ready to change society at large when they had achieved personal enlightenment. Nothing should get between them and that aim. But in reality, Heard's sociable nature, and his desire to convince people of his recipe for international harmony, meant that the community became a popular destination for anyone in California interested in social change, spiritual growth, or out-of-the-ordinary ventures.

In the end, it was the visitors rather than Trabuco's participants who carried Heard's ideas out into the world, giving the community a resonance far beyond its boundaries. They ranged from the anthropologist and scholar of Eastern religion W. Y. Evans-Wentz to the poet and pacifist William Stafford.[59] Commonweal, a leading Catholic journal, dispatched a correspondent, Anne Fremantle, to Trabuco to investigate what was going on: she concluded that Heard was running something like a Quaker meeting with yoga classes, and that his efforts were a 'sign for this century', which was turning away from organized, orthodox religion to something more individualistic.[60]

Trabuco College also became a haunt for the constellation of English intellectuals and artists who had set up in America during the early 1940s. Maria Huxley, who was a regular guest along with her husband, ran into so many old friends from England there that she came to think of the place as an English country-house party that had somehow become stranded abroad – a view perhaps helped along by the community's spartan food and inadequate heating.[61] One of the longer-standing English visitors was Iris Tree, a free-spirited Bloomsbury poet who had been painted by Augustus John and Vanessa Bell between the wars. Not quite committing to the rigorous neo-brahmin lifestyle, she nonetheless relished the escape from convention, taking over the cooking – which improved drastically, to general relief – writing hymns, and wandering with the goats and deer in the surrounding hills in a picturesque red skirt and scarf.

Other visitors to Trabuco College went on to shape the counterculture and the wider spiritual landscape. The Englishman Alan Watts stayed for a few days; his bestselling book The Way of Zen (1957) would help popularize Buddhism in 1960s America, and make him a famed guru of the New Age.[62] It was a visit to Trabuco College that prompted Huston Smith to begin the research that would result in *The Religions of Man* (1958), one of the most influential books on comparative religion. Bill Wilson, the spiritually minded co-founder of Alcoholics Anonymous, turned up to consult Heard on the development of his organization.[63] Heard, inevitably, encouraged him not to run it as a large, centralized structure, but in small units akin to generating cells – advice that Wilson took, giving Alcoholics Anonymous the unique, cellular organization that it retains to the present day.

Few of the original twenty-five neo-brahmins stayed living in Trabuco Canyon for long. Participants were particularly put off by the rule of absolute celibacy that Heard imposed, even on married couples, insisting that sexual desire was an egotistical addiction which must be sublimated to spiritual ends (an extreme view that may have stemmed from his lifelong struggle to accept his own homosexuality).[64] But those who left the community were replaced by others, eager to become 'the shock troops of a new dispensation', as one young navy ensign and neo-brahmin put it.[65] For residents and visitors alike, Trabuco was a place of deep enchantment in those early years – described, like Gurdjieff's institute, as 'something out of *Alice in Wonderland*', although not necessarily for the reasons Heard intended.[66]

For some, the appeal of the community was less about self-enlightenment or social salvation than about relinquishing personal responsibility. Maria Huxley showed the attractions of Trabuco's strict regime when she described it as utterly relaxing: after having to think so hard about how to live for most of her life, all choice was suddenly taken out of her hands by Heard. 'Bells rang *for me*, reading was done *for me*, all decisions and responsibilities carried *for me*.'[67] This response to the community was far from what Heard wanted: participants were supposed to be learning how to lead, not how to surrender their individual freedom in order to follow. But the atmosphere of the community didn't leave much room for the exercise of leadership by anyone but himself.

Others were drawn to Trabuco by the stream of famous visitors. Miriam King, a young Stanford graduate who joined the community straight out of university, was held spellbound by the exchanges at the religious seminars between leading Hindu, Buddhist and other spiritual thinkers that Heard organized and chaired. She particularly admired the relationship between Heard and Huxley, as through this period they remained close companions in their spiritual questing. Huxley stayed at Trabuco for days at a time, exchanging ideas with Heard and using the library to compile selections from religious texts and the writings of seers, philosophers and prophets. He would publish these in the groundbreaking book *The Perennial Philosophy*, which – like Heard's practical utopia – emphasized the commonalities between the major religions of the world.[68] Felix Greene, one evening, made the mistake of accepting Huxley's help in the kitchen while preparing food for thirty. He was subjected to a long lecture on natural gas and its influence on civilization, at the end of which Huxley turned from the stove towards him, plaintively asking, 'How do you light this thing?'[69]

During the Second World War, Trabuco College burned brightly as a centre of spiritual idealism. It did not offer a perfect pattern for a better way of life, as Heard sometimes hoped; it could hardly have been expected to do so, since Heard almost only ever focused his attention on the spiritual plane. Nor did it send fully trained 'neo-brahmins' out into the world to lead others. Where it worked best was as a laboratory for ideas. Trabuco College was a medley of expatriate English intelligentsia, Eastern spiritual teachers and a wide range of idealistic Americans. Its atmosphere – vibrant, intellectually inclusive, endlessly experimental – inspired conversations and concepts that would become articles, books, organizations, movements, psychological treatments and future communal settlements. The experimentation in Trabuco Canyon helped lay the foundation for California to become the centre for alternative cultures in the 1960s and 70s. The future of the state was being acted out in miniature across the community's grounds, as the inhabitants of Trabuco College melded Eastern spirituality and Western psychology, vegetarianism and yoga, guru worship and communal living.

*

The difficulties of life at Trabuco College began to manifest themselves through the 1940s. Like the other practical utopias of the period, the community struggled to stay financially afloat, to balance its theoretical aims with the realities of day-to-day subsistence, and to keep itself relevant as the world moved deeper into all-consuming war. But of all the problems with the running of Trabuco College, the largest was Heard himself.

Heard was naturally disposed to the role of freewheeling intellectual and guru that he had adopted in England in the 1920s and 30s. A man of limitless energies, a fervent believer in esoteric ideas, and an eloquent, inspiring conversationalist, he had the ability to convince people he was attuned to the spiritual. It was this that had led so many of those seeking a new path in the interwar years to adopt him as a guide. Isherwood described how impressive Heard was when he sat motionless, long fingers pressed together in his lap, pale blue eyes staring into the distance, his expression that of 'a radio operator with headphones over his ears, receiving a message which the people around him couldn't hear'.[70]

But managing a community called for considerably more than a spiritual aura and rhetorical prowess. Accounts needed to be balanced, buildings maintained and people fed. Small squabbles had to be soothed before they grew larger, and neo-brahmins encouraged when they showed signs of becoming disenchanted with the rigours of life at Trabuco College. Heard was fastidiously resistant to wasting his time on such 'mundanities'. For him, the good life meant a total focus on spiritual progress. He did not compensate for his lack of interest in the administrative side of communal life by introducing clear rules and regulations in the mode of Eberhard Arnold with the Bruderhof, or the Elmhirsts in forming a trust and company structure for Dartington Hall. He valued liberty more than anything, both his own and that of others, and he feared that any formal institutionalization might compromise that. The consequence of this was that as Trabuco College emerged from the excitement of its early years, it came to feel more like a random, disorganized gathering of individuals than a united, coherently functioning community.

Heard's character posed an additional problem. Many of those who joined Trabuco College were expecting charismatic leadership along the lines of what G. I. Gurdjieff supplied at the Institute for the Harmonious Development of Man. They wanted a guru who took a controlling role in their lives. But Heard saw his fellow

neo-brahmins as collaborators and equals on the path to enlightenment, not as disciples whose every waking moment he was
responsible for directing. He might enjoy magnetizing them for an
hour or two during a lecture, or setting them a daily timetable, but
he usually liked to retreat with his books to study and think – and
he expected others to do the same. In this he was perhaps most like
Mushanokōji Saneatsu: his individualism risked leaving a vacuum at
the heart of the community. Leonard Elmhirst, who was observing
Trabuco College with fascination from Devon, thought that Heard
expected too much of the people who joined him. Most of the
community's participants, Elmhirst guessed, 'had but the dimmest
idea of what to do with their minds in the three daily meditation
periods' and were driven only by 'a vague groping for "something"
other than church doctrine'.[71] In the absence of clear spiritual and
practical guidance from Heard, inhabitants began to act out – like
the woman who took the austere Trabuco regime to its extreme
and began to eat mud.[72]

Heard's lifelong habit of private spiritual seeking was deeply
engrained. As Trabuco College began to throw up more problems
– dissatisfied inhabitants, bills to be paid, mice overrunning the
kitchen – his response was to retreat deeper into his old ways. In
theory, he continued to believe in the value of community life as a
way of perfecting his world-redeeming religion and nurturing its
missionaries. But in reality, he spent more and more time on his
own, reading and meditating – in part to escape his disappointment
at his followers' failure to advance themselves spiritually. His bursts
of engagement with his fellow communards tended to be short-lived:
he would pick a favourite inhabitant to lavish with pedagogical
attention, but he was then liable to drop them shortly after – 'often',
as Maria Huxley observed, 'making the dropped favourite despair
of everything and leave Trabuco and God; forgetting that God and
Gerald were not the same thing'.[73] By the middle of the 1940s, the
sense of unity at Trabuco College, so carefully fostered by group
meals, meditation, lectures and shared practical labour in the early
days, had almost completely atrophied.

The years after the war ushered in one of America's great
economic booms. Consumer capitalism became the order of the day
– a swing back, in a sense, to the individualistic materialism that

had dominated before the First World War. A large number of affluent, casual Californians arrived at Trabuco College hoping to discover better ways of living than the dominant one flourishing in the outside world. But while they were interested in spiritualism, they had little sympathy with the community's principles of extreme asceticism, and were put off by the absence of organized community life or any obvious leader. Heard, by this time, was too much taken up with his own research to think about reconfiguring Trabuco College to suit the changing times.

With its leader in private retreat, Trabuco's population grew smaller and smaller. Felix Greene fell in love with another inhabitant, Elena Lindeman, and, unwilling to abide by the rule of celibacy, left the community in order to marry her. Without Greene's practical and administrative skills, Trabuco College fell quickly into debt. Once the project's greatest advocate, Greene wrote after his departure that it had become 'a much more morbid place than we can realise while we are there. Sick, a little unreal.'[74] The community was stuck in a time warp. Its rigorous regime, designed to fit Heard's idiosyncratic third morality and to weather the apocalypse of world war, was disconnected from the reality of prosperous, post-war America. In 1949, with funds running out and followers nearly all departed, Heard closed the community and donated the property to the Vedanta Society. It functions today as a Hindu monastery – still full of people preoccupied with pursuing the spiritual good life, but without the burning aspiration to transform the world.

*

Gerald Heard stayed on in America until his death in 1971. He and Aldous Huxley both became influential gurus in the countercultural scene of the 1960s. The 'Mystical Expatriates of Southern California', as they were called by Alan Watts, lectured on college campuses, on the radio and at the growing number of centres for alternative spirituality in California. Both continued to publish extensively.[75] Although the times had changed, their fundamental ideas never did – their view continued to be that people should open themselves up to a larger, transcendent reality; should learn, as Huxley wrote, that 'all is in all'.[76] Once people discovered this, a new harmonious unity of humankind would be achieved. In addition to the many techniques the two friends had advocated for achieving such unity throughout the 1930s and 40s – Buddhist meditation, Hindu philosophy, psychology and communal living – they began to promote the use of LSD, mescaline and other psychedelic drugs. Huxley's *The Doors of Perception*, a book that made mescaline famous, presented drug-taking as a way to access 'the miracle, moment by moment, of naked existence' as experienced by Adam in the Garden of Eden.[77] This line of investigation paved the way for the 'psychedelic renaissance' of the twenty-first century, and for the researchers today who are looking into hallucinogens as a serious therapeutic treatment for conditions such as depression, anxiety and addiction.[78]

Huxley's last novel, *Island*, is the story of a utopia. He wrote it as a counterbalance to *Brave New World*, and it became a handbook among those starting communes in Vermont and California, Colorado and New Mexico in the 1960s.[79] The book, fuelled by the writer's experiences at Dartington Hall in the 1920s and Trabuco College in the 1940s, describes an island where the population lives in non-materialistic and cooperative harmony, using a drug called *moksha* to further their spiritual enlightenment. Heard, too, drew on his communitarian experimentation between the 1920s and 40s to counsel the next generation. Michael Murphy and Dick Price, two young Americans, were prompted by one of his hours-long monologues – covering, as Murphy remembered, 'the Old Testament, the New Testament, Buddhism, Christianity, evolutionary theory, the whole works' – to start a residential retreat on the Californian coast.[80] The Esalen Institute, as Murphy and Price called their community, became the world headquarters of the 'human potentiality movement', promoting a blend of psychology and esoteric Eastern spiritualism that captivated the countercultural idealists of the 1960s.[81]

Trabuco College was short-lived and small in scale, but it seemed to many who stayed there that it was a place of vital importance. 'I began to feel I had at last reached the company of the angels,' wrote one American who visited in 1945.[82] Here was a community for those who sought a mode of life based on promoting peace and spiritual enlightenment: it offered beauty and an 'elevated' atmosphere; the comradeship of other seekers; and, above all, a magnetic leader whose 'bursts of insight and arcane memorabilia' were at once educative and inspiring.[83] While it lasted, Trabuco College worked as a catalyst for new ways of thinking about how to be and what to believe, radiating ideas out into the world and, in some cases, changing the lives of its participants – as one wrote – 'completely and for good'.[84] After it closed, the memory of Trabuco College became a touchstone for the idealists of 1960s counterculture, shaping the next generation's experiments with self-actualization, the fusing of scientific and spiritual ideas, and back-to-the-land communal living.

CONCLUSION

RADICALLY DIFFERENT WAYS OF BEING

Today, the weeds grow high in Atarashiki Mura, and there is no one walking along its narrow paths. Each small home has a vitrine outside the front door, displaying a painting of a chrysanthemum, or a hand-built ceramic vase, or a calligraphic rendition of Mushanokōji Saneatsu's six-point manifesto. The community's flag – four colours representing international unity, surrounded by blue for the sea – flaps above the derelict water pump in the main square. At the bottom of the village I find a farmer enjoying a beer and a roll-up, crouched beside his rusting blue pickup truck, looking out over the fields. When I ask if he lives in Atarashiki Mura he looks confused for a moment, then shakes his head, smiling. No. He just rents the land from the New Villagers. They've grown too old to farm.

The land that was once the Harmonious Institute for the Development of Man has been divided in two. The priory houses a set of upmarket apartments; expensive cars are locked behind the high iron fence. The gardens are still accessible though, part of the grounds of a nursing home, somewhat overgrown. I stumble on the remnants of Gurdjieff's sauna – bent iron, crumbling stone, the smell of damp earth. A man with a pipe in his mouth approaches me. 'You know the Fourth Way?' He is disappointed when I am not a follower. He used to be one himself, he tells me, but now not so much. 'Gurdjieff was a great man, though,' he insists. I follow him into the nursing home, where it turns out he is the receptionist. From behind the large desk in the foyer he prints me out the pamphlet that he's compiled for the pilgrims who appear every few months.

In the Bruderhof's dining hall in East Sussex, men in hoodies and women in ankle-length dresses and trainers eat at long trestle tables. I talk to two girls in their late teens. Both speak in the unique accent – part German, part American – that is heard everywhere in the community, the result of a century of international living. After the meal the weather forecast is read out from the internet for the twenty-two other Bruderhof settlements. One of the girls tells me that she misses her family in upstate New York, but that you go where the community sends you. She and her friend seem to know exactly why it is that they are living in this place: they are representatives of a different social order, pointing the way towards the kingdom of God.

While some of the utopian communities of the interwar years have survived, most have not – and those that continue are not the vital forces for social change they once were. These experiments in living all ended up facing a similar set of problems. Their founders tended to have a greater talent for theorizing than for practical action; they were skilled at identifying the shortcomings of the world as it was and conjuring up alluring alternatives with words, but less talented at organizing people and funds into functional, enduring systems. There were tensions between the ideals of cooperation, egalitarianism and democracy, and the practice of elitism and hierarchy. There was the constant struggle to reconcile a vision of a world that renounced materialism with the crushingly practical financial requirements needed to keep a community going. The last great hurdle for all of these places was time itself, the difficulty of remaining relevant as the historical context that inspired an initial burst of idealism ran up against a changed reality – a new dominant social philosophy and a new set of hopes and fears.

The end of the Second World War brought with it a surge in the birth rate – producing the closely grouped 'baby boomer' generation that reached maturity after the war, and fuelled the next wave of practical utopia-building.[1] At first glance, the communities of the 1960s bear a striking resemblance to those established between the wars. They consisted of small groups separating themselves off from the mainstream to pursue radically different lifestyles – lifestyles that often incorporated back-to-the-landism and the promotion of spiritual and creative self-realization. Yet the practical utopians of the 1960s were, like the idealists of the interwar period, reacting against the prevailing ideologies of their time. Communards in this period lived in the shadow of the Cold War and Vietnam, but they had not experienced the realities of a full-blown international conflict like the First World War. Rather than searching for alternative social models that would promote pacifism and internationalism, they tended to be driven more by a desire for self-liberation and self-actualization.[2] 'The personal is political' ran one popular catchphrase.[3] Their communities aimed to free people – women in particular – from the conformity of nuclear families and nine-to-five jobs, from patriarchy and bureaucracy, from career ladders and the pressure to consume.

And, by the 1960s, mass production had led to widespread ownership of radios and televisions, while travel – even travel by air – became relatively affordable. As with the idealists of the 1920s and 30s, these technological advances broadened the possibilities of social dreaming. Westerners jetted to retreats in India and returned the next month with an arsenal of new ideas. Images of counter-cultural pursuits – Woodstock, civil rights marches, colourfully dressed youths with flowers in their hair living in communes – were beamed into the homes of millions, creating a sense of an internationally shared social experience. The result of this mass communication was that the 1960s felt like a global revolutionary moment – even though the vast majority of ordinary working people were getting on with their day-to-day lives.

Countercultural living had a mass reach that was entirely different to the appeal of the small, eclectic communities of the interwar years. In America alone, there were thousands of active settlements by the end of the 1960s, together involving over half a million people.[4] Among the most famous of these was Drop City in southern Colorado, which proclaimed itself an entirely new civilization. Its inhabitants took new names, lived in geodesic structures inspired by the futurist architect Richard Buckminster Fuller, and embraced sexual freedom, drugs and radical politics. Another well-known community was the 'universal' township of Auroville in south India, which aimed to promote human unity and the 'transformation of consciousness' by rejecting money, religion and government.[5] Representatives from 124 nations attended its inauguration, bringing flags and soil from their homeland. In Britain, one of the more colourful experiments was in a hotel on Eel Pie Island on the River Thames, which participants turned into a commune. It housed a hundred or so artists and would-be artists, who dedicated themselves to creative pursuits, discussing anarchism and making love in a designated 'sex room', until, at the end of the decade, the building burned down.

Much of what seemed new and original in this wave of counter-culture was an extension of experiments begun in the interwar years – just as the experiments of the interwar years were themselves indebted to the idealistic thinkers and social models that came before them: to Leo Tolstoy and his estate at Yasnaya Polyana; to William Morris's ideal of the medieval craft community; to Sir Horace Plunkett and the Irish cooperative movement; to Jesus Christ and the early Church. Practical utopianism, though always of its time, never ceases to draw from and contribute to a larger, historical network of social dreaming, with utopian experiments of every era inflecting those of later ages, each successive generation of idealists finding something new to admire in what has gone before.

*

The utopians in the wake of the First World War tackled the great problems of their time: how to prevent another war; how to promote harmony and understanding between East and West; how to cultivate responsible citizenship and balance local and international identities; how to benefit from science without being led by it; how to lead a holistically fulfilling life amid the imperatives of industrial, capitalist modernity. The solutions they came up with might now seem comical, dysfunctional and even faintly horrifying – like their fix-ation on psychological shocks, or on connecting with the 'super-consciousness'. But these men and women nonetheless produced ideas that were useful at the time and that, later on, gradually percolated into the wider world.

The example of planned community living, for instance, became an inspiration for the international community development move-ment that took off after the Second World War. The holism of Dartington Hall fed into Britain's welfare state. The low-impact lifestyle of the Bruderhof and Atarashiki Mura prefigured the

environmental movement. Tagore's ideal of liberal, practical education influenced the school system of the whole of India. Even Heard
and Huxley's embrace of psychedelics and Gurdjieff's promotion of
full wakefulness rather than 'unconscious' living found their way
into mainstream psychological discourse and the business methods
of Silicon Valley.[6] The people who passed through these social experiments picked up ideas and then reworked and re-enacted them in
other settings. At the same time, the very existence of such radical
communities conveyed, even to those who never saw them at first
hand, a message about the possibility of the world being otherwise
than it was.

Idealists around the world are still building and joining practical
utopias. Faced with the spectre of ecological catastrophe, many
contemporary utopians experiment with low-impact, non-
consumerist modes of communal living that do no damage to the
natural world. In the mountains of Asturias in northern Spain, a
group of sixty or so Spanish, French, Danish and German men and
women have set up the remote commune of Matavenero, where
they live as self-sufficiently as possible, growing their own food,
building their own houses, and consuming very little.[7] The twenty-
strong community of Suderbyn is located on a Swedish island in the
Baltic Sea, and their ambition is to model a circular system for food
and energy production by deploying a geodesic dome greenhouse
and a biogas digestor.[8] Larger initiatives include the community of
Toyosato in Japan, whose several hundred participants aim to show
how a fulfilling life can be built on the back of sustainable farming
and cooperation, no hard currency and minimal possessions.[9]

Today's utopians are just as much preoccupied by the 'practical'
side of utopianism as those of the interwar period. Pure idealism
must be set aside to address the mundane problems of communal
living: how to share tools, cars, living space and childcare; how to
balance communal bank accounts at the same time as building solar
panels and composting toilets.[10] But these communards are still
dedicated to creating real-life models of the 'good place' that they
hope will influence the world at large. They attend conferences,
speak at universities, and protest at antiglobalization rallies.[11] They
organize community tours, educational programmes and youth
exchanges. They publish extensively: blueprints for eco-friendly

buildings, vegan recipe books, academic papers on sustainability. Taking advantage of the internet and social media, they link their small settlements together with other similarly minded endeavours through online platforms and international associations, allowing their ambitions, experiences and techniques to be shared world-wide. Toyosato, for instance, is one of more than seventy low-impact communities that form the Yamagishi movement, which stretches from Japan to Australia, Brazil, Switzerland and the United States. The twenty-first century's 'ecotopians' hope that by connecting local communities to global networks they can inspire other would-be communards as well as national governments to change their behaviour.

Practical utopianism is fruitful in unpredictable ways. Utopians inspire because they refuse to accept the shortcomings of the world or the impossibility of change. They demand more – whether, like the interwar idealists in this book, it is more cooperation, more equality, more spiritual and creative meaning; or, like twenty-first-century community-builders, a more egalitarian and sustainable deployment of the world's resources. Utopians identify the urgent problems of the day and devote their lives to finding solutions. It is hard not to admire that combination of idealism, optimism and practical dedication. Criticizing the status quo is rarely enough to create real change – whether that criticism comes in the form of marches, petitions, policy papers or satirical tweets. What we need are laboratories to devise, test and demonstrate new ideas and systems; concrete experiments that prove the viability of what other-wise would remain nothing more than an alluring set of ideas. While few practical utopias last for long, utopian living is extraordinarily generative. It creates openings in the fabric of society, inspires change, reminds us that it is possible to reach beyond the dominant assump-tions of our day and discover radically different ways of being.

We live in an age teeming with dystopian fears. Our cultural imagination is haunted by visions of drought and untenably high temperatures, of artificial intelligence becoming uncontrollable, of mounting inequality and discrimination, of moral decay and apoca-lyptic disaster. The global coronavirus outbreak has contributed hugely to the sense that things cannot continue as they are, that society is at breaking point and urgently needs to be reformed. The anxiety of our age is not so different from that of the interwar years. The inescapable horrors of that time – of conflict, inequality and pandemic – seemed just as unprecedented and insurmountable. One response then was resignation, submission, turning away from the fate of the collective in favour of private pleasures. But others dreamed of a better future for society, and dared to try to turn their dreams into reality. A world without them would have been a poorer place.

The stories of the utopians of the interwar years are an inspiration, and give a sense of how new ideas are born and seep out into the world. But today more than ever, we need our own forms of practical idealism, the prototypes and experiments that can help us grapple with the questions of contemporary existence. What would it mean to live in a carbon-neutral society? How can we oppose the rising tides of populism, hyper-individualism and inequality? Is there a way to address our growing distrust of politicians and the democratic process? A way to reform the opaque machinations of the technological corporations that dominate our day-to-day lives? A way to strengthen community in an age of individualism and social fragmentation? Utopians have always refused to accept current definitions of what is possible, and have infused the world with new, optimistic energy. That is why we need them now.

ACKNOWLEDGEMENTS

I would like to thank, in no particular order: my agent, Sophie Scard; George Morley, Marissa Constantinou, Laura Carr and everyone at Picador/Macmillan who helped this book on its way; Rachael Beale and Fraser Crichton, for their rigorous editing; Alexandra Harris, Jennifer Kabat, Lena Schipper and Jules Evans – generous, insightful readers of early drafts; Peter Mandler, Stella Tillyard, Laura Carter and Lucy Delap, for their steady encouragement and open-mindedness about how to do history; the staff of the Dartington Hall archives in Exeter, and of the Humanities Reading Rooms in the British Library; Marianne Wright, Bernard Hibbs and those who kindly shared their knowledge of the Bruderhof community with me; David Anderson, for his collegiate spirit in helping me access journals; Tessa Morris-Suzuki, Kazuyo Yasuda, Chika Tonooka, David Plath and Yoko Yamashita, without whose assistance I would not have been able to write about Atarashiki Mura; John Roger Barrie, open-handed in his help with my research on Gerald Heard; Kevin Mount, a fount of wisdom on Dartington Hall; Hilary Platt, who supported me in finding my own path; the Society of Authors/K Blundell Trust, for providing a grant that allowed me more time for writing; my parents, Rachel Watson and John Sanderson, and my husband, Luke, with whom I feel privileged to have shared this project and so much else.

The Utopians was inspired by my grandfather, John Watson, and is dedicated to my son James, who was born as I finished it.

BIBLIOGRAPHY

ARCHIVES

British Library Newspaper Archives
Dartington Hall Archives, Devon Record Office
Eduard Lindeman Archives, Columbia University
Nancy Wilson Ross Archives, Harry Ransom Center, University of Texas
L. S. Penrose Papers, UCL, Special Collections
Hubble Papers, Huntington Digital Library

INTRODUCTION: 'The Art of Living Together in Harmony'

Belling, Catherine, 'Overwhelming the Medium: Fiction and the Trauma of Pandemic Influenza in 1918', *Literature and Medicine* 28 (2009), 55–81

Blücher, Princess Evelyn, *An English Wife in Berlin* (London, 1920)

Bregman, Rutger, *Utopia for Realists*, trans. Elizabeth Manton (New York, 2017)

Clark, Christopher, *The Sleepwalkers: How Europe Went to War in 1914* (London, 2012)

Collins, Steven, 'Monasticism, Utopias and Comparative Social Theory', *Religion* 18 (1988), 101–35

Das, Santanu, 'The Indian Sepoy and the First World War', https://www.bl.uk/world-war-one/articles/the-indian-sepoy-in-the-first-world-war#note1 [accessed 20 July 2020]

Dehner, George, *Influenza: A Century of Science and Public Health Response* (Pittsburgh, PA, 2012)

Gilman, Charlotte Perkins, *Herland* (London, 2015 [1915])

Gorman, Daniel, *The Emergence of International Society in the 1920s* (Cambridge, 2012)

Grandin, Greg, *Fordlandia: The Rise and Fall of Henry Ford's Forgotten Jungle City* (London, 2010)

Hewitson, Mark, 'Princes' Wars, Wars of the People, or Total War? Mass Armies and the Question of a Military Revolution in Germany, 1792–1815', *War in History* 20 (2013), 452–90

Huxley, Aldous, *Brave New World* (London, 1932)

—'Ozymandias', in *Adonis and the Alphabet, and Other Essays* (London, 1956)

Jenkins, Philip, *The Great and Holy War* (New York, 2014)

Jennings, Chris, *Paradise Now: The Story of American Utopianism* (New York, 2016)

Kern, Stephen, *The Culture of Time and Space, 1880–1918* (Cambridge, 1983)

Kumar, Krishnan, *Utopia and Anti-Utopia in Modern Times* (Oxford, 1987)

Landau, Rom, *God Is My Adventure: A Book on Modern Mystics, Masters and Teachers* (London, 1935)

Levitas, Ruth, *The Concept of Utopia* (Witney, 2011 [1990])

Macaulay, Rose, *What Not* (London, 2019 [1918])

More, Thomas, *Libellus vere aureus, nec minus salutaris quam festivus, de optimo rei publicae statu deque nova insula Utopia* (A Little, True Book, As Beneficial As It Is Enjoyable, About How Things Should Be In The New Island Utopia) (Cambridge, 2002 [1516])

Omissi, David, *Indian Voices of the Great War: Soldiers' Letters, 1914–18* (Basingstoke, 1999)

Pragnell, Vera, *The Story of the Sanctuary* (Steyning, 1928)

Rhodes, Cecil, *The Last Will and Testament of Cecil John Rhodes*, ed. W. T. Stead (London, 1902)

Rodgers, Daniel T., *Atlantic Crossings: Social Politics in a Progressive Age* (Cambridge, MA, 1998)

Scheler, Max, *Person and Self-Value: Three Essays*, trans. Manfred S. Frings (Dordrecht; Boston; Lancaster, 1987)

Shaw, Jane, *Octavia, Daughter of God: The Story of a Female Messiah and Her Followers* (London, 2011)

Spinney, Laura, *Pale Rider: The Spanish Flu of 1918 and How It Changed the World* (London, 2017)

Sutcliffe, Steven, *Children of the New Age: A History of Alternative Spirituality* (London, 2002)

Thomson, Mathew, *Psychological Subjects: Identity, Culture and Health in Twentieth-Century Britain* (Oxford, 2006)

Tooze, Adam, 'A Small Village in the Age of Extremes: The Häusern Experiment', unpublished paper, 2014, 1–29

Vaughan, Victor C., *A Doctor's Memories* ([n.p.], 2007 [1926])

ONE: 'Life in its Completeness' on the Plains of Bengal: Rabindranath Tagore's Santiniketan-Sriniketan

Alam, Fakrul and Radha Chakravarty (eds), *The Essential Tagore* (Cambridge, MA; London, 2011)

Bhattacharya, Sabyasachi, *Rabindranath Tagore: An Interpretation* ([n.p.], 2011)

Bose, Mandakranta, 'Indian Modernity and Tagore's Dance', *University of Toronto Quarterly* 77 (2008), 1085–94

Chattopadhyay, Madhumita, 'Rabindranath Tagore's Model of Rural Reconstruction: A Review', *International Journal of Research and Analytical Reviews* 5 (2018), 142–6

Choudhuri, Inder Nath, *Indian Renaissance and Rabindranath Tagore* (New Delhi, 2019)

Clout, Hugh and Iain Stevenson, 'Jules Sion, Alan Grant Ogilvie and the Collège des Ecossais in Montpellier: A Network of Geographers', *Scottish Geographical Journal* 120 (2004), 181–98

Cohen, Matthew Isaac, *Performing Otherness: Java and Bali on International Stages, 1905–1952* (Basingstoke, 2010)

Colman, Gould P., *Education and Agriculture: A History of the New York State College of Agriculture at Cornell University* (Ithaca, NY, 1963)

Das, Sisir Kumar (ed.), *The English Writings of Rabindranath Tagore: A Miscellany*, vol. 3 (New Delhi, 1996)

Dasgupta, Sugata, *A Poet and a Plan. Tagore's Experiments in Rural Reconstruction* (Calcutta, 1962)

Das Gupta, Uma, *Santiniketan and Sriniketan* (Calcutta, 1983)

——'Santiniketan', in Mushirul Hasan (ed.), *Knowledge, Power & Politics: Educational Institutions in India* (New Delhi, 1998)

——'In Pursuit of a Different Freedom: Tagore's World University at

Santiniketan', *Indian International Centre Quarterly* 29 (2002–3), 25–38

——*Rabindranath Tagore: A Biography* (Oxford, 2004)

——'Tagore's Ideas of Social Action and the Sriniketan Experiment of Rural Reconstruction, 1922–41', *University of Toronto Quarterly* 77 (2008), 992–1004

——'Rabindranath's Experiments with Education, Community and Nation at His Santiniketan Institutions', in Sanjukta Dasgupta and Chinmoy Guha (eds), *Tagore at Home in the World* (New Delhi, 2013)

Dutta, Krishna and Andrew Robinson, *Rabindranath Tagore: The Myriad-minded Man* (Bloomsbury, 1995)

——*Selected Letters of Rabindranath Tagore* (Cambridge, 1997)

Elmhirst, Leonard K., *Rabindranath Tagore: Pioneer in Education. Essays and Exchanges Between Rabindranath Tagore and L. K. Elmhirst* (London, 1961)

——*Poet and Plowman* (Calcutta, 1975)

Ghosh, Santidev, 'Sikshasatra and Naitalimi Education', in Santosh Chandra Sengupta (ed.), *Rabindranath Tagore: Homage from Visva-Bharati* (Visva-Bharati, 1962), 121–37

Green, Gretchen, *The Whole World & Company* (New York, 1936)

Hazareesingh, Kissoonsingh (ed.), *A Rich Harvest: The Complete Tagore/Elmhirst Correspondence and Other Writings* (Mauritius, 1992)

Immerwahr, Daniel, *Thinking Small: The United States and the Lure of Community Development* (Cambridge, MA; London, 2015)

Kripalani, Krishna, *Rabindranath Tagore. A Biography* (London, 1962)

Lal, Prem Chand, *Reconstruction and Education in Rural India* (London, 1932)

Makherjee, Usha, 'Sriniketan Experiment in Rural Reconstruction', *Economic Weekly*, 25 October 1952, 1107–9

Mosley, Oswald, *My Life* (London, 2006 [1968])

O'Connell, Kathleen M., 'Education at Santiniketan: 1902–1920', *Indian International Centre Quarterly* 38 (2011), 18–31

Omissi, David, *Indian Voices of the Great War: Soldiers' Letters, 1914–18* (Basingstoke, 1999)

Ray, Satyajit, 'Final Testimony', *Guardian*, London, 1 August 1991

Robinson, Sandra (ed.), *Discourses of Empire and Commonwealth* (Leiden, 2016)

Tagore, Rabindranath, *Gitanjali* (London, 1918 [first published in Sanskrit in 1910; first published in English in 1912])

——*Personality* (London, 1917)

——*Glimpses of Bengal* (London, 1921)

——*Creative Unity* (London, 1922)

——*Tagore, Centenary Volume, 1861–1961*, S. Radhakrishnan and others (eds) (New Delhi, 1961)

——*A Compilation of Selected Speeches, Letters and Songs of Tagore*, trans. Chiranjiv Kaviraj (Agartala, 1969)

——*Collected Poems and Plays of Rabindranath Tagore* ([Hong Kong], 1977 [1936])

——*My Life in My Words*, Uma Das Gupta (ed.) (New Delhi, 2006)

Tagore, Rathindranath, *On the Edges of Times* (Calcutta, 1981)

Williams, Louise Blakeney, 'Overcoming the 'Contagion of Mimicry': The Cosmopolitan Nationalism and Modernist History of Rabindranath Tagore and W. B. Yeats', *American Historical Review* (2007), 69–100

TWO: 'A New Manor Which May Be the Unit of the New England': Dorothy and Leonard Elmhirst's Dartington Hall

Adams, Henry, *The Education of Henry Adams* (Boston; New York, 1918)

Bonham-Carter, Victor, *Dartington Hall: History of an Experiment* (London, 1958)

——*Land and Environment: The Survival of the English Countryside* (Rutherford, NJ, 1971)

Butler, Lise, 'Michael Young, the Institute of Community Studies, and the Politics of Kinship', *Twentieth Century British History* 26 (2015), 203–24

Brassley, Paul, Jeremy Burchardt and Lynne Thompson (eds), *The English Countryside between The Wars: Regeneration or Decline?* (New York, 2006)

Brassley, Paul, David Harvey, Matt Lobley and Michael Winter, 'Accounting for Agriculture: The Origins of the Farm Management Survey', *Agricultural History Review* 61 (2013), 135–53

Brown, Jane, *Angel Dorothy: How an American Progressive Came to Devon* (London, 2017)

Colman, Gould P., *Education and Agriculture: A History of the New York State College of Agriculture at Cornell University* (Ithaca, NY, 1963)

Cornford, Thomas, 'The English Theatre Studios of Michael Chekhov and Michel Saint-Denis, 1935–65', unpublished PhD thesis, University of Warwick, 2012

Croly, Herbert, *The Promise of American Life* (Cambridge, MA, 1965 [1909])

—*Willard Straight* (New York, 1925)

Curry, W. B., *The School and a Changing Civilisation* (London, 1934)

De la Iglesia, Maria, *Dartington Hall School: Staff Memories of the Early Years* (Exeter, 1996)

Delap, Lucy and Sue Morgan (eds), *Men, Masculinities and Religious Change in Twentieth-Century Britain* (Basingstoke, 2013)

Dewey, John, *Democracy and Education: An Introduction to the Philosophy of Education* (New York, 1999 [1916])

Diner, Steven J., *A Very Different Age: Americans of the Progressive Era* (New York, 1998)

Elmhirst, Dorothy and Leonard, *Prospectus* (Totnes, 1926)

Elmhirst, Leonard, *Faith and Works at Dartington* (Totnes, 1937)

Godley, Andrew and Bridget Williams, 'Democratizing Luxury and the Contentious 'Invention of the Technological Chicken' in Britain', *The Business History Review* 83 (2009), 267–90

Gould, Karolyn, 'The Modest Benefactor', *Cornell Alumni News* 3 (1975), 19–21

Green, Martin, *Mountain of Truth: The Counterculture Begins, Ascona, 1900–1920* (Hanover; London, 1989)

Gribble, David, *That's All Folks: Dartington Hall School Remembered* (Crediton, 1987)

Hall, Lesley A., "A City that We Shall Never Find'? The Search for a Community of Fellow Progressive Spirits in the UK between the Wars', *Family & Community* 18 (2015), 24–36

Hardy, Dennis, *Utopian England: Community Experiments, 1900–1945* (London, 2000)

Harrison, Rachel Esther, 'Dorothy Elmhirst and the Visual Arts at Dartington Hall 1925–1945', unpublished PhD thesis, University of Plymouth, 2002

Hazelgrove, Jenny, *Spiritualism and British Society between the Wars* (Manchester, 2000)

Heard, Gerald, 'The Dartington Experiment', *Architectural Review* 449 (1934), 119–122

Huxley, Aldous, *Those Barren Leaves* (London, 1925)

Jeremiah, David, 'Dartington – a Modern Adventure', in Samuel Smiles (ed.), *Going Modern and Being British: Art, Architecture and Design in Devon c. 1910–60* (Exeter, 1998)

Kidel, Mark, *Beyond the Classroom. Dartington's Experiments in Education* (Devon, 1990)

King, Greg, *A Season of Splendor: The Court of Mrs Astor in Gilded Age New York* (Hoboken, NJ, 2009)

Leach, Bernard, *A Potter's Book* ([n.p.], 1940)

Light, Alison, *Mrs Woolf and the Servants: The Hidden Heart of Domestic Service* (London, 2007)

Mandler, Peter, *The Fall and Rise of the Stately Home* (New Haven, CT, 1997)

Murray, Nicholas, *Aldous Huxley* (London, 2002)

Neima, Anna, 'Dartington Hall and Social Reform in Interwar Britain', unpublished PhD thesis, University of Cambridge, 2019

Nicholas, Larraine, *Dancing in Utopia: Dartington Hall and its Dancers* (Alton, 2007)

Owen, Alex, *The Darkened Room: Women, Power and Spiritualism in Late Victorian England* (London, 1989)

Pinder, John (ed.), *Fifty Years of Political and Economic Planning: Looking Forward, 1931–1981* (London, 1981)

Pevsner, Nikolaus, *Devon* (Harmondsworth, 1989 [1952])

Rauchways, Eric, 'A Gentleman's Club in a Woman's Sphere: How Dorothy Whitney Straight Created The New Republic', *The Journal of Women's History* 11 (1999), 60–85

Ritschel, Daniel, *The Politics of Planning: The Debate on Economic Planning in Britain in the 1930s* (Oxford, 1997)

Sandel, Michael, *Democracy's Discontent: America in Search of a Public Philosophy* (London, 1996)

Sharp, Martin, 'Michael Chekhov: The Dartington years' (DVD, Palomino Films, 2002)

Swanberg, W. A., *Whitney Father, Whitney Heiress* (New York, 1980)

Young, Michael, *The Elmhirsts of Dartington: The Creation of a Utopian Community* (London, 1982)

THREE: Self-Realization in the Mountains of Japan: Mushanokōji Saneatsu's Atarashiki Mura

Arnold, Matthew, 'Culture and its Enemies', *Cornhill Magazine* 16 (1867), 36–53

Bird, Isabella, *Unbeaten Tracks in Japan* (London, 1880)

Borland, Janet, 'Capitalising on Catastrophe: Reinvigorating the Japanese State with Moral Values through Education following the 1923 Great Kantō Earthquake', *Modern Asian Studies* 40 (2006), 875–907

Daruvala, Susan, *Zhou Zuoren and an Alternative Chinese Response to Modernity* (Cambridge, MA, 2000)

Dodd, Stephen, *Writing Home: Representations of the Native Place in Modern Japanese Literature* (Cambridge, MA, 2004)

Duke, Benjamin, *The History of Modern Japanese Education: Constructing the National School System, 1872–1890* (New Brunswick, NJ, 2009)

Gordon, Andrew, *A Modern History of Japan: From Tokugawa Times to the Present* (New York, 2009 [2003])

Fowler, Edward, *The Rhetoric of Confession: Shishōsetsu in Early Twentieth-Century Japanese Fiction* (Berkeley, CA; Oxford, 1988)

Frederick, Sarah, 'Yamakawa Kikue and Edward Carpenter: Translation, Affiliation, and Queer Internationalism', in Julia C. Bullock, Ayako Kano and James Welker (eds), *Rethinking Japanese Feminisms* (Hawai'i, HI, 2018)

Harootunian, Harry, *Overcome by Modernity: History, Culture, and Community in Interwar Japan* (Princeton, NJ, 2000)

Hay, Stephen N., *Asian Ideas of East and West: Tagore and His Critics in Japan, China and India* (Cambridge, MA, 1970)

Hayford, Charles W., *To the People: James Yen and Village China* (New York, 1991)

Ima-Izumi, Yoko, 'The Female Voice in Blake Studies in Japan, 1910s–1930s', in Steve Clark and Masashi Suzuki (eds), *The Reception of Blake in the Orient* (London, 2006)

Keaveney, Christopher T., *Beyond Brushtalk: Sino-Japanese Literary Exchange in the Interwar Period* (Hong Kong, 2009)

Keene, Donald, *Dawn to the West: Japanese Literature of the Modern Era*, vol. 3 (New York, 1998)

Kikuchi, Yuko, *Japanese Modernisation and Mingei Theory: Cultural Nationalism and Oriental Orientalism* (New York, 2004)

Kohl, Stephen W., Yoko Matsuoka McClain and Ryoko Toyama McClellan, *The White Birch School (Shirakabaha) of Japanese Literature: Some Sketches and Commentary* (Oregon, 1975)

Konishi, Sho, *Anarchist Modernity: Cooperatism and Japanese Russian Intellectual Relations in Modern Japan* (Cambridge, MA, 2013)

—'Ordinary Farmers Living Anarchist Time: Arishima Cooperative Farm in Hokkaido, 1922–1935', *Modern Asian Studies* 47 (2013), 1845–87

Kusakabe, Madoka, 'Saka Ineko and Kirabayashi Taiko: The Café and *Jokyū* as a State for Social Criticism', unpublished PhD thesis, University of Oregon, 2011

Leach, Bernard, *Beyond East and West: Memoirs, Portraits and Essays* (London, 1978)

Lebra, Takie Sugiyama, *Above the Clouds: Status Culture of the Modern Japanese Nobility* (Berkeley, CA; Oxford, 1993)

Lins, Ulrich, 'Esperanto as a Language and Idea in China and Japan', *Language Problems and Language Planning* 32 (2008), 47–60

Long, Hoyt, 'Farmers' Art in an Age of Cosmopolitan Agrarianism', in *On Uneven Ground: Miyazawa Kenji and the Making of Place in Modern Japan* (Stanford, CA, 2012), 159–91

Macleod, Calum, 'From Our Correspondent: Crushed Dreams of Utopia in Rural China', *The Times*, 2 May 2016

Maeda, Hayao, *One Hundred Years of Atarashiki Mura* (Japanese edition, Tokyo, 2017), extracts translated by Kazuyo Yasuda

Maeterlinck, Maurice, *Wisdom and Destiny*, trans. Alfred Sutro (New York, 1901)

Minohara, Tosh, Tze-ki Hon and Evan Dawley (eds), *The Decade of the Great War: Japan and the Wider World in the 1910s* (Leiden, 2014)

Mochizuki, Yoshikhiro, 'Rediscovering Musha-ism: The Theory of Happiness in the Early Works of Mushanokōji Saneatsu', unpublished Masters thesis, University of Hawai'i, 2005

Moeran, Brian, 'Bernard Leach and the Japanese Folk Craft Movement: The Formative Years', *Journal of Design History* 2 (1989), 139–144

Morris-Suzuki, Tessa, *The Technological Transformation of Japan: From the Seventeenth to the Twenty-first Century* (New York, 1994)

—'Invisible Politics', *Humanities Australia* 5 (2014), 53–7

—'A Century of Social Alternatives in a Japanese Mountain Community', in *New Worlds from Below: Informal Life Politics and Grassroots Action in Twenty-first-century Northeast Asia* (Australia, 2017), 5176

—'Beyond Utopia: New Villages and Living Politics in Modern Japan and across Frontiers', *History Workshop Journal* 85 (2018), 47–71

—*Japan's Living Politics* (Cambridge, 2020)

Mortimer, Maya, *Meeting the Sensei: The Role of the Master in Shirakaba Writers* (Leiden, 2000)

—'Mushanokōji Saneatsu: Luzern', *Asiatische Studien: Zeitschrift der Schweizerischen Asiengesellschaft* 58 (2004), 479–90, at 481

Morton, Leith, *Divided Self: A Biography of Arishima Takeo* (Sydney, 1989)

[n.a.], 'Atarashiki mura in Interwar Japan', https://rekolektiv.wordpress.com/essays/historical-essays/atarashiki-mura-in-interwar-japan/ [accessed 20 August 2020]

Ning, Ou, 'Utopia', in Christian Sorace, Ivan Franceschini and Nicholas Loubere (eds), *Afterlives of Chinese Communism: Political Concepts from Mao to Xi* (Acton, Australia, 2019), 309–13

—'Autonomy: Utopia or Realpolitik', in Hou Hanru (ed.), *Zizhiqu: Autonomous Regions* (Guangzhou, 2013)

Partner, Simon, *Toshié: A Story of Village Life in Twentieth-Century Japan* (Berkley; London, 2004)

Plath, David W., 'The Fate of Utopia: Adaptive Tactics in Four Japanese Groups', *American Anthropologists* 68, 1152–63

Roden, Donald, *Schooldays in Imperial Japan: A Study in the Culture of a Student Elite* (Berkeley, CA; London, 1980)

Rahav, Shakhar, 'How Shall We Live?: Chinese Communal Experiments after the Great War in Global Context', *Journal of World History* 26 (2015), 521–48

Rapley, Ian, 'When Global and Local Culture Meet: Esperanto in 1920s Rural Japan', *Language Problems and Language Planning* 37 (2013), 179–96

Solnit, Rebecca, *A Paradise Built in Hell: The Extraordinary Communities that Arise in Disasters* (London; New York, 2009)

Tipton, Elise, *Modern Japan: A Social and Economic History* (London, 2002)

Tonooka, Chika, 'Reverse Emulation and the Cult of Japanese Efficiency in Edwardian Britain', *The Historical Journal* 60 (2017), 95–119

Weisenfeld, Gennifer, *MAVO: Japanese Arts and the Avant-Garde, 1905–1931* (Berkeley, CA; Los Angeles, CA; London, 2002)

Yiu, Angela, 'The Intellectual and Literary Contexts of a Taishō Utopian Village', *Japan Review* 20 (2008), 203–30

—'From Utopia to Empire: Atarashikimura and *A Personal View of the Great East Asia War* (1942)', *Utopian Studies* 19 (2008), 213–32

Young, A. Morgan, *Japan Under Taishō Tennō 1912–1926* (London, 1928)

FOUR: The Forest Philosophers of Fontainebleau: G. I. Gurdjieff's Institute for the Harmonious Development of Man

Anderson, Margaret, *My Thirty Years' War: An Autobiography* (London, 1930)

—*Little Review Anthology* (New York, 1953)

—*The Unknowable Gurdjieff* (New York, 1991)

Baker, Rob, 'No Harem: Gurdjieff and the Women of the Rope', *Gurdjieff International Review* 1.2 (1997–98), 39–45

Bechhofer-Roberts, C. E., *In Denikin's Russia and the Caucasus, 1919–1920* (London, 1921)

—'The Forest Philosophers', *Century Magazine* CVIII (1), May 1924

Bell, Mary C., 'Some Memories of the Prieuré', September 1949, *Gurdjieff International Review* 1 (1998), https://www.gurdjieff.org/bell.htm [accessed 20 August 2020]

Bennett, John, *Gurdjieff: Making a New World* (London, 1973)

—*Witness: The Autobiography of John Bennett* (London, 1974 [1961])

Black, Ian E., *A Friend in France* (Jonathan Cape, 1941)

Bryce, James, *Transcaucasia and Ararat, Being Notes of a Vacation Tour in the Autumn of 1876* (London, 1877)

Butkovsky-Hewitt, Ann, *With Gurdjieff in St Petersburg and Paris* (London, 1978)

Carswell, J., *Lives and Letters: A. R. Orage, Beatrice Hastings, Katherine Mansfield, John Middleton Murry, S. S. Koteliansky, 1906–1957* (London, 1978)

Clarke, Peter B., *Encyclopaedia of New Religious Movements* (London, 2006)

Coates, Chris, 'How Many Arks Does It Take?', in Timothy Miller (ed.), *Spiritual and Visionary Communities: Out to Save the World* (London; New York, 2013)

Cott, Nancy F., 'Revisiting the Transatlantic 1920s: Vincent Sheean vs. Malcolm Cowley', *The American Historical Review* 118 (2013), 46–75

De Hartmann, Thomas, *Our Life with Mr Gurdjieff* (New York, 1964)

Dearborn, Mary V., *Mistress of Modernism: The Life of Peggy Guggenheim* (Boston, MA; New York, 2004)

Diment, Galya, *A Russian Jew of Bloomsbury: The Life and Times of Samuel Koteliansky* (Montreal; Kingston, 2011)

Ertas, Sebnem, 'The Changing Physical Environment of Kars City After the 93 War', in Recep Efe, Lia Matchavariani, Abdulkadir Yaldir and Laszio Levai (eds), *Developments in Science and Engineering* ([Bulgaria], 2016), 612–24

Figes, Orlando, *A People's Tragedy, the Russian Revolution, 1891–1924* (London, 2017 [1996])

Fitzgerald, F. Scott, *This Side of Paradise* (Cambridge, 2012 [1920])

Ford, Hugh, *Four Lives in Paris* (San Francisco, 1987)

Gibbon, Monk, *The Masterpiece and the Man: Yeats as I Knew Him* (London, 1959)

Gurdjieff, G. I., *The Herald of Coming Good: First Appeal to Contemporary Humanity* (Paris, 1933)

—*Beelzebub's Tales to His Grandson: All and Everything* (London, 2000 [1950])

—*Meetings with Remarkable Men* (New York, 2002 [1963])

—*Life is Real Only Then, When 'I Am'* (London, 1999 [1974])

Hoffman, Maud, 'Taking the Life Cure in Gurdjieff's School', *New York Times*, 10 February 1924

Hulme, Kathryn, *Undiscovered Country* (London, 1966)

Kafian, Adele, 'Looking Back to the Last Days of Katherine Mansfield', *Adelphi*, October 1946

Kenworthy, Scott M., *The Heart of Russia: Trinity-Sergius, Monasticism, and Society after 1825* (New York; Oxford, 2010)

Kimber, Gerri and Claire Davison (eds), *The Diaries of Katherine Mansfield* (Edinburgh, 2016)

Landau, Rom, *God Is My Adventure: A Book on Modern Mystics, Masters and Teachers* (London, 1935)

Lappin, Linda, 'The Ghosts of Fontainebleau', *Southwest Review* 87 (2002), 29–48

Lipsey, Roger, *Gurdjieff Reconsidered: The Life, the Teachings, the Legacy* (Boulder, CO, 2019)

Lottman, Herbert R., *Man Ray's Montparnasse* (New York, 2011)

Luhan, Mabel Dodge, *Lorenzo in Taos* (Santa Fe, NM, 2007 [1932])

Mairet, Philip, *Autobiographical and Other Papers* (Manchester, 1981)

Moore, James, *Gurdjieff and Mansfield: The Initiation of the Priestess* (London, 1980)

—*Gurdjieff: A Biography* (Shaftesbury, 1999 [1991])

Munson, Gorham, 'Black Sheep Philosophers', *Gurdjieff International*

Review 1998 (3), https://www.gurdjieff.org/munson1.htm [accessed 20 February 2019]

Nott, C. S., *Teachings of Gurdjieff: The Journal of a Pupil* (London, 1961)

O'Sullivan, Vincent and Margaret Scott (eds), *The Collected Letters*, vol. 5 (Oxford, 2008)

Osborne, Huw, *The Rise of the Modernist Bookshop: Books and the Commerce of Culture in the Twentieth Century* (London, 2015)

Ouspensky, P. D., *Tertium Organum: The Third Canon of Thought, a Key to Enigmas of the World*, trans. E. Kadloubovsky and the author (London, 1981 [1912])

—*In Search of the Miraculous. Fragments of an Unknown Teaching* (London, 1950)

Owen, Alex, *The Place of Enchantment: British Occultism and the Culture of the Modern* (Chicago, IL; London, 2004)

Pamuk, Orhan, *Snow*, trans. Maureen Freely (London, 2004)

Patterson, William Patrick, *Ladies of the Rope: Gurdjieff's Special Left Bank Women's Group* (Fairfax, CA, 1999)

Pauwels, Louis, *Gurdjieff* (Isle of Man, 1964)

Peters, Fritz, *Boyhood with Gurdjieff* (New York, 1964)

Petsche, Johanna J. M., 'A Gurdjieff Genealogy: Tracing the Manifold Ways the Gurdjieff Teaching Has Travelled', *International Journal for the Study of New Religions* 4 (2013), 72–4

Pogson, Beryl, *Maurice Nicoll: A Portrait* (London, 1961)

Post, Jerrold M., 'Narcissism and the Charismatic Leader-Follower Relationship', *Political Psychology* 7 (1986), 675–88

Rudnick, Lois Palken, *Mabel Dodge Luhan: New Woman, New Worlds* (Albuquerque, NM, 1984)

Saurat, Denis, 'Visite à Gourdjieff', *La Nouvelle Revue Française*, November 1933

Schorer, Mark, *Sinclair Lewis: An American Life* (New York, 1961)

Seymour-Smith, Martin, *The 100 Most Influential Books Ever Written* (New York, 1998)

Taylor, Paul Beekman, *Gurdjieff and Orage: Brothers in Elysium* (York Beach, ME; [UK], 2001)

—*Gurdjieff's America: Mediating the Miraculous* ([UK], 2004)

Tchekhovitch, Tcheslaw, *Gurdjieff: A Master in Life* (Toronto, 2006)

—'Théâtre des Champs-Elysées', *Le Temps*, 15 December 1923

Tomalin, Claire, *Katherine Mansfield: A Secret Life* (Harmondsworth, 2003)

Webb, James, *Harmonious Circle: The Lives and Works of G. I. Gurdjieff, P. D. Ouspensky and Their Followers* (New York, 1980)

Wolfe, Edwin, *Episodes with Gurdjieff* (Birmingham, AL, 2002 [1973])

—'Further Episodes with Gurdjieff', *Gurdjieff International Review* 6 (2003), https://www.gurdjieff.org/grossman2.htm. [accessed 20 August 2020]

Young, James Carruthers, 'An Experiment at Fontainebleau: A Personal Reminiscence', *British Journal of Medical Psychology* 7 (1927), 447–61

FIVE: Seeking the Kingdom of God in Rural Germany: Eberhard and Emmy Arnold's Bruderhof

Arnold, Annemarie, *Youth Movement to Bruderhof: Letters and Diaries of Annemarie Arnold née Wächter, 1926–1932* (Rifton, NY; Robertsbridge, UK, 1986)

Arnold, Eberhard, *The War: A Call to Inwardness* (Gotha, 1914)

—*Why We Live in Community* (Rifton, NY, 1995 [1925])

—'Life's Task', translated from Eberhard Arnold, transcript, 8 October 1933 (Bruderhof Historical Archive EA163) and Eberhard Arnold, transcript, 18 March 1932 (Bruderhof Historical Archive EA4), in *Called to Community: The Life Jesus Wants for His People*, Charles E. Moore (ed.) (Walden, NY, 2016)

—*God's Revolution: Justice, Community, and the Coming Kingdom* (Walden, NY; Robertsbridge, UK; Elsmore, Australia, 1997)

Arnold, Eberhard and Emmy, *Seeking for the Kingdom of God*, selected and edited from earlier sources by Heini and Annemarie Arnold (New York, 1974)

Arnold, Eberhard and Emmy von Hollander, *Love Letters* (Rifton, NY, 2007)

Arnold, Emmy, *Torches Together* (Rifton, NY, 1964)

—*A Joyful Pilgrimage: My Life in Community* (Farmington, PA; Robertsbridge, UK, 1999)

Barth, Emmy, *No Lasting Home: A Year in the Paraguayan Wilderness* (Walden, NY; Robertsbridge, UK, 2009)

—*An Embassy Besieged: The Story of a Christian Community in Nazi Germany* (Eugene, OR, 2010)

Baum, Markus, *Against the Wind: Eberhard Arnold and the Bruderhof* (London, 1998)

Crouthamel, Jason, *The Great War and German Memory: Society, Politics and Psychological Trauma, 1914–1945* (Exeter, 2009)

Bruderhof, the, *Foundations of Our Faith & Calling* (Walden, NY; Robertsbridge, UK, 2014)

—*The Plough*, vol. 1, no. 3 (1953)

Hutterian Brethren (eds), *Brothers Unite: An Account of the Uniting of Eberhard Arnold and the Rhön Bruderhof with the Hutterian Church* (Ulster Park, NY, 1988)

Janzen, Rod, 'The Hutterites and the Bruderhof: The Relationship between an Old Order Religious Society and a Twentieth-Century Communal Group', *Mennonite Quarterly Review* 79 (2005), 505–44

Jenkins, Philip, *The Great and Holy War: How World War I Became a Religious Crusade* (New York, 2014)

Keegan, John, *The First World War* (London, 1998)

Koven, Seth, *The Match Girl and the Heiress* (Oxford, 2015)

MacCarthy, Fiona, *Eric Gill* (London, 1989)

Macintyre, Ben, *Forgotten Fatherland: The Search for Elisabeth Nietzsche* ([n.p.], 1992)

Meier, Hans, *The Dissolution of the Rhön Bruderhof in Retrospect* (Rifton, NY, 1979)

Mommsen, Peter, *Homage to a Broken Man: The Life of J. Heinrich Arnold – A True Story of Faith, Forgiveness, Sacrifice, and Community* (Robertsbridge, UK, 2004)

[n.a.], *Memories of Our Early Years* (Rifton, NY, pamphlet 197309, [n.d.]), vol. 1

Oved, Yaacov, *The Witness of the Brothers: A History of the Bruderhof* (London, 2017)

Peck, Robert N., 'An Ex-Member's View of the Bruderhof Communities from 1948–1961', in Gorman Beauchamp, Kenneth Roemer and Nicholas D. Smith (eds), *Utopian Studies* I (Lanham, MD, 1987), 111–22

Randall, Ian M., "Church Community is a Gift of the Holy Spirit': The Spirituality of the Bruderhof Community', *Centre for Baptist History and Heritage Studies*, Occasional Papers vol. 10 (Oxford, 2014)

—*The Christian Peace Experiment: The Bruderhof Community in Britain, 1933–1942* (Eugene, OR, 2018)

Rubin, Julius H., *The Other Side of Joy: Religious Melancholy Among the Bruderhof* (Oxford, 2000)

—'Contested Narratives: A Case Study of the Conflict between a New Religious Movement and its Critics', http://www.perefound.com/jr_cn.html, [n.d.] [accessed 18 August 2020]

Stephan, Karen H. and G. Edward Stephan, 'Religion and the Survival of Utopian Communities', *Journal for the Scientific Study of Religion* 12 (1973), 89–100

The Times, 'From Our Special Correspondent', 6 September 1938, 'The Cotswold Bruderhof – German Peasant Colony'

Tyldesley, Michael, *No Heavenly Delusion? A Comparative Study of Three Communal Movements* (Liverpool, 2003)

Wayland-Smith, Ellen, *Oneida: From Free Love Utopia to Well-Set Table* (New York, 2016)

Williams, John Alexander, *Turning to Nature in Germany: Hiking, Nudism and Conservation, 1900–1940* (Stanford, CA, 2007)

Zablocki, Benjamin, *The Joyful Community* (Baltimore, MD, 1971)

SIX: California Dreaming: Gerald Heard's Trabuco College

Ackerley, J. R., *My Father and Myself* (London, 1968)

Anderson, Walter Truett, *The Upstart Spring: Esalen and the American Awakening* (Reading, MA, 1983)

Bedford, Sybille, *Aldous Huxley: A Biography*, vols 1 and 2 (London, 1973 and 1974)

Burke, Flannery, *From Greenwich Village to Taos: Primitivism and Place at Mabel Dodge Luhan's* (Lawrence, KS, 2008)

Clay, Alexa, 'Utopia Inc', *Aeon*, 28 February 2017 [accessed 13 August 2020]

Dunaway, David King, *Huxley in Hollywood* (Bloomsbury, 1990 [1989])

Eros, Paul, "One of the Most Penetrating Minds in England': Gerald Heard and the British Intelligentsia of the Interwar Period', unpublished PhD thesis, University of Oxford, 2011

Falby, Alison, *Between the Pigeonholes: Gerald Heard, 1889–1971* (Newcastle, 2008)

Freeden, Michael, 'Eugenics and Progressive Thought: A Study in Ideological Affinity', *Historical Journal* 22 (1979), 645–71

Freemantle, Anne, 'Heard Melodies', *The Commonweal* 43 (25 January 1946), 384–5

Gardiner, Juliet, "Searching for the Gleam': Finding Solutions to the Political and Social Problems of 1930s Britain', *History Workshop Journal* 72 (2011), 103–17

Heard, Gerald, *The Ascent of Humanity: An Essay on the Evolution of Civilization from Group Consciousness Through Individuality to Super-Consciousness* (London, 1929)

—'Men and Books', review of *Letters of George III* by B. Dobrée and *Government in Business* by Stuart Chase, *Time and Tide*, 9 November 1935, 1619–20

— The Significance of the New Pacifism', in Gerald K. Hibbert (ed.), *The New Pacifism* (London, 1936)

—*The Third Morality* (New York, 1937)

—*Pain, Sex and Time: A New Hypothesis of Evolution* (London, 1939)

—'The Poignant Prophet', *The Kenyon Review* 27 (1965), 49–70

Holtby, Winifred, 'The Art of Science', review of *This Surprising World: A Journalist Looks at Science, Time and Tide* XIII, 9 June 1932, 771

Huxley, Aldous, *Eyeless in Gaza* (London, 2004 [1936])

—*Ends and Means: An Enquiry into the Nature of Ideals and into the Methods Employed for their Realization* (London, 1946 [1937])

—(ed.), *An Encyclopaedia of Pacifism* (London, 1937)

—*The Perennial Philosophy* (New York, 1945)

—*The Doors of Perception* (San Francisco, CA, 1954)

—'Ozymandias, the Desert Utopia That Failed', in *Tomorrow and Tomorrow and Tomorrow and Other Essays* (New York 1956)

—*Island* (London, 2005 [1962])

Isherwood, Christopher (ed.), *Vedanta for the Western World* (London, 1948)

—*Diaries*, vol. 1: 1939–1960, ed. Katherine Bucknell (London, 1996)

King, Miriam, 'Life at Trabuco', [n.d.], https://www.geraldheard.com/writings-and-recollections/2017/8/2/life-at-trabuco [accessed 20 August 2020]

Knox, Ronald, *Broadcast Minds* (London, 1932)

Kripal, Jeffrey J., *Esalen: America and the Religion of No Religion* (Chicago, 2007)

Lash, Joseph P., *Eleanor and Franklin* (London, 1972)

Lattin, Don, *Distilled Spirits* (Berkeley, CA; Los Angeles, CA, 2012)

Lewis, Jeremy, *Shades of Greene: One Generation of the English Family*
    (London, 2011)

Maloney, C. J., *Back to the Land: Arthurdale, FDR's New Deal, and the Costs
    of Economic Planning* (Hoboken, NJ, 2011)

Mitchinson, Naomi, *You May Well Ask: A Memoir, 1920–1940* (London, 1979)

Murphy, Michael, 'Totally on Fire', [n.d.], https://www.geraldheard.
    com/writings-and-recollections/2017/8/2/totally-on-fire [accessed
    19 August 2020]

Murray, Nicholas, *Aldous Huxley: An English Intellectual* (London, 2003)

Overy, Richard, *The Morbid Age: Britain between the Wars* (London, 2009)

Parker, Peter, *Isherwood: A Life* (London, 2004)

Renwick, Chris, *British Sociology's Lost Biological Roots: A History of
    Futures Past* (Basingstoke, 2012)

Robb, David, 'Brahmins from Abroad: English Expatriates and Spiritual
    Consciousness in Modern America', *American Studies* 26 (1985),
    45–60

Sessa, Ben, *The Psychedelic Renaissance: Reassessing the Role of Psychedelic
    Drugs in 21st Century Psychiatry and Society* (London, 2017)

Smith, Grover (ed.), *Letters of Aldous Huxley* (London, 1969)

Stievermann, Jan, Philip Goff, Detlef Junker, *Religion and the
    Marketplace in the United States* (Oxford, 2015)

Veysey, Laurence R., *The Communal Experience: Anarchist and Mystical
    Communities in Twentieth-Century America* (Chicago, IL; London, 1973)

Watts, Alan, *In My Own Way: An Autobiography 1915–1965* (New York,
    1973)

Webb, Beatrice, *My Apprenticeship*, vol. 1 (London, 1926)

Williams, Louise Blakeney, 'Overcoming the 'Contagion of Mimicry':
    The Cosmopolitan Nationalism and Modernist History of
    Rabindranath Tagore and W. B. Yeats', *American Historical Review*
    (2007), 69–100

Whisenhunt, Donald W., *Utopian Movements and Ideas of the Great
    Depression: Dreamers, Believers, and Madmen* (Lanham, MD, 2013)

Yogeshananda, Swami, 'Trabuco College Tryout', [n.d.], https://www.
    geraldheard.com/writings-and-recollections/2017/8/2/trabuco-
    college-tryout [accessed 20 August 2020]

Zahn, Franklin, 'Temporary Monk', 1984, https://www.geraldheard.
    com/writings-and-recollections/2017/8/2/temporary-monk
    [accessed 20 August 2020]

CONCLUSION: Radically Different Ways of Being

Callenbach, Ernest, "Ecotopia' in Japan?', *Communities Magazine* 131 (2006), 42–9

Hanisch, Carol, 'The Personal Is Political' (first published in 1970), reprinted in *Radical Feminism: A Documentary Reader*, Barbara A. Crow (ed.) (New York, 2000), 113-7

Jacoby, Russell, *The End of Utopia: Politics and Culture in an Age of Apathy* (New York, 1999)

Jones, Landon, *Great Expectations: America and the Baby Boom Generation* (New York, 1980)

Kumar, Krishnan, 'The End of Socialism? The End of Utopia? The End of History?', in Krishnan Kumar and Stephen Bann (eds), *Utopias and the Millennium* (London, 1993)

—'The Ends of Utopia', *New Literary History* 41 (2010), 549–69

Lockyer, Joshua, "We Try to Create the World That We Want': Intentional Communities Forging Liveable Lives in St Louis', working paper 2011, 3

Lofton, Kathryn, 'Considering the Neoliberal in American Religion', in Jan Stievermann, Philip Goff and Detlef Junker (eds), *Religion and the Marketplace in the United States* (Oxford; New York, 2015), 269–288

Marantz, Andrew, 'Silicon Valley's Crisis of Conscience: Where Big Tech Goes to Ask Deep Questions', *New Yorker*, 19 August 2019

Oved, Yaacov, *Globalization of Communes, 1950–2010* (New Brunswick, NJ, 2013)

Wallmeier, Philip, 'Exit as Critique. Communes and Intentional Communities in the 1960s and Today', *Historical Social Research* 42 (2017), 147–171

Zablocki, Benjamin, *Alienation and Charisma* (New York, 1980)

NOTES

INTRODUCTION: 'The Art of Living Together in Harmony'

1 (Luke 17:12), Eberhard Arnold quoted in Baum, *Against the Wind: Eberhard Arnold and the Bruderhof* (London, 1998), 28
2 Leonard Elmhirst to Dorothy Elmhirst, 6 March 1925, LKE/DWE/12/A, Dartington Hall Archives
3 Christopher Clark, *The Sleepwalkers: How Europe Went to War in 1914* (London, 2012), xxi
4 This figure is for the Imperial Wars, 1805–15. Mark Hewitson, 'Princes' Wars, Wars of the People, or Total War? Mass Armies and the Question of a Military Revolution in Germany, 1792–1815', *War in History* 20 (2013), 452–90, at 453
5 Philip Jenkins, *The Great and Holy War* (New York, 2014), 29–31
6 Jenkins, *Holy War*, 45
7 David Omissi, *Indian Voices of the Great War: Soldiers' Letters, 1914–18* (Basingstoke, 1999), 43
8 Victor C. Vaughan, *A Doctor's Memories* ([n.p.], 2007 [1926]), 383–4
9 Laura Spinney, *Pale Rider: The Spanish Flu of 1918 and How It Changed the World* (London, 2017)
10 George Dehner, *Influenza: A Century of Science and Public Health Response* (Pittsburgh, PA, 2012), 48
11 Catherine Belling, 'Overwhelming the Medium: Fiction and the Trauma of Pandemic Influenza in 1918', *Literature and Medicine* 28 (2009), 55–81
12 D. H. Lawrence to Lady Cynthia Asquith, November 1915, quoted in Krishnan Kumar, *Utopia and Anti-Utopia in Modern Times* (Oxford, 1987), 380–1
13 Quoted in Santanu Das, 'The Indian Sepoy and the First World War', https://www.bl.uk/world-war-one/articles/the-indian-sepoy-in-the-first-world-war#note1 [accessed 20 July 2020]

14 Cecil Rhodes, *The Last Will and Testament of Cecil John Rhodes*, ed. W. T. Stead (London 1902), 190

15 Greg Grandin, *Fordlandia: The Rise and Fall of Henry Ford's Forgotten Jungle City* (London, 2010)

16 The Land of Cockaigne was commonly referred to in medieval myth. It was described, for example, in the thirteenth-century English poem 'The Land of Cockayne', which satirized monastic life.

17 Thomas More, *Libellus vere aureus, nec minus salutaris quam festivus, de optimo rei publicae statu deque nova insula Utopia* (A Little, True Book, As Beneficial As It Is Enjoyable, About How Things Should Be In The New Island Utopia) (Cambridge, 2002 [1516])

18 [n.a.], 'Atarashiki mura in Interwar Japan', [n.d.], https://rekolektiv. wordpress.com/essays/historical-essays/atarashiki-mura-in-interwar-japan/ [accessed 11 February 2020]

19 Jane Shaw, *Octavia, Daughter of God: The Story of a Female Messiah and Her Followers* (London, 2011)

20 Charlotte Perkins Gilman, *Herland* (London, 2015 [1915]); Rose Macaulay, *What Not* (London, 2019 [1918])

21 Aldous Huxley, 'Ozymandias', in *Adonis and the Alphabet, and Other Essays* (London, 1956), 100

ONE: 'Life in its Completeness' on the Plains of Bengal: Rabindranath Tagore's Santiniketan-Sriniketan

1 All quotations in this paragraph are from Rabindranath Tagore, 'The Schoolmaster' (1924), in Sisir Kumar Das (ed.), *The English Writings of Rabindranath Tagore: A Miscellany*, vol. 3 (New Delhi, 1996), 508–9

2 Footnote to an article published in Charles Dickens' journal, *All the Year Round*, 5 April 1862, 80

3 There was a precursor to Brahmo Samaj, Brahmo Sabha, which was founded in 1825 by the intellectual Raja Rammohun Roy. Debendranath Tagore helped transform this scholarly association into a mass movement for social and moral reform in the 1840s.

4 Krishna Dutta and Andrew Robinson, *Rabindranath Tagore: The Myriad-minded Man* (Bloomsbury, 1995), 46

5 Tagore to Leonard Elmhirst, 19 December 1937, quoted in Kissoonsingh Hazareesingh (ed.), *A Rich Harvest: The Complete Tagore/Elmhirst Correspondence and Other Writings* (Mauritius, 1992)

6 Fakrul Alam and Radha Chakravarty (eds), *The Essential Tagore* (Cambridge, MA; London, 2011), 93

7 Dutta and Robinson, *Tagore*, 230

8 Ibid., *Tagore*, 67

9   Tagore's wife's original name was Bhabatarini, but shortly after the
    marriage it was changed to Mrinalini, either by Tagore or by his family
    – a symbol of the expectation that the young girl could be modelled to
    her new family's wishes. Krishna Kripalani, *Rabindranath Tagore. A
    Biography* (London, 1962), 185

10 The British Raj enacted measures to prevent female infanticide, raise the
    age of consent and outlaw child marriage. Some Indian nationalist
    reformers – including many belonging to Brahmo Samaj – also cham-
    pioned measures supporting women's rights, but others resisted the
    imposition of 'Western' standards on their country's culture.

11 Rathindranath Tagore, *On the Edges of Times* (Calcutta, 1981), 36

12 Rabindranath Tagore, *Glimpses of Bengal* (London, 1921), 18;
    Rathindranath Tagore, *Edges*, 19

13 Rathindranath Tagore, *Edges*, 34

14 Rabindranath Tagore, quoted in Uma Das Gupta, *Rabindranath Tagore: A
    Biography* (Oxford, 2004), 11

15 Rathindranath Tagore, *Edges*, 28

16 Rabindranath Tagore, quoted in Das Gupta, *Tagore*, 32

17 For much of the time when Tagore was working as a zamindar, his wife
    and children stayed with his extended family at Jorasanko. In 1898, he
    brought them all to his estate house in Shelidah, East Bengal, in large
    part because he wanted to supervise his children's education. His chil-
    dren were called Renuka, Shamindranath, Meera, Rathindranath and
    Madhurilata.

18 Rathindranath Tagore, 'Father as I Knew Him', in *Tagore, Centenary Volume,
    1861–1961* (New Delhi, 1961) [edited by S. Radhakrishnan and others],
    53–4

19 Tagore, quoted in Das Gupta, *Tagore*, 5

20 Early on, the school was known alternately as Brahmacharyashram,
    Ashram Vidyalaya and Santiniketan Vidyalaya. It was only renamed Patha
    Bhavana in the 1920s, but it is called this throughout the chapter to
    avoid confusion.

21 Dutta and Robinson, *Tagore*, 136

22 The idea of Tagore as the first international literary celebrity is used by
    Amit Chaudhuri – 'Foreword', Alam and Chakravarty (eds), *The Essential
    Tagore*, x

23 David Omissi, *Indian Voices of the Great War: Soldiers' Letters, 1914–18*
    (Basingstoke, 1999)

24 Rabindranath Tagore, *Gitanjali* (London, 1918 [first published in Sanskrit
    in 1910; first published in English in 1912])

25 Alam and Chakravarty (eds), *The Essential Tagore*, 186

26 Krishna Dutta and Andrew Robinson, *Selected Letters of Rabindranath
    Tagore* (Cambridge, 1997), 188

27 The exception was Japan. Tagore's reception there is discussed in chapter 3.

28 Rabindranath Tagore to Rathindranath Tagore, quoted in Dutta and Robinson, *Tagore*, 204

29 Rabindranath Tagore, *Creative Unity* (London, 1922), 171–2

30 Tagore quoted in Uma Das Gupta, 'Tagore's Ideas of Social Action and the Sriniketan Experiment of Rural Reconstruction, 1922–41', *University of Toronto Quarterly* 77 (2008), 992–1004, at 992

31 Leonard K. Elmhirst, *Poet and Plowman* (Calcutta, 1975), 58

32 Tagore quoted in Dutta and Robinson, *Tagore*, 143

33 Quoted in Das Gupta, *Tagore*, 31

34 Daniel Gorman, *The Emergence of International Society in the 1920s* (Cambridge, 2012)

35 Sir Patrick Geddes had started his own 'world university' – the Collège des Ecossais in Montpellier, France – as an 'international hall of residence whose occupants would promote world citizenship'. He tried unsuccessfully to get Tagore to join. Hugh Clout and Iain Stevenson, 'Jules Sion, Alan Grant Ogilvie and the Collège des Ecossais in Montpellier: A Network of Geographers', *Scottish Geographical Journal* 120 (2004), 181–98, at 182

36 Dutta and Robinson, *Selected Letters*, 291

37 Tagore quoted in Leonard Elmhirst, *Rabindranath Tagore: Pioneer in Education. Essays and Exchanges between Rabindranath Tagore and L. K. Elmhirst* (London, 1961), 45

38 Rabindranath Tagore, 'On Some Educational Questions', 1919, quoted in Sisir Kumar Das (ed.), *The English Writings of Rabindranath Tagore: A Miscellany*, vol. 3 (New Delhi, 1996 [1968]), 748

39 Gretchen Green, *The Whole World & Company* (New York 1936), 149

40 'Luxury's Noose' was the title of an essay written by Tagore in 1906. Inder Nath Choudhuri, *Indian Renaissance and Rabindranath Tagore* (New Delhi, 2019), 265

41 Prem Chand Lal, *Reconstruction and Education in Rural India* (London, 1932), 43

42 Tagore, *A Compilation of Selected Speeches, Letters and Songs of Tagore*, trans. Chiranjiv Kaviraj (Agartala, 1969), 44; Kathleen M. O'Connell, 'Education at Santiniketan: 1902–1920', *Indian International Centre Quarterly* 38 (2011), 18–31

43 Quoted in Alam and Chakravarty (eds), *The Essential Tagore*, 43

44 Tagore had already tried admitting girls to Patha Bhavana in 1908, but had quickly ended the experiment after a complicated romantic entanglement between two of the students. He returned to the idea with renewed enthusiasm in the 1920s.

45 Rabindranath Tagore, *Personality* (London, 1917), 116

46 Das Gupta, 'In Pursuit of a Different Freedom', 33

47 Satyajit Ray, 'Final Testimony', *Guardian*, London, 1 August 1991

48 Giuseppe Tucci, 'Recollections of Tagore', *Tagore, Centenary Volume*, 59

49 Dutta and Robinson, *Tagore*, 134

50 Uma Das Gupta, 'Rabindranath's Experiments with Education, Community and Nation at His Santiniketan Institutions', in Sanjukta Dasgupta and Chinmoy Guha (eds), *Tagore at Home in the World* (New Delhi, 2013), 281

51 Mandakranta Bose, 'Indian Modernity and Tagore's Dance', *University of Toronto Quarterly* 77 (2008), 1085–94; Matthew Isaac Cohen, *Performing Otherness: Java and Bali on International Stages, 1905–1952* (Basingstoke, 2010), 166

52 Elmhirst, *Poet and Plowman*, 58

53 Lal, *Reconstruction and Education*, 50

54 Dutta and Robinson, *Tagore*, 134

55 Das Gupta, 'In Pursuit of a Different Freedom', 36

56 Dutta and Robinson, *Tagore*, 231

57 Quoted in Kripalani, *Tagore*, 214; Sabyasachi Bhattacharya, *Rabindranath Tagore: An Interpretation* ([n.p.], 2011), 139

58 Oswald Mosley, *My Life* (London, 2006 [1968]), 105

59 Dutta and Robinson, *Tagore*, 283

60 Rathindranath Tagore, *Edges*, 158–9

61 Tagore to Leonard Elmhirst, 18 April 1923, quoted in Das Gupta, *Tagore*, 101

62 Alam and Chakravarty (eds), *The Essential Tagore*, 117

63 L. K. Elmhirst, *Essays and Exchanges*, 27

64 In the 1910s, Tagore's son Rathindranath and an English missionary, Charles Freer Andrews, had experimented with transforming Sriniketan into a centre for reviving the local villages. But their efforts collapsed because of their lack of clear strategy. Other plans for the site – including one for Zionists from Palestine to settle there and work with local farmers – were never launched at all. Dutta and Robinson, *Tagore*, 331

65 Leonard Elmhirst had been recommended to Tagore by Sam Higginbottom, an English missionary devoted to rural community development in India who founded the Allahabad Agricultural Institute in 1919.

66 Tagore quoted in Dutta and Robinson, *Tagore*, 149

67 Elmhirst, *Poet and Plowman*, 81

68 Nirad Chaudhuri quoted in Dutta and Robinson, *Tagore*, 326; see also 332–3

69 Chand Lal, *Reconstruction and Education*, 56

70 Rabindranath Tagore read Horace Plunkett and A. E.'s [a pseudonym used by George William Russell] *The National Being* (1916) on Irish cooperative living (Louise Blakeney Williams, 'Overcoming the 'Contagion of Mimicry': The Cosmopolitan Nationalism and Modernist History of Rabindranath Tagore and W. B. Yeats', *American Historical Review* (2007), 69–100, at 97).

71 Gould P. Colman, *Education and Agriculture: A History of the New York State College of Agriculture at Cornell University* (Ithaca, NY, 1963)

72 Das Gupta, *Tagore*, 33

73 Green, *The Whole World*, 116

74 Elmhirst, *Poet and Plowman*, 18

75 Elmhirst, *Pioneer in Education*, 23

76 Elmhirst diary entry, 24 February 1922, *Poet and Plowman*, 127. Tagore, now in his sixties, even adopted this new arrangement for himself, digging a trench in his Santiniketan garden. Twenty-seven years later, when Elmhirst went back to visit Santiniketan-Sriniketan, the students' gardens were dotted with 'little thatched sentry boxes' which he was told were 'Elmhirst latrines'; 'Could I have a greater compliment?' he commented. *Poet and Plowman*, 125.

77 Tagore to C. F. Andrews, 1921, quoted in Dutta and Robinson, *Tagore*, 329; 18–19; Tagore to Elmhirst, March 1922, quoted in Elmhirst, *Poet and Plowman*, 145

78 Tagore to Elmhirst, 3 September 1932, LKE/TAG/9/A, Dartington Hall Archives. Unless specified otherwise, all archival references in this chapter are to this collection.

79 Daniel Immerwahr, *Thinking Small: The United States and the Lure of Community Development* (Cambridge, MA; London, 2015)

80 Tagore to Leonard, 13 November 1922, LKE/TAG/9/A

81 Tagore, quoted in Dutta and Robinson, *Tagore*, 124

82 Green, *The Whole World*, 127–30

83 Leonard Elmhirst to Dorothy Elmhirst, 2 April 1922, quoting a letter received from Tagore, LKE/DWE/10/G

84 Arthur Geddes to Leonard Elmhirst, 24 April 1923, LKE/IN/6/D

85 Tagore, quoted in Dutta and Robinson, *Tagore*, 333–4

86 Tagore, 1908, quoted in Uma Das Gupta, 'In Pursuit of a Different Freedom: Tagore's World University at Santiniketan', *Indian International Centre Quarterly* 29 (2002–3), 25–38, at 31

87 Siksha-Satra began at Santiniketan, because that was where its main teacher lived, but it was soon afterwards moved to join the institute for rural regeneration at Sriniketan.

88 Tagore quoted by Santidev Ghosh, 'Sikshasatra and Naitalimi Education', in Santosh Chandra Sengupta (ed.), *Rabindranath Tagore: Homage from Visva-Bharati* (Visva-Bharati, 1962), 121–37, at 121

89 Dutta and Robinson, *Selected Letters*, 490; Kripalani, *Tagore*, 8

90 Arthur Geddes to Leonard Elmhirst, 24 April 1923, LKE/IN/6/D

91 Quoted in Dutta and Robinson, *Tagore*, 17

92 Ibid., 87

93 Elmhirst, *Poet and Plowman*, 40

94 Tagore to Leonard Elmhirst, 18 April 1923 quoted in Das Gupta, *Tagore*, 101

95   Dutta and Robinson, *Selected Letters*, 175
96   Ibid., 493
97   Ibid., 281
98   Elmhirst, *Poet and Plowman*, 20
99   Dutta and Robinson, *Tagore*, 323
100 Ibid., 364
101 Uma Das Gupta, 'Santiniketan', in Mushirul Hasan (ed.), *Knowledge, Power & Politics: Educational Institutions in India* (New Delhi, 1998), 292–3
102 Wilmot Perera visited Santiniketan-Sriniketan in 1932. Tagore went to see the newly established Sri Palee ('where beauty reigns') in Ceylon in 1934. The institute, which originally aimed at rural reconstruction, is now a government college.
103 Usha Makherjee, 'Sriniketan Experiment in Rural Reconstruction', *Economic Weekly*, 25 October 1952, 1107–9; Madhumita Chattopadhyay, 'Rabindranath Tagore's Model of Rural Reconstruction: A Review', *International Journal of Research and Analytical Reviews* 5 (2018), 142–6
104 Rabindranath Tagore, *Collected Poems and Plays of Rabindranath Tagore* (Macmillan, 1977 [1936]), 16

TWO: 'A New Manor Which May Be the Unit of the New England': Dorothy and Leonard Elmhirst's Dartington Hall

1   Gerald Heard, 'The Implication of Dartington Hall, to a Visitor', *News of the Day*, supplement to the 500th number, 13 March 1934, MC/S4/42/F1, Dartington Hall Archives. Unless specified otherwise, all the following archival references are to this collection.
2   David Gribble, *That's All Folks: Dartington Hall School Remembered* (Crediton, 1987), 25
3   Aldous Huxley quoted in Nicholas Murray, *Aldous Huxley* (London, 2002), 449
4   Leonard, 'Plymouth Playgoers' Circle', 10 March 1935, LKE/G/S8/A
5   Dartington's activities were regularly reported in short columns in the *Western Morning News*, *Exeter and Plymouth Gazette*, *Western Times* and *Western Daily Press* (British Library Newspaper Archives). Articles in national publications included Sir William Beach Thomas, 'Dartington Hall – A Great Rural Experiment', *Listener*, 29 November 1933, 809–13; Gerald Heard, 'The Dartington Experiment'; Christopher Hussey, 'High Cross Hill, Dartington, Devon', *Country Life*, 11 February 1933, 144–9. The estate also appeared in the *New York Herald Tribune*, among other American newspapers, and in H. J. Massingham's book, *Country* – Dartington was 'recapturing the art of living as a self-dependent local community' (London, 1934), 132.

6   Aldous Huxley, *Those Barren Leaves* (London, 1925), 35
7   Gordon Russell to Dorothy, 21 October 1931, DWE/G/9/A
8   W. A. Swanberg, *Whitney Father, Whitney Heiress* (New York, 1980)
9   Greg King, *A Season of Splendor: The Court of Mrs Astor in Gilded Age New York* (Hoboken, NJ, 2009)
10 Henry Adams, *The Education of Henry Adams* (Boston, MA; New York, 1918), 26
11 Dorothy, [n.d.], Sunday evening talk, 'Background and foreground – a personal pattern', DWE/S/1/E
12 Jane Brown, *Angel Dorothy: How an American Progressive Came to Devon* (London, 2017), 30. Dorothy inherited three-tenths of William Collins Whitney's property.
13 Brown, *Angel Dorothy*, 19
14 Dorothy described this later to Leonard, 15 July 1931, LKE/DWE/12/E
15 Swanberg, *Whitney Father*, 198–201. For discussions of 'trust-busting' reform, see Michael Sandel, *Democracy's Discontent: America in Search of a Public Philosophy* (London, 1996), 211–21, and Steven J. Diner, *A Very Different Age: Americans of the Progressive Era* (New York, 1998).
16 Karolyn Gould, 'The Modest Benefactor', *Cornell Alumni News* 3 (1975), 19–21
17 Dorothy quoted in Swanberg, *Whitney Father*, 224
18 Whitney Straight quoted in Eric Rauchways, 'A Gentleman's Club in a Woman's Sphere: How Dorothy Whitney Straight Created *The New Republic*', *The Journal of Women's History* 11 (1999), 60–85, at 79
19 Herbert Croly, *Willard Straight* (New York, 1925)
20 Herbert Croly, *The Promise of American Life* (Cambridge, MA, 1965 [1909])
21 Leonard, 'A Friday', notebook, September 1920; notebook, 16 August 1923, LKE/G/S17/C
22 Michael Young, *The Elmhirsts of Dartington: The Creation of a Utopian Community* (London, 1982)
23 Gerald Heard to Leonard, 11 November 1924, LKE/G/17/E
24 Leonard to Dorothy, 27 October 1920, LKE/DWE/10/A
25 Dorothy's reaction was recalled in a letter from Leonard to Dorothy, 22 August 1955, quoted in Young, *The Elmhirsts*, 75.
26 For these letters, see file LKE/DWE
27 Dorothy to Leonard, 24 October 1921, LKE/DWE/10/D
28 Brown, *Angel Dorothy*, 104
29 Leonard to Dorothy, 29 July 1924, LKE/DWE/11/E
30 Leonard to Eduard Lindeman, box 2, Eduard Lindeman Archives, Columbia University
31 Leonard to Dorothy, 12 December 1924, LKE/DWE/12/A
32 Leonard Elmhirst to Richard Elmhirst, 25 June 1923, quoted in Young, *The Elmhirsts*, 95

33   Rabindranath Tagore to Leonard Elmhirst, in Krishna Dutta and
     Andrew Robinson, *Selected Letters of Rabindranath Tagore* (Cambridge,
     1997), 11
34   Peter Mandler, *The Fall and Rise of the Stately Home* (New Haven, CT,
     1997)
35   Young, *The Elmhirsts*, 104
36   Leonard to Dorothy, 6 March 1925, LKE/DWE/12/A
37   Leonard to Mrs S. K. Ratcliffe, 4 March 1929, LKE/G/26/A
38   Brown, *Angel Dorothy*, 110
39   'Report of meeting held to discuss plans and purposes of Dartington
     school', 11 September 1926, and 'Third meeting to discuss school',
     September 1926, T/DHS/A/1/A
40   John Dewey, *Democracy and Education: An Introduction to the Philosophy of
     Education* (New York, 1999 [1916])
41   Leonard to Dorothy, 12 December 1924, LKE/DWE/12/A
42   Dorothy to Eduard Lindeman, 9 June 1925, box 2, Eduard Lindeman
     Archives, Columbia University
43   Dorothy, diary, 24 September 1926, DWE/G/S7/E/7
44   Leonard in 'Second meeting for school', T/DHS/A/1/Al; Book of
     Juniors' Friday meetings, 1 June 1928–June 1931, T/DHS/A/3/B
45   Gribble (ed.), *That's All Folks*, *passim*
46   Dorothy, note on the school, [1927], T/DHS/A/1/A
47   Ibid.
48   Leonard to Anna Bogue, 24 June 1927, DWE/US/2/B
49   Dorothy to Helen Page, 16 March 1927, DWE/G/8/E
50   Leonard to Dorothy, 19 May 1923, LKE/DWE/11/C; Leonard, 'Report
     on Education Experiment, Dartington Hall, September to December,
     1926', DWE/DHS/1
51   Dougie Hart quoted in Gribble (ed.), *That's All Folks*, 17
52   Robert Cowan gathered the gossip he had heard locally in a report for
     Dartington's sales manager James Harrison, 27 January 1936,
     T/PP/P/1/G.
53   R. A. Edwards, 'Dartington: A report for the Bishop of the Diocese',
     January 1948, DWE/G/S3/G
54   Ibid.; Francis Acland to Leonard, 10 October 1936, LKE/DEV/1/B
55   Dorothy to Frances Livingtone, 11 February 1927, DWE/G/7/A
56   Paul Brassley, Jeremy Burchardt and Lynne Thompson (eds), *The English
     Countryside between the Wars: Regeneration or Decline?* (New York, 2006)
57   Leonard to Seebohm Rowntree, 29 December 1921 [extract], LKE/
     IN/24/A; Gould P. Colman, *Education and Agriculture: A History of the
     New York State College of Agriculture at Cornell University* (Ithaca, NY, 1963)
58   Andrew Godley and Bridget Williams, 'Democratizing Luxury and the
     Contentious 'Invention of the Technological Chicken' in Britain', *The
     Business History Review* 83 (2009), 267–90

59   The farm buildings featured in architectural and farming journals and
     several were reproduced in the Agricultural Research Council's farm at
     Stafford.

60   Michael Young interview with Mrs Crook, 23 August 1977, T/HIS/
     S20/D

61   Dorothy to Leonard, 25 April 1926, LKE/DWE/6/B

62   Dorothy to Leonard, 30 August 1936, LKE/DWE/6/B

63   Dorothy to R. A. Edwards, 2 August 1942, DWE/G/S3/G

64   Dorothy, 'Notes on talk by Bill Sheldon', [n.d.], DWE/G/S7/E/7

65   Raymond O'Malley to Michael Young, 5 January 1983, T/HIS/S20/D

66   Beatrice Straight to Nancy Wilson Ross, 7 June 1936, 156/2, Nancy
     Wilson Ross Archives, Harry Ransom Center, University of Texas

67   *News of the Day*, 9 October 1928, T/PP/EST/1-8; 'Education committee
     minutes', 25 October 1929, T/DHS/A/4/C

68   Martin Sharp, 'Michael Chekhov: The Dartington Years' (DVD, Palomino
     Films, 2002)

69   Victor Bonham-Carter, *Land and Environment: The Survival of the English
     Countryside* (Rutherford, NJ, 1971), 142

70   Dorothy to Anna Bogue, 7 October 1930, DWE/US/2/F

71   [n.a.], 'The New Rural England', *The Architect and Building News*,
     30 June, 14 July, 21 July 1933

72   Krishna Dutta and Andrew Robinson, *Rabindranath Tagore: The Myriad-
     minded Man* (Bloomsbury, 1995), 292

73   George E. G. Catlin to Leonard, 7 September 1925, LKE/G/4/E

74   Leonard to Joe Lash, describing the visit for Lash's biography of Eleanor
     Roosevelt, 18 October 1969, LKE/USA/4/A; Dr Alfred Striemer to
     Leonard, 29 August 1937, LKE/LAND/1/I

75   Leonard Elmhirst, untitled note, [n.d.], LKE/G/S8/B

76   This complaint came from J. W. B. Butterworth, a worker in the plant
     nursery, who sent a letter to Leonard, 22 February 1937, LKE/
     DEV/1/D.

77   T/PP/EST/1-8 and G. H. Thurley's answer to a 1931 estate question-
     naire, T/PP/P/1/E

78   Leonard to Frederic Bartlett, 2 January 1934, LKE/G/S8/D

79   Frederic Bartlett to Leonard, 22 February 1935, LKE/G/13/B

80   Ibid.

81   David Jeremiah, 'Dartington Hall – a Landscape of an Experiment in
     Rural Reconstruction', in Brassley et al (eds), *The English Countryside*,
     116–131

82   Leonard to Nikolaus Pevsner, quoted in Nikolaus Pevsner, *Devon*
     (Harmondsworth, 1989 [1952]), 314

83   Transcription of Sunday evening meeting, 23 September 1928,
     LKE/G/31/A

84   Leonard to Dorothy, 29 March 1926, LKE/DWE/12/D

85 William St John Pym, response to 1931 Dartington questionnaire,
    T/PP/P/1/E

86 Rachel Esther Harrison, 'Dorothy Elmhirst and the Visual Arts at
    Dartington Hall 1925–1945', unpublished PhD, University of Plymouth,
    2002, 76 and 80–1

87 Michael Young's interview with Marjorie Fogden, 15 September 1976,
    T/HIS/S22

88 William St John Pym, response to 1931 Dartington questionnaire,
    T/PP/P/1/E

89 See, for example, Alison Light, *Mrs Woolf and the Servants: The Hidden
    Heart of Domestic Service* (London, 2007)

90 Gerald Heard, 'The Implication of Dartington Hall, to a Visitor', *News of
    the Day*, supplement to the 500th number, 13 March 1934, MC/S4/42/
    F1

91 Reminiscences of Herbert Mills, a local man who worked on the estate,
    21 January 1970, LKE/G/31/E

92 14 July 1929, Leonard notebook, 1928–32, LKE/G/S17/C/23

93 Ibid.

94 Dorothy to Anna Bogue, 22 October 1931, DWE/US/1/A

95 Leonard, note on Dartington's financial structure, January 1931,
    LKE/G/S11A

96 Leonard, notes, 17 May 1936, LKE/G/S9/A. This was a private limited
    company with an initial capital of £65,000, later raised to £125,000.
    Leonard had 64,999 shares and Fred Gwatkin one. Dorothy had none.
    The trust began in 1931 as three trusts – one holding the land, one
    managing the school, one promoting research and holding shares in the
    company – but in 1932 they were merged into one, the Dartington Hall
    Trust.

97 Dorothy to Eduard Lindeman, 14 May [1925?], box 2, Eduard Lindeman
    Archives

98 Maurice Punch, 'W. B. Curry (1900–1962): A Re-assessment',
    T/DHS/B/1/I

99 Gerald Heard to Margaret Isherwood, 17 December 1933, DWE/G/6A

100 Leonard to John Mountford, 11 December 1933, LKE/LAND/2/B

101 *News of the Day*, 13 December 1927, T/PP/EST/1/001

102 M. K. Gandhi showed a polite interest in visiting, but ultimately said he
    was too busy. Leonard to Gandhi, 24 September 1931; Gandhi to
    Leonard, 30 September 1931, LKE/IN/6/B

103 Leonard, 'The role of agricultural economists in the promotion of world
    order', 30 June–3 July 1939, LKE/LAND/9/A

104 PEP first met in March 1931 under the chairmanship of Sir Basil Blackett.
    The group's members included biologist Julian Huxley, Bank of England
    director Basil Blackett and environmentalist Max Nicholson. They often
    spent weekends at Dartington, discussing the future of the country over

cream teas. They approved of the estate, which they saw as doing in miniature what they wanted to do on a national scale – rethinking all the aspects of the way society worked. The think tank published reports, broadsheets, and a journal, *Planning*, and was active until 1978, when it merged with the Centre for Studies in Social Policy to form the Policy Studies Institute. (John Pinder (ed.), *Fifty Years of Political and Economic Planning: Looking Forward, 1931–1981* (London, 1981)).

105 Dorothy to Ruth Morgan, May 1928, quoted in Harrison, 'Dorothy Elmhirst and the Visual Arts', 126

106 Goldsworthy ('Goldie') Lowes Dickinson was one of the many scholars drawn into political activism by the horror of the First World War. His fervent internationalism and his atheistic freethinking rubbed off on both Gerald Heard and Leonard – though leading them in very different directions.

107 Alex Owen, *The Darkened Room: Women, Power and Spiritualism in Late Victorian England* (London, 1989); Lucy Delap and Sue Morgan (eds), *Men, Masculinities and Religious Change in Twentieth-Century Britain* (Basingstoke, 2013)

108 Gerald Heard to Leonard Elmhirst, 6 December 1934, LKE/G/17/E

109 Notes from 17 November 1934 meeting, LKE/G/S9/A; Gerald Heard to Dorothy, 9 August 1934, DWE/G/6A

110 [n.a.], notes from Sunday evening meeting, 25 February, LKE/G/9/A

111 Leonard quoted by Gerald Heard in a letter to Margaret Isherwood, 8 October 1934, DWE/6/F2; Gerald Heard to Dorothy, 30 September 1932, DWE/G/5/D

112 Gerald Heard, 'The Dartington Experiment', *Architectural Review* 449 (1934), 119–122

113 'The basis of fixing rent for the Dartington Hall Artificial Insemination Centre', 1944, T/AG ECON/1/B

114 Paul Brassley, David Harvey, Matt Lobley and Michael Winter, 'Accounting for Agriculture: the Origins of the Farm Management Survey', *Agricultural History Review* 61 (2013), 135–53

115 Author interview with Etain Todds (née Kabraji), 17 May 2015

116 Leonard, 'Confidential memo', 29 December 1937, LKE/G/S8

117 *News of the Day*, 25 June 1937, T/PP/EST/1/019

118 James Harrison to W. K. Slater, 29 February 1936, T/DHS/B/18/A

119 Gerald Heard to the Elmhirsts, 2 November 1935, LKE/G/17/E

120 W. B. Curry to Chris Martin, 24 October 1934, T/DHS/B/20/A; W. B. Curry to Hans Oppenheim, 25 September 1941, T/DHS/B/20/B

121 William Sheldon to the Elmhirsts, 7 May 1935, DWE/G/9/E; Young, *The Elmhirsts*, 177–9

122 W. B. Curry to W. K. Slater, 22 February 1936, T/DHS/B/18/A

123 Gerald Heard to Margaret Isherwood, 17 May 1935, DWE/G/6A; Gerald Heard to Margaret Isherwood, 17 December 1933, DWE/G/6A

124 Michael Young interview with Ronald Anderson, 8 October 1977,
     T/HIS/S20/D

125 Brown, *Angel Dorothy*, 170–1

126 Dorothy, 'My talk in the Barn Theatre on the eve of my departure for
     Chekhov in America', DWE/A/15

127 Ibid.

128 Dorothy to Leonard, 9 April 1939, T/HIS/S22/B

129 Michael Chekhov stayed in America during the war, later moving to
     Hollywood and becoming a guru to stars including Marilyn Monroe.

130 Young, *The Elmhirsts*, 344

131 In spite of this endowment, by the first decades of the twentieth century
     Dartington Hall Trust had fallen deep into debt – a debt trustees sought
     to reduce by selling off assets, including paintings, residential property
     and sites for housing development.

132 Schumacher College was founded by social and environmental activist
     Satish Kumar. It offers courses on subjects ranging from sustainability to
     spiritual holism, and draws internationally recognized figures including
     James Lovelock, originator of the Gaia hypothesis, and writer Roger
     Deakin.

133 Leonard to Dorothy, 26 August 1931, LKE/DWE/12/E

THREE: Self-Realization in the Mountains of Japan: Mushanokōji Saneatsu's Atarashiki Mura

1 There are two alternate spelling for his surname, Mushanokōji and
   Mushakōji. Although the latter is technically correct, the former is more
   commonly used.

2 Zhou Zuoren quoted in Christopher T. Keaveney, *Beyond Brushtalk: Sino-
   Japanese Literary Exchange in the Interwar Period* (Hong Kong, 2009), 91

3 Angela Yiu, 'The Intellectual and Literary Contexts of a Taishō Utopian
   Village', *Japan Review* 20 (2008), 203–30, at 208

4 Elise Tipton, *Modern Japan: A Social and Economic History* (London, 2002),
   41

5 Chika Tonooka, 'Reverse Emulation and the Cult of Japanese Efficiency
   in Edwardian Britain', *The Historical Journal* 60 (2017), 95–119

6 Her maiden name was Kadenokōji Naruko.

7 Viscount Mushanokōji Saneyo quoted in Stephen W. Kohl, Yoko
   Matsuoka McClain and Ryoko Toyama McClellan, *The White Birch School
   (Shirakabaha) of Japanese Literature: Some Sketches and Commentary* (Oregon,
   1975), 43

8 Takie Sugiyama Lebra, *Above the Clouds: Status Culture of the Modern
   Japanese Nobility* (Berkeley, CA; Oxford, 1993), 83–5

9 Peers' School – *Gakushūin*. This school was controlled by the Imperial
   Household Ministry rather than the Education Ministry, like most other

government schools, and was intended to educate those who would serve the emperor.

10 Benjamin Duke, *The History of Modern Japanese Education: Constructing the National School System, 1872–1890* (New Brunswick, NJ, 2009)

11 Mushanokōji's autobiography, *Aru Otoko* (*A Certain Man*, 1923), quoted in Maya Mortimer, *Meeting the Sensei: The Role of the Master in Shirakaba Writers* (Leiden, 2000), 19–20

12 Mushanokōji, *Aru Otoko* (*A Certain Man*, 1923) quoted in Hayao Maeda, *One Hundred Years of Atarashiki Mura* (Japanese edition, Tokyo, 2017), extract translated by Kazuyo Yasuda, chapter 2, section 1, para. 2

13 'Tei' is the name given to the cousin in Mushanokōji's autobiography.

14 Quoted in Mortimer, *Meeting*, 21; Yiu, 'Intellectual and Literary Contexts', 207

15 Tolstoy became the most translated figure in modern Japan. Sho Konishi, *Anarchist Modernity: Cooperatism and Japanese Russian Intellectual Relations in Modern Japan* (Cambridge, MA, 2013), 95

16 The *burakumin* or 'hamlet people' were an outcast community in the feudal era, made up of those associated with 'impure' professions – undertakers, executioners and butchers – those tainted by stigma, and their descendants. Traditionally they lived in their own segregated hamlets. The feudal caste system was formally dissolved in 1869, but the discrimination against this group continued.

17 Maya Mortimer, 'Mushanokōji Saneatsu: Luzern', *Asiatische Studien Zeitschrift der Schweizerischen Asiengesellschaft* 58 (2004), 479–90, at 481

18 Ibid., 482

19 Ibid.

20 Tessa Morris-Suzuki, *The Technological Transformation of Japan: From the Seventeenth to the Twenty-First Century* (New York, 1994), chapter 4

21 Donald Roden, *Schooldays in Imperial Japan: A Study in the Culture of a Student Elite* (Berkeley, CA; London, 1980), 95

22 Mortimer, *Meeting*, 51

23 An anti-war pamphlet by Tolstoy, *Bethink Yourselves*, was published in *Heimin Shimbun* on 7 August 1904. The influence of Tolstoy's pacifism was so great among Japan's young intellectuals generally that, after the Russo-Japanese War, the Home Ministry was driven to ban the consumption of the writer's work in schools and public places. Sho Konishi, *Anarchist Modernity*, 135

24 Quoted in Mortimer, 'Luzern', 482

25 Fortnight Group – *Jūyokkakai*

26 Keene, *Dawn*, 451

27 Maurice Maeterlinck, *Wisdom and Destiny*, trans. Alfred Sutro (New York, 1901), 173

28 Mushanokōji's *Jiko no Tame*, quoted in Mortimer, *Meeting*, 142

29 Mushanokōji in *Shirakaba* (1912), quoted in Gennifer Weisenfeld, *MAVO:*

Japanese Arts and the Avant-Garde, 1905–1931 (Berkeley, CA; Los Angeles, CA; London, 2002), 22

30   Mushanokōji's *'Kare ga Sanjū no Toki'* – 'Himself at the Age of Thirty' – was published in 1915.

31   Edward Fowler, *The Rhetoric of Confession: Shishōsetsu in Early Twentieth-Century Japanese Fiction* (Berkeley, CA; Oxford, 1988), 128

32   Madoka Kusakabe, 'Saka Ineko and Kirabayashi Taiko: The Café and *Jokyū* as a State for Social Criticism', unpublished PhD, University of Oregon, 2011

33   Mortimer, *Meeting*, 27, 65; Donald Keene, *Dawn to the West: Japanese Literature of the Modern Era*, vol. 3 (New York, 1998), 5–6

34   Keaveney, *Beyond Brushtalk*, 84

35   Mushanokōji in *Shirakaba* (1912), quoted in Weisenfeld, *MAVO*, 22

36   Roden, *Schooldays in Imperial Japan*, 194

37   Fowler, *The Rhetoric of Confession*, 132

38   Tessa Morris-Suzuki, 'A Century of Social Alternatives in a Japanese Mountain Community', in *New Worlds from Below: Informal Life Politics and Grassroots Action in Twenty-First-Century Northeast Asia* (Australia, 2017), 51–76

39   Tipton, *Modern Japan*, 86

40   Quoted from Mushanokōji, *A Good-Natured Person* (1910). Yoko Ima-Izumi, 'The Female Voice in Blake Studies in Japan, 1910s–1930s', in Steve Clark and Masashi Suzuki (eds), *The Reception of Blake in the Orient* (London 2006), 198

41   Bernard Leach had spent part of his childhood in Hong Kong and Japan, before going to school in England. He returned to Japan in 1909 to learn about Japanese art, and became close to various members of the White Birch Group, particularly Yanagi Sōetsu (Brian Moeran, 'Bernard Leach and the Japanese Folk Craft Movement: The Formative Years', *Journal of Design History* 2 (1989), 139–144).

42   Bernard Leach, *Beyond East and West: Memoirs, Portraits and Essays* (London, 1978), 218

43   Kohl, McClain and McClellan, *White Birch School of Japanese Literature*, 48

44   Keene, *Dawn*, 443

45   Tosh Minohara, Tze-ki Hon and Evan Dawley (eds), *The Decade of the Great War: Japan and the Wider World in the 1910s* (Leiden, 2014), 6; A. Morgan Young, *Japan under Taishō Tennō 1912–1926* (London, 1928), 110–19

46   Quoted in Mortimer, *Meeting*, 106

47   'A Young Man's Dream' – 'Aru Seinen no Yume', 1916–17

48   For details of Rabindranath Tagore's reception in Japan, see Stephen N. Hay, *Asian Ideas of East and West: Tagore and His Critics in Japan, China and India* (Cambridge, MA, 1970)

49   Quoted in Tessa Morris-Suzuki, *Japan's Living Politics* (Cambridge, 2020), 63

50 Quoted in Mortimer, *Meeting*, 30

51 Yuko Kikuchi, *Japanese Modernisation and Mingei Theory: Cultural Nationalism and Oriental Orientalism* (New York, 2004)

52 From *Kare no Seishun Jidai* (His Era of Youth) by Mushanokōji Saneatsu, quoted in Maeda, *One Hundred Years*, extract translated by Kazuyo Yasuda, chapter 2, section 1, para. 3

53 The principles and plan in this and the following paragraph are taken from Mushanokōji Saneatsu, 'Stepping into a New Life' (Atarashiki Seikatsu ni Hairu Michi) and 'Dialogue Concerning the New Village' (Atarashiki Mura nit suite no Taiwa), both quoted in Kikuchi, *Japanese Modernisation*, 30; and from Mushanokōji Saneatsu, 'The Spirit of Atarashiki-mura', quoted in Maeda, *One Hundred Years*, extract translated by Kazuyo Yasuda, chapter 2, section 4.

54 Morris-Suzuki, *Japan's Living Politics*, 72

55 Mortimer, *Meeting*, 31

56 Kan Kikuchi, 'Kantan na Shikyo' (Easy Death), quoted in Maeda, *One Hundred Years*, extract translated by Kazuyo Yasuda, chapter 3, section 1, para. 4 and 7

57 The full argument between Arishima Takeo and Mushanokōji Saneatsu is laid out in Leith Morton, *Divided Self: A Biography of Arishima Takeo* (Sydney, 1989), 136–7. The quotes in the paragraph are paraphrased from this book.

58 Keene, *Dawn*, 452

59 Mushanokōji Saneatsu, 'Atarashiki Mura no Shomondo' ('Small Interview about Atarashiki Mura') in the first issue of members' magazine *Atarashiki Mura*, quoted in Maeda, *One Hundred Years*, extract translated by Kazuyo Yasuda, chapter 2, section 1, para. 5–6

60 Simon Partner, *Toshié: A Story of Village Life in Twentieth-Century Japan* (California, 2004)

61 Isabella Bird, *Unbeaten Tracks in Japan* (London, 1880); Partner, *Toshié*

62 Mushanokōji Saneatsu, 'The Earth' ('Tochi', 1920), quoted in Stephen Dodd, 'Satō Haruo: The Fantasy of Home', in *Writing Home: Representations of the Native Place in Modern Japanese Literature* (Cambridge, MA, 2004), 149

63 From *Mushanokōji Saneatsu, Tochi* (The Earth) quoted in Maeda, *One Hundred Years*, extract translated by Kazuyo Yasuda, prologue, para. 11

64 These plans are summarized from the three dialogues written by Mushanokōji on the village, laid out in Angela Yiu, 'From Utopia to Empire: Atarashikimura and *A Personal View of the Great East Asia War* (1942)', *Utopian Studies* 19 (2008), 213–32

65 Kikuchi, *Japanese Modernisation*, 27, 31

66 Matthew Arnold, 'Culture and its Enemies', *Cornhill Magazine* 16 (1867), 36–53; Yiu, 'Intellectual and Literary Contexts', fn. 8

67 Mushanokōji quoted in Mortimer, *Meeting*, 29

68   Yiu, 'Intellectual and Literary Contexts', 218; Maeda, *One Hundred
     Years*, extract translated by Kazuyo Yasuda, chapter 3, section 1, para.
     2 and 3

69   Kawashima Denkichi (1897–1955); Himori Shinichi (1900–59). Himori,
     who became one of the lovers of Mushanokōji's wife Miyagi Fusako,
     went on to act in seventy films between 1925 and 1959.

70   Tessa Morris-Suzuki, 'Beyond Utopia: New Villages and Living Politics in
     Modern Japan and across Frontiers', *History Workshop Journal* 85 (2018),
     47–71, at 55; Maeda, *One Hundred Years*, extract translated by Kazuyo
     Yasuda, chapter 3, section 3, para 7–8

71   Arishima Takeo, 'The Liberation of Artistic Production' – *Geijutsu Seisaku
     no Kaihō*, 1918, quoted in Morton, *Divided Self*, 99

72   Mushanokōji quoted in Morris-Suzuki, 'Beyond Utopia', 54; Maeda, *One
     Hundred Years*, extract translated by Kazuyo Yasuda, chapter 2, section 1,
     para. 5–6

73   Kikuchi, *Japanese Modernisation*, 31

74   Maeda, *One Hundred Years*, extract translated by Kazuyo Yasuda, chapter 3,
     section 5, para. 5; Yiu, 'Intellectual and Literary Contexts'

75   *Kōfuku Mono*, 'The Happy Man', 1919, quoted in Mortimer, *Meeting*, 176

76   Quoted in Keene, *Dawn*, 453

77   *Kōfuku Mono*, 'The Happy Man', 1919, quoted in Mortimer, *Meeting*, 176

78   Mortimer, *Meeting*, 30

79   Mushanokōji quoted in Maeda, *One Hundred Years*, extract translated by
     Kazuyo Yasuda, chapter 2, section 4

80   Mortimer, *Meeting*, 211

81   Yamakawa Hitoshi, *Shakaishugisha no Shakaikan* (the View of Society by a
     Socialist), quoted in Maeda, *One Hundred Years*, extract translated by
     Kazuyo Yasuda, chapter 3, section 1, para. 5

82   [n.a.], 'Atarashiki mura in Interwar Japan', https://rekolektiv.wordpress.
     com/essays/historical-essays/atarashiki-mura-in-interwar-japan/
     [accessed 20 August 2020]

83   Maeda, *One Hundred Years*, extract translated by Kazuyo Yasuda, chapter 3,
     section 3, para. 4

84   Atarashiki Mura today has a small gallery that gives a glimpse of the
     community's art through the last century. There is also a museum dedi-
     cated to the memory of Mushanokōji Saneatsu, which displays some of
     his painting and calligraphy.

85   Quoted in Morris-Suzuki, 'A Century of Social Alternatives', 59. See
     also Tessa Morris-Suzuki, 'Invisible Politics', *Humanities Australia* 5
     (2014), 53–72

86   Maeda, *One Hundred Years*, extract translated by Kazuyo Yasuda, chapter 1,
     section 5, para. 6

87   Tomeo Sagoya joined the village at the age of fourteen, together with his
     older brother Iwao (Maeda, *One Hundred Years*, extract translated by

Kazuyo Yasuda, chapter 2, section 3, para. 2). Prime Minister
Hamaguchi Osachi was shot in Tokyo Station in November 1930 and
died of his wounds the following August.

88 Keene, *Dawn*, 457

89 Denkichi Kawashima, quoted in Maeda, *One Hundred Years*, extract translated by Kazuyo Yasuda, chapter 3, section 3, para. 3

90 Ibid., chapter 3, section 2, para. 6 and section 5, para. 2

91 Keene, *Dawn*, 452

92 Maeda, *One Hundred Years*, extract translated by Kazuyo Yasuda, chapter 3,
section 3, para. 2

93 Yiu, 'Intellectual and Literary Contexts', 208

94 Morris-Suzuki, 'Beyond Utopia', 55

95 'New Farm Village' (*Atarashiki Nōson*); 'Community Loving Society'
(*Aikyōkai*). Hoyt Long, 'Farmers' Art in an Age of Cosmopolitan
Agrarianism', in *On Uneven Ground: Miyazawa Kenji and the Making of Place
in Modern Japan* (Stanford, CA, 2012), 159–91

96 *Asahi Shinbun*, 19 October 1919, quoted in Morris-Suzuki, 'Beyond
Utopia', 55

97 Ibid., 56

98 Sarah Frederick, 'Yamakawa Kikue and Edward Carpenter: Translation,
Affiliation, and Queer Internationalism', in Julia C. Bullock, Ayako Kano
and James Welker (eds), *Rethinking Japanese Feminisms* (Hawai'i, HI,
2018), 191

99 Keaveney, *Beyond Brushtalk*; Susan Daruvala, *Zhou Zuoren and an Alternative
Chinese Response to Modernity* (Cambridge, MA, 2000), 50–1

100 Zhou Zuoren was sceptical of Tagore's spiritual idealism: it was far from
the dominant mood of realism among China's intellectuals, most of
whom were chiefly interested in importing materialist doctrines from
Communist Russia. Hay, *Asian Ideas*, 198–9.

101 Zhou Zuoren quoted in Keaveney, *Beyond Brushtalk*, 91

102 Ibid., 90

103 Charles W. Hayford, *To the People: James Yen and Village China* (New York,
1991); Shakhar Rahav, 'How Shall We Live?: Chinese Communal
Experiments after the Great War in Global Context', *Journal of World
History* 26 (2015), 521–48; Keaveney, *Beyond Brushtalk*, 75, 91–3;
Daruvala, *Zhou Zuoren*, 50–1

104 Morris-Suzuki, 'Beyond Utopia', 58

105 Ou Ning, 'Utopia' in Christian Sorace, Ivan Franceschini and Nicholas
Loubere (eds), *Afterlives of Chinese Communism: Political Concepts from Mao
to Xi* (Acton, Australia, 2019), 309–13

106 Esperanto ('one who hopes') was a language created in the late nineteenth century by L. L. Zamenhof, who hoped that a language
unattached to a nation would foster international peace and understanding. It was hugely popular among Chinese and Japanese intellectual

groups. By the mid-1920s, Japan had the highest number of Esperanto speakers of any non-European country. Mushanokōji, *Atarashiki mura no seikatsu*, 'Life in the New Village', quoted in Morris-Suzuki, *New World from Below*, 60. Ulrich Lins, 'Esperanto as a Language and Idea in China and Japan', *Language Problems and Language Planning* 32 (2008), 47–60; Ian Rapley, 'When Global and Local Culture Meet: Esperanto in 1920s Rural Japan', *Language Problems and Language Planning* 37 (2013), 179–96.

107 Maeda, *One Hundred Years*, extract translated by Kazuyo Yasuda, chapter 3, section 5, para. 4

108 'To a Chinese Brethren' (*Aru Shina no kyodai ni*, 1919), based on a translation in Yiu, 'From Utopia to Empire', 225

109 Morton, *Divided Self*; Sho Konishi, 'Ordinary Farmers Living Anarchist Time: Arishima Cooperative Farm in Hokkaido, 1922–1935', *Modern Asian Studies* 47 (2013), 1845–87; Keene, *Dawn*, 488

110 Morris-Suzuki, 'Beyond Utopia', 55

111 Janet Borland, 'Capitalising on Catastrophe: Reinvigorating the Japanese State with Moral Values through Education following the 1923 Great Kantō Earthquake', *Modern Asian Studies*, 875–907, at 881

112 Rebecca Solnit, *A Paradise Built in Hell: The Extraordinary Communities that Arise in Disasters* (London; New York, 2009)

113 Ibid., 898

114 David W. Plath, 'The Fate of Utopia: Adaptive Tactics in Four Japanese Groups', *American Anthropologists* 68, 1152–63, at 1154

115 Most of the New Villagers agreed to be relocated; just two households, including Mushanokōji's first wife Fusako and her second husband, remained in Hyūga. Morris-Suzuki, 'Beyond Utopia', 64

116 Mushanokōji visited Europe for the first time in 1936. Staying in Berlin with his brother Kintomo, who by now was Japan's ambassador to the Third Reich, he shook the Führer's hand. 'Truth alone does not unite people', he wrote afterwards. 'It is also necessary for someone to penetrate into the very heart of people's mentality and elicit unanimous enthusiasm.' (Quoted in Mortimer, *Meeting*, 37.) Mushanokōji's romantic fascination with sweeping social visions lent charismatic dictatorship a fatal appeal.

117 Yiu, 'From Utopia to Empire', *passim*

118 Yoshikhiro Mochizuki, 'Rediscovering Musha-ism: the Theory of Happiness in the Early Works of Mushanokōji Saneatsu', unpublished thesis, University of Hawai'i, 2005, 1

119 Quoted in Maeda, *One Hundred Years*, extract translated by Kazuyo Yasuda

120 Morris-Suzuki, *Japan's Cultural Politics*, 76

121 Ibid., 38

122 Morris-Suzuki, 'Beyond Utopia', 57

123 Morris-Suzuki, *Japan's Cultural Politics*, 80

124 Ou Ning's village was closed down in 2016 after the authorities cut off

the water and electricity. (Ou Ning, 'Autonomy: Utopia or Realpolitik', in Hou Hanru (ed.), *Zizhiqu: Autonomous Regions* (Guangzhou, 2013); Calum Macleod, 'From Our Correspondent: Crushed Dreams of Utopia in Rural China', *The Times*, 2 May 2016)

FOUR: The Forest Philosophers of Fontainebleau: G. I. Gurdjieff's Institute for the Harmonious Development of Man

1 James Bryce, *Transcaucasia and Ararat, Being Notes of a Vacation Tour in the Autumn of 1876* (London, 1877), 114, chapter 3. Orhan Pamuk's novel *Snow* (London, 2004, trans. Maureen Freely) gives a glimpse of Kars in more recent times.

2 Sebnem Ertas, 'The Changing Physical Environment of Kars City After the 93 War', in Recep Efe, Lia Matchavariani, Abdulkadir Yaldir and Laszio Levai (eds), *Developments in Science and Engineering* ([Bulgaria], 2016), 612–24

3 Alexandropol is known now as Gyumri. For speculations on the first, scantily documented years of G. I. Gurdjieff's life, see James Webb, *Harmonious Circle: The Lives and Works of G. I. Gurdjieff, P. D. Ouspensky and Their Followers* (New York, 1980) and James Moore, *Gurdjieff: A Biography* (Shaftesbury, 1999 [1991]).

4 While Georgiades was the original name of Gurdjieff's father, it is likely he altered it to Gurdjian when moving in Armenian society. Gurdjieff is the Russian rendering of Gurdjian (Webb, *Harmonious Circle*, 26). See Moore, *Gurdjieff*, 9, fn. 1 for an extensive discussion of Gurdjieff's possible birth date. A likely guess, based on Gurdjieff's memoirs, is 1866.

5 Scott M. Kenworthy, *The Heart of Russia: Trinity-Sergius, Monasticism, and Society after 1825* (New York; Oxford, 2010), 169–220

6 G. I. Gurdjieff, *Beelzebub's Tales to His Grandson: All and Everything* (London, 2000 [1950]), 732

7 P. D. Ouspensky, *In Search of the Miraculous. Fragments of an Unknown Teaching* (London, 1950), 36; John Bennett, *Gurdjieff: Making a New World* (London, 1973), 83

8 Gurdjieff, *Meetings, passim*

9 Others speculate that he was only able to move between countries so easily because he was acting as a spy for the Tsar. Moore, *Gurdjieff*, 27; Rom Landau quoted in Louis Pauwels, *Gurdjieff* (Isle of Man, 1964), 40–1

10 Webb, *Harmonious Circle*, 40–81

11 See, for example, Rom Landau, *God Is My Adventure: A Book on Modern Mystics, Masters and Teachers* (London, 1935)

12 Orlando Figes, *A People's Tragedy, the Russian Revolution, 1891–1924* (London, 2017 [1996])

13   Bennett quoted in Gorham Munson, 'Black Sheep Philosophers', *Gurdjieff International Review* 1998 (3), https://www.gurdjieff.org/munson1.htm [accessed 20 February 2019]

14   Thomas de Hartmann, *Our Life with Mr Gurdjieff* (New York, 1964), 4–7

15   Paul Beekman Taylor, *Gurdjieff America: Mediating the Miraculous* ([UK], 2004), 140; Ann Butkovsky-Hewitt, *With Gurdjieff in St Petersburg and Paris* (London, 1978), 143

16   Moore, *Gurdjieff*; Ouspensky, *In Search*, *passim*

17   Fritz Peters, *Boyhood with Gurdjieff* (New York, 1964), 195–6

18   John Bennett, *Witness: The Autobiography of John Bennett* (London, 1974 [1961]), 110; Webb, *Harmonious Circle*, 140

19   Ouspensky, *In Search*, 40

20   Ibid., 317

21   Butkovsky-Hewitt, *With Gurdjieff*, 67

22   Although Julia Osipovna Ostrowska was called Gurdjieff's 'wife', she was always known as Madame Ostrowska and they may never have been legally married. Webb, *Harmonious Circle*, 137

23   Butkovsky-Hewitt, *With Gurdjieff*, 86

24   Gladys Alexander's notes quoted in Bennett, *Gurdjieff*, 217

25   Butkovsky-Hewitt, *With Gurdjieff*, 93; Ouspensky, *In Search*, 12

26   Butkovsky-Hewitt, *With Gurdjieff*, 71–2

27   Kathryn Hulme, *Undiscovered Country* (London, 1966), 41

28   Ouspensky, *In Search*, chapter 6

29   P. D. Ouspensky, *Tertium Organum: The Third Canon of Thought, a Key to Enigmas of the World*, trans. E. Kadloubovsky and the author (London, 1981 [1912])

30   Ouspensky, *In Search*, 12

31   Gurdjieff, 'The Material Question', in *Meetings with Remarkable Men* (New York, 2002 [1963]), 277

32   Tcheslaw Tchekhovitch, *Gurdjieff: A Master in Life* (Toronto, 2006), 49

33   Peters, *Boyhood*, 195–6 – the source of all further quotes in this paragraph

34   Ouspensky, *In Search*, 52 and *passim*

35   Ibid.

36   Ibid.

37   Gurdjieff quoted in Chris Coates, 'How Many Arks Does It Take?', in Timothy Miller (ed.), *Spiritual and Visionary Communities: Out To Save The World* (London; New York, 2013), 177–90, at 177

38   Bennett, *Witness*, 110

39   Lady Rothermere also funded T. S. Eliot's literary magazine *Criterion*. Pauwels, *Gurdjieff*, 147.

40   The Home Office did grant Gurdjieff permission to settle, but not his followers, which made it impossible for him to stay and carry on his work. Moore, *Gurdjieff*, 154–71

41   For a detailed discussion of Mansfield's motivations for joining Gurdjieff,

see Claire Tomalin, *Katherine Mansfield: A Secret Life* (Harmondsworth, 2003), 591 and *passim*; Gerri Kimber and Claire Davison (eds,) *The Diaries of Katherine Mansfield* (Edinburgh, 2016), 171.

42   Katherine Mansfield to J. M. Murry, 23 October 1922, Vincent O'Sullivan and Margaret Scott (eds), *The Collected Letters*, vol. 5 (Oxford, 2008), 307

43   De Hartmann, *Our Life*, 101; Katherine Mansfield to J. M. Murry, 21 October 1922, O'Sullivan and Scott (eds), *Collected Letters,* vol. 5, 304–5

44   Galya Diment, *A Russian Jew of Bloomsbury: The Life and Times of Samuel Koteliansky* (Montreal; Kingston, 2011), 119

45   Vincent O'Sullivan and Margaret Scott (eds), *The Collected Letters of Katherine Mansfield* (Oxford, 1984–2008), vol. 4, 82–3

46   Katherine Mansfield to J. M. Murry, 21 October 1922, O'Sullivan and Scott (eds), *Collected Letters*, vol. 5, 304–5

47   Although no documents certify Gurdjieff's paternity, he is believed to have had seven children with various of his followers, including Nicholas de Val and Cynthia (called Dushka) Howarth. Webb, *Harmonious Circle*, 317; Peters, *Boyhood* (New York, 1964), 19

48   Orage quoted in Roger Lipsey, *Gurdjieff Reconsidered: The Life, the Teachings, the Legacy* (Boulder, CO, 2019), 67

49   Quoted in James Moore, *Gurdjieff and Mansfield: The Initiation of the Priestess* (London, 1980); Moore, *Gurdjieff*, 173

50   Katherine Mansfield to J. M. Murry, 21 October 1922, O'Sullivan and Scott (eds), *Collected Letters*, vol. 5, 304–5

51   Toomer, quoted in Webb, *Harmonious Circle*, 282; C. E. Bechhofer-Roberts, 'The Forest Philosophers', *Century Magazine* CVIII (1), New York, May 1924, 173

52   C. S. Nott, *Teachings of Gurdjieff: The Journal of a Pupil* (London, 1961), 45; Paul Beekman Taylor, *Gurdjieff and Orage: Brothers in Elysium* (York Beach, ME; [UK], 2001), 32

53   Katherine Mansfield to J. M. Murry, 21 October 1922, O'Sullivan and Scott (eds), *Collected Letters*, vol. 5, 310

54   Ibid.

55   Katherine Mansfield to J. M. Murry, 27 October 1922, O'Sullivan and Scott (eds), *Collected Letters*, vol. 5, 310; to S. S. Koteliansky, 19 October 1922, 303–4

56   Olgivanna's full name was Olga Ivanovna Lazovich Hinzenberg. Bennett, *Gurdjieff*, 157–8; Mansfield quoted in Pauwels, *Gurdjieff*, 295

57   Adele Kafian, 'Looking Back to the Last Days of Katherine Mansfield', *Adelphi*, October 1946

58   Katherine Mansfield to J. M. Murry, 12 November 1922, O'Sullivan and Scott (eds), *Collected Letters*, vol. 5, 323

59   Nott, *Teachings*, 55

60   Mansfield to J. M. Murry, 21 October 1922, O'Sullivan and Scott (eds),
     Collected Letters, vol. 5, 304–5; Nott, *Teachings*; Mary C. Bell, 'Some
     memories of the Prieuré', September 1949, *Gurdjieff International Review*
     1 (1998), https://www.gurdjieff.org/bell.htm [accessed 20 August
     2020]

61   Bennett, *Gurdjieff*, 157–8

62   Ibid.

63   Quoted in Hugh Ford, *Four Lives in Paris* (San Francisco, 1987), 278

64   Katherine Mansfield to J. M. Murry, 27 October 1922, O'Sullivan and
     Scott (eds), *Collected Letters*, vol. 5, 310

65   James Carruthers Young, 'An Experiment at Fontainebleau: A Personal
     Reminiscence', *British Journal of Medical Psychology* 7 (1927), 447–61;
     Bell, 'Some Memories of the Prieuré'

66   Orage quoted in Lipsey, *Gurdjieff Reconsidered*, 67

67   Maud Hoffman, 'Taking the Life Cure in Gurdjieff's School', *New York
     Times*, 10 February 1924

68   Mansfield to J. M. Murry, 12 November 1922, O'Sullivan and Scott
     (eds), *Collected Letters*, vol. 5, 322

69   Mansfield to Murry, December 1922, ibid., 338

70   Mansfield to Murry, 27 October 1922, ibid., 310

71   Galya Diment, *A Russian Jew of Bloomsbury: The Life and Times of Samuel
     Koteliansky* (Montreal; Kingston, 2011), 121

72   Katherine Mansfield to J. M. Murry, 12 November 1922, O'Sullivan and
     Scott (eds), *Collected Letters*, vol. 5, 323

73   Gurdjieff, *Meetings with Remarkable Men*, 285

74   Margaret Anderson, *My Thirty Years' War: An Autobiography* (London, 1930),
     256–7; Herbert R. Lottman, *Man Ray's Montparnasse* (New York, 2011),
     203; Moore, *Gurdjieff*, 175

75   Webb, *Harmonious Circle*, 32; Nott, *Teachings*, 30

76   Bennett, *Gurdjieff*, 139

77   Mabel Dodge Luhan, *Lorenzo in Taos* (Santa Fe, NM, 2007 [1932]), 128

78   Gladys Alexander's notes, quoted by Bennett, *Gurdjieff*, 146

79   Mansfield quoted in Pauwels, *Gurdjieff*, 297; Moore, 193

80   Mark Schorer, *Sinclair Lewis: An American Life* (New York, 1961), 378

81   Nott, *Teachings*, 56

82   Peters, *Boyhood*, 81; Edwin Wolfe, *Episodes with Gurdjieff* (Birmingham,
     AL, 2002 [1973])

83   Quoted in Pauwels, *Gurdjieff*, 177

84   Mathew Thomson, *Psychological Subjects: Identity, Culture and Health in
     Twentieth-Century Britain* (Oxford, 2006)

85   L. S. Penrose, 'Observations on Gurdjieff's Institute', Penrose/2/3/13,
     UCL, Special Collections. Penrose's diagnosis echoes the psychological
     dangers that come with any community reliant on a strong leader.
     Followers in these situations often project their own desire for

conviction and certainty onto a charismatic personality. They then begin to narcissistically identify with that person – and in so doing risk losing their sense of self. Jerrold M. Post, 'Narcissism and the Charismatic Leader–Follower Relationship', *Political Psychology* 7 (1986), 675–88

86   Beryl Pogson, *Maurice Nicoll: A Portrait* (London, 1961); Young, 'An Experiment at Fontainebleau'

87   Pogson, *Maurice Nicoll*, 80

88   Initially an address to the British Psychological Society, this was later published in the first edition of the literary journal *The New Adelphi*, edited by John Middleton Murry, husband to Katherine Mansfield. J. Carswell, *Lives and Letters: A. R. Orage, Beatrice Hastings, Katherine Mansfield, John Middleton Murry, S. S. Koteliansky, 1906–1957* (London, 1978), 174–93

89   Pauwels, *Gurdjieff*, 135

90   Moore, *Gurdjieff*, 195

91   Gurdjieff, *Life is Real Only Then, When 'I Am'*, 30

92   Ian E. Black, *A Friend in France* (Jonathan Cape, 1941), 19; 'Théâtre des Champs-Elysées', *Le Temps*, 15 December 1923

93   The Sunwise Turn bookshop was founded in 1916 by Madge Jenison and Mary Mowbray-Clarke. Jessie Dwight bought into the venture later on. Huw Osborne, *The Rise of the Modernist Bookshop: Books and the Commerce of Culture in the Twentieth Century* (London, 2015)

94   F. Scott Fitzgerald, *This Side of Paradise* (Cambridge, 2012 [1920]), 260

95   Daniel T. Rodgers, *Atlantic Crossings: Social Politics in a Progressive Age* (Cambridge, MA, 1998); Nancy F. Cott, 'Revisiting the Transatlantic 1920s: Vincent Sheean vs. Malcolm Cowley', *The American Historical Review* 118 (2013), 46–75

96   Margaret Anderson, *The Unknowable Gurdjieff* (New York, 1991), 111

97   Moore, *Gurdjieff*, 202

98   Taylor, *Gurdjieff's America*, 40–1

99   Moore, *Gurdjieff*, 199

100 Taylor, *Brothers in Elysium*, 46

101 Webb, *Harmonious Circle*, 27

102 Fritz, *Boyhood*, 65

103 Lois Palken Rudnick, *Mabel Dodge Luhan: New Woman, New Worlds* (Albuquerque, NM, 1984), 228

104 De Hartmann, *Our Life*, 135

105 Fritz Peters, *Boyhood*, 7–9. Fritz Peters, Margaret Anderson's nephew, came from a broken home in New York and had been adopted by Jane Heap before being brought to France.

106 Nott, *Teachings*, 80

107 Webb, *Harmonious Circle*, 291; Peters, *Boyhood*, 15

108 Moore, *Gurdjieff*, 207

109   De Hartmann, *Our Life*, 139
110   Anderson, *Unknowable Gurdjieff*, 28
111   Peters, *Boyhood*, 76
112   Margaret Anderson, *Little Review Anthology* (New York, 1953), 353
113   Munson, 'Black Sheep Philosophers'
114   Pogson, *Maurice Nicoll*, 87
115   Moore, *Gurdjieff*, 212; Peters, *Boyhood*, 152–5
116   G. I. Gurdjieff, *Beelzebub's Tales to His Grandson* (London, 2000 [1950])
117   Peters, *Boyhood*, 30; Nott, *Teachings*, 127
118   Edwin Wolfe, 'Further Episodes with Gurdjieff', *Gurdjieff International Review* 6 (2003), https://www.gurdjieff.org/grossman2.htm [accessed 20 August 2020]; Bennett, *Gurdjieff*, 274
119   In the end, the *All and Everything* trilogy consisted of *Beelzebub's Tales to His Grandson* (1950), *Meetings with Remarkable Men (or An Objectively Impartial Criticism of the Life of Man)* (1963) and *Life is Real Only Then, When 'I Am'* (London, 1999 [1974])
120   *Beelzebub's Tales to His Grandson* would even be included by one literary critic, Martin Seymour-Smith, in a list of *The 100 Most Influential Books Ever Written* (New York, 1998), 447–52.
121   Moore, *Gurdjieff*, 245
122   Webb, *Harmonious Circle*, 420
123   Taylor, *Gurdjieff's America*, 28
124   Moore, *Gurdjieff*, 249; Webb, *Harmonious Circle*, 426
125   Hulme, *Undiscovered Country*, 69; Monk Gibbon, *The Masterpiece and the Man: Yeats as I Knew Him* (London, 1959), 91
126   Moore, *Gurdjieff*, 249
127   Hulme, *Undiscovered Country*, 70
128   Moore, *Gurdjieff*, 68
129   Moore, *Gurdjieff*, 262; William Patrick Patterson, *Ladies of the Rope: Gurdjieff's Special Left Bank Women's Group* (Fairfax, CA, 1999), 97
130   Kathryn Hulme quoted in Rob Baker, 'No Harem: Gurdjieff and the Women of the Rope', *Gurdjieff International Review* 1.2 (1997–98), 39–45. Online posting 27 January 2002
131   Webb, *Harmonious Circle*, 448
132   Johanna J. M. Petsche, 'A Gurdjieff Genealogy: Tracing the Manifold Ways the Gurdjieff Teaching Has Travelled', *International Journal for the Study of New Religions* 4 (2013), 72–4
133   Katherine Mansfield to J. M. Murry, 10 November 1922, O'Sullivan and Scott (eds), *Collected Letters*, vol. 5, 319
134   Mansfield to Murry, 27 October 1922, ibid., 310

FIVE: Seeking the Kingdom of God in Rural Germany: Eberhard and Emmy Arnold's Bruderhof

1   John Keegan, *The First World War* (London, 1998), 423
2   The World Council of Churches was officially inaugurated in 1948 but its roots lay in various ecumenical movements that were triggered by the First World War.
3   Acts 4:32–37
4   The name Bruderhof was only used to describe the community for the first time in 1926, but for ease of reference this name is used throughout the chapter.
5   For current information about the Bruderhof and its various communities, see https://www.bruderhof.com.
6   Markus Baum, *Against the Wind: Eberhard Arnold and the Bruderhof* (London, 1998), 3–4. Eberhard Arnold's mother Elisabeth, née Voight, was from a family of scholars. His father, Carl Franklin, was the son of Swiss and American missionaries.
7   Eberhard and Emmy Arnold, *Seeking for the Kingdom of God*, selected and edited from earlier sources by Heini and Annemarie Arnold (New York, 1974), 23–5
8   Eberhard lectured with the Young Men's Christian Association; led Bible study classes with the Christian Student Movement; and helped the Salvation Army deliver 'soup, soap and salvation', as the slogan ran, to the working classes.
9   Emmy von Hollander was born in 1885 in Riga, Latvia – part of the Russian Empire – into a German Baltic family involved in administration and academia. In 1890 the family emigrated to Halle in Germany where her father was appointed professor of law at the university.
10 Emmy Arnold, *A Joyful Pilgrimage: My Life in Community* (e-book, Farmington, PA; Robertsbridge, UK, 1999), 6
11 Baum, *Against the Wind*, 21
12 Ibid., 33
13 Eberhard Arnold and Emmy von Hollander, *Love Letters* (Rifton, NY, 2007), 57
14 Eberhard's doctoral thesis was titled 'Nietzsche's Religious Development and Christianity'. It appeared in print in 1910 as *Early Christian and Anti-Christian Elements in the Development of Friedrich Nietzsche*. For an English précis, see Baum, *Against the Wind*, 56–9.
15 Emmy Arnold, *Joyful Pilgrimage*, 11
16 Germany had Protestant and Catholic regions. The Kaiser was the constitutional head of the Protestant Church.
17 Although the war drew enthusiasm from many religious leaders, there were also those who saw it as diametrically opposed to their faith. In Britain, for example, the pacifist Fellowship of Reconciliation, set up in

1914 to promote international harmony, had attracted over 7,000 members by the end of the war. Ian M. Randall, *A Christian Peace Experiment: The Bruderhof Community in Britain, 1933–1942* (Eugene, OR, 2018), 22–3; Philip Jenkins, *The Great and Holy War: How World War I Became a Religious Crusade* (New York, 2014)

18 Martin Luther posted his Ninety-Five Theses at Wittenberg on 31 October 1517.

19 In 1913, Eberhard was diagnosed with tuberculosis and the entire family retreated to a cottage in the Tyrolean Alps to wait for him to recover – which he did, but with permanently weakened lungs.

20 Quoted in Baum, *Against the Wind*, 82

21 Eberhard Arnold, *The War: A Call to Inwardness* (Gotha, 1914). This was later republished, with the militant nationalism erased, as *Innerland: A Guide into the Heart and Soul of the Bible*.

22 Emmy Arnold, *Joyful Pilgrimage*, 29

23 Eberhard Arnold, 'Über den Sinn des Krieges' ('On the Meaning of War'), in *Der Wahreitszeuge* (September 1915), quoted in Baum, *Against the Wind*, 83

24 Eberhard and Emmy Arnold, *Seeking for the Kingdom of God*, 236

25 Ibid., 236

26 Emmy Arnold, *A Joyful Pilgrimage*, 29

27 Yaacov Oved, *The Witness of the Brothers: A History of the Bruderhof* (London, 2017), 48

28 Baum, *Against the Wind*, 73

29 Emmy Arnold, *A Joyful Pilgrimage*, 35

30 Ibid., 38

31 Baum, *Against the Wind*, 82

32 Quoted in Randall, *Christian Peace Experiment*, 18

33 *Gemeinde* is here translated as 'church-community', although there is no direct equivalent in English. The word was used by Eberhard Arnold to signify a church congregation that was a true, united spiritual fellowship.

34 Peter Mommsen, *Homage to a Broken Man: The Life of J. Heinrich Arnold – A True Story of Faith, Forgiveness, Sacrifice, and Community* (Robertsbridge, UK, 2004), 13

35 Baum, *Against the Wind*, 77, 82; Emmy Barth, *An Embassy Besieged: The Story of a Christian Community in Nazi Germany* (Eugene, OR, 2010), 10–11

36 The Arnolds' children were Emy-Margret (born 1911); Eberhard-Heinrich, known as Hardy (1912); Johann Heinrich, known as Heini (1913); Hans-Hermann (1916); and Monika (1918).

37 John Alexander Williams, *Turning to Nature in Germany: Hiking, Nudism and Conservation, 1900–1940* (Stanford, CA, 2007)

38 Emmy Arnold, *Joyful Pilgrimage*, 35

39 Julius H. Rubin, *The Other Side of Joy: Religious Melancholy Among the*

Bruderhof (Oxford, 2000), 50; Emmy Arnold, *Joyful Pilgrimage*, 46

40 Barth, *Embassy*, 21

41 For the story of the Shakers, the Oneida Community and other nine-teenth-century American utopias, see Chris Jennings, *Paradise Now: The Story of American Utopianism* (New York, 2016).

42 Ian M. Randall, "Church Community is a Gift of the Holy Spirit': The Spirituality of the Bruderhof Community', *Centre for Baptist History and Heritage Studies*, Occasional Papers vol. 10 (Oxford, 2014); The Bruderhof, *Foundations of Our Faith & Calling* (Walden, NY; Robertsbridge, UK, 2014)

43 Oved, *Witness*, 20

44 Baum, *Against the Wind*, 133

45 Oved, *Witness*, 70

46 Emmy Arnold, *Joyful Pilgrimage*, 81

47 Ibid., 41

48 'Life's Task' (translated from Eberhard Arnold, transcript, 8 October 1933 (Bruderhof Historical Archive EA 163), and Eberhard Arnold, transcript, 18 March 1932 (Bruderhof Historical Archive EA4)), in *Called to Community: The Life Jesus Wants for His People*, Charles E. Moore (ed.) (Walden, NY, 2016)

49 Ibid.

50 John Hoyland quoted in Baum, *Against the Wind*, 172

51 Emmy Arnold, 'Community Is Born: The Founding of the Bruderhof', 18 June 2020, translated from the German and adapted by Emmy Barth Maendel, https://www.plough.com/en/topics/community/intentional-community/community-is-born [accessed 14 August 2020]

52 Oved, *Witness*, 16

53 Emmy Arnold, *Joyful Pilgrimage*, 61

54 Ibid., 46

55 Rubin, *Other Side*, 52

56 Emmy Arnold, *Joyful Pilgrimage*, 46

57 Baum, *Against the Wind*, 179

58 Eberhard quoted in Baum, *Against the Wind*, 141

59 Eberhard Arnold, *Why We Live in Community* (Rifton, NY, 1995 [1925]), 15

60 Barth, *Embassy*, 15

61 Ibid.

62 This religious joy, and its flip side of spiritual crisis, is a phenomenon that has been observed among other groups dedicated to restoring biblical communal religion, including the Mennonites, and Moravians. Rubin, *Other Side*

63 Barth, *Embassy*, 19

64 Ibid., 15

65 Ibid.

66 Emmy Arnold, *Joyful Pilgrimage*, 42

67 Baum, *Against the Wind*, 143; Emmy Arnold, *Torches Together* (Rifton, NY, 1964), 80–1

68 Oved, *Witness*, 31; Matthew 18:15–20

69 Michael Tyldesley, *No Heavenly Delusion? A Comparative Study of Three Communal Movements* (Liverpool, 2003), 60

70 Hans-Joachim Schoeps quoted in Baum, *Against the Wind*, 174

71 Emmy Arnold, 'Community Is Born: The Founding of the Bruderhof', 18 June 2020, translated from the German and adapted by Emmy Barth Maendel, https://www.plough.com/en/topics/community/intentional-community/community-is-born [accessed 14 August 2020]

72 *The Plough*, vol. 1, no. 3 (1953), 7–9

73 Benjamin Zablocki, *The Joyful Community* (Baltimore, 1971), 76; Emmy Arnold, *Torches Together*, 62

74 Notes of members' meeting, 1935, draft translation by Bruderhof Historical Archive, EA 35/77

75 Oved, *Witness*, 68

76 Emmy Arnold, *Torches Together*, 121

77 Emmy Arnold, *Joyful Pilgrimage*, 99

78 Zablocki, *Joyful Community*, 76

79 Emmy Arnold, *Joyful Pilgrimage*, 92

80 Most of the Hutterites had moved from the United States to Canada during the First World War, facing hostility because of their refusal to join the armed forces. The story of the relationship between the Hutterites and Bruderhof is told in *Brothers Unite: An Account of the Uniting of Eberhard Arnold and the Rhön Bruderhof with the Hutterian Church*, translated and edited by the Hutterian Brethren (Ulster Park, NY, 1988).

81 *Brothers Unite*, 13

82 The Hutterites, fleeing religious persecution in Europe, crossed the Atlantic in 1874 to try their luck in America. The American professor J. G. Evert reported to Eberhard that the Hutterites he had met were 'not very sympathetic to me, as they reject culture'. Randall, *Christian Peace Experiment*, 30.

83 Emmy Arnold, *Joyful Pilgrimage*, 92 and 100

84 Oved, *Witness*, 51

85 Emmy Arnold, 'Community Is Born: The Founding of the Bruderhof', 18 June 2020, translated from the German and adapted by Emmy Barth Maendel, https://www.plough.com/en/topics/community/intentional-community/community-is-born [accessed 14 August 2020]

86 Oved, *Witness*, 67; Eberhard quoted in Emmy Arnold, *Joyful Pilgrimage*, 106

87 Eberhard quoted in Baum, *Against the Wind*, 198

88 *Brothers Unite*, 165

89 Emmy Arnold, *Joyful Pilgrimage*, 113

90 Rubin, *Other Side*, 66–7

91 Emmy Arnold, *Joyful Pilgrimage*, 112
92 Baum, *Against the Wind*, 199–200
93 Emmy Arnold, *Joyful Pilgrimage*, 114
94 Ibid., 54
95 Rod Janzen, 'The Hutterites and the Bruderhof: The Relationship between an Old Order Religious Society and a Twentieth-Century Communal Group', *Mennonite Quarterly Review* 79 (2005), 505–44
96 Such criticisms have come, in particular, from an organization of ex-Bruderhof members called Keep In Touch. See Julius H. Rubin, 'Contested Narratives: A Case Study of the Conflict between a New Religious Movement and its Critics', http://www.perefound.com/jr_cn.html, [n.d.], [accessed 18 August 2020]
97 Barth, *Embassy*, 23
98 Ibid., 26
99 Ibid., 223
100 Emmy Arnold, *Joyful Pilgrimage*, 130
101 Statement from 26 March 1933, Eberhard Arnold, *God's Revolution: Justice, Community, and the Coming Kingdom* (Walden, NY; Robertsbridge, UK; Elsmore, Australia, 1997), 52
102 Emmy Arnold, *Joyful Pilgrimage*, 132
103 There is unfortunately no indication of whether the letter to Hitler was actually read. Barth, *Embassy*, 233
104 Ibid.
105 Ibid.
106 Ibid., 45
107 Emmy Arnold, *Joyful Pilgrimage*, 139
108 Quoted in Barth, *Embassy*, 245
109 Emmy Arnold, *Joyful Pilgrimage*, 155
110 Hans Meier, *The Dissolution of the Rhön Bruderhof in Retrospect* (Rifton, NY, 1979), 2–4
111 Seth Koven, *The Match Girl and the Heiress* (Oxford, 2015)
112 The previous owner of the farm happened to be the son of Colonel Reginald Dyer, who was responsible for the massacre of hundreds of unarmed people at Amritsar in India in 1919. The event was a key factor in turning Rabindranath Tagore towards practical utopianism. The history of the Cotswold Bruderhof is recounted by Randall in *Christian Peace Experiment*.
113 Emmy Arnold, *Joyful Pilgrimage*, 158
114 Randall, *Christian Peace Experiment*, 70; Extract from *The Times*, 'From our Special Correspondent', 6 September 1938, 'The Cotswold Bruderhof – German Peasant Colony'
115 Fiona MacCarthy, *Eric Gill* (London, 1989)
116 Oved, *Witness*, 100
117 W. H. Garbett to Leonard Elmhirst, [n.d.], LKE/LAND/1/I, Dartington Hall Archives

118 Elisabeth Nietzsche was joined in Paraguay by her husband Bernhard
    Förster and fourteen impoverished German families who had been
    vetted for their racial purity. Most of the settlers died of hunger and
    disease. Förster committed suicide and Elisabeth returned to Germany
    in 1893. Ben Macintyre, *Forgotten Fatherland: The Search for Elisabeth
    Nietzsche* ([n.p.], 1992); John Gimlette, *At the Tomb of the Inflatable Pig:
    Travels Through Paraguay* (New York, 2005)

119 Emmy Barth, *No Lasting Home: A Year in the Paraguayan Wilderness* (Walden,
    NY; Robertsbridge, UK, 2009). A few of the Bruderhof members who
    were left behind to wind up the Cotswold farm began a new community
    in Shropshire.

120 Acts 4:32–37

121 Eberhard Arnold, transcript, 8 October 1933 (Bruderhof Historical
    Archive EA 163), and Eberhard Arnold, transcript, 18 March 1932
    (Bruderhof Historical Archive EA4), translated from the German

122 Karen H. Stephan and G. Edward Stephan, 'Religion and the Survival of
    Utopian Communities', *Journal for the Scientific Study of Religion* 12
    (1973), 89–100

SIX: California Dreaming:
Gerald Heard's Trabuco College

1 This evening is recalled by Gerald Heard in 'The Poignant Prophet', *The
  Kenyon Review* 27 (1965), 49–70.

2 Aldous Huxley fictionalized his transition from cynical detachment to
  social and spiritual commitment through the experiences of Anthony
  Beavis in *Eyeless in Gaza* (1936).

3 Sunday evening talk given at Dartington by Aldous Huxley, 10 February
  1935, LKE/G/18/A, Dartington Hall Archives. All archival references
  in this chapter are to this repository, unless specified otherwise.

4 See, for example, Juliet Gardiner, "Searching for the Gleam': Finding
  Solutions to the Political and Social Problems of 1930s Britain', *History
  Workshop Journal* 72 (2011), 103–17, and Richard Overy, *The Morbid Age:
  Britain between the Wars* (London, 2009)

5 Gerald Heard to Leonard Elmhirst, 6 December 1934, LKE/G/17

6 Gerald Heard, *Pain, Sex and Time: A New Hypothesis of Evolution* (London,
  1939), 2; Gerald Heard, 'Men and Books', review of *Letters of George III*
  by B. Dobrée and *Government in Business* by Stuart Chase, *Time and Tide*, 9
  November 1935, 1619–20

7 Heard was christened Henry Fitzgerald Heard, but he was known as
  Gerald.

8 Beatrice Webb, *My Apprenticeship*, vol. 1 (London, 1926), 153

9 Having gone to America for his health as a young man, Sir Horace

Plunkett (1854–1932) acquired many of his ideas on rural reform in a decade spent ranching in Wyoming. On his return to his family estate in Ireland, he pursued the cause of agricultural cooperation, founding the Irish Agricultural Organisation Society and influencing the development of the cooperative movement throughout the world.

10 Rabindranath Tagore read Horace Plunkett and A. E.'s [a pseudonym used by George William Russell] *The National Being* (1916) on Irish cooperative living (Louise Blakeney Williams, 'Overcoming the 'Contagion of Mimicry': The Cosmopolitan Nationalism and Modernist History of Rabindranath Tagore and W. B. Yeats', *American Historical Review* (2007), 69-100, at 97); Daniel T. Rodgers, *Atlantic Crossings: Social Politics in a Progressive Age* (Cambridge, MA, 1998), 321.

11 Gerald Heard's book on flying saucers, *Is Another World Watching? The Riddle of the Flying Saucers* (1950), speculated that these alien spaceships were piloted by bees from Mars, who were anxious about humankind's use of atomic weapons, since these risked destabilizing the solar system. In spite of its eccentricity, it resonated with Heard's lifelong preoccupation with pacifism and building bridges between societies. His detective stories were published under the pseudonym H. F. Heard.

12 Ronald Knox, *Broadcast Minds* (London, 1932), 34

13 Naomi Mitchinson, *You May Well Ask: A Memoir, 1920–1940* (London, 1979), 107

14 Gerald Heard, *The Ascent of Humanity: An Essay on the Evolution of Civilization from Group Consciousness Through Individuality to Super-Consciousness* (London, 1929)

15 Heard, 'Poignant Prophet', 56

16 The ideas in this paragraph are taken from Gerald Heard's *The Third Morality* (New York, 1937).

17 Leonard Elmhirst to Gerald Heard, 26 December 1934, LKE/G/17

18 Notes from 17 November 1934 meeting, LKE/G/S9/A; Gerald Heard to Dorothy, 9 August 1934, DWE/G/6A

19 Gerald Heard to Margaret Isherwood, 1932, DWE/6/F1

20 Gerald Heard to Margaret Isherwood, 15 February 1934, DWE/G/6; Gerald Heard to Dorothy Elmhirst, 30 September 1932, DWE/G/5

21 Gerald Heard to Margaret Isherwood, 17 December 1933, DWE/G/6A

22 Sybille Bedford, *Aldous Huxley: A Biography*, vol. 1 (1973, London), 388

23 Quoted in Aldous Huxley (ed.), *An Encyclopaedia of Pacifism* (London, 1937), 89-90

24 Eros, Paul, "One of the Most Penetrating Minds in England': Gerald Heard and the British Intelligentsia of the Interwar Period', unpublished PhD thesis, University of Oxford, 2011, 180

25 Gerald Heard, 'The Significance of the New Pacifism', in Gerald K. Hibbert (ed.), *The New Pacifism* (London, 1936), 17

26 Eros, 'Heard', 10

27 Aldous Huxley, *Ends and Means: An Enquiry into the Nature of Ideals and into the Methods Employed for their Realization* (London, 1946 [1937]), 273

28 Aldous Huxley, *Brave New World* (London, 1932)

29 Eros, 'Heard', 199

30 Grover Smith (ed.), *Letters of Aldous Huxley* (London, 1969), 398

31 Eros, 'Heard', 199

32 Ibid.

33 Gerald Heard to Julian Huxley, quoted in Richard Overy, *The Morbid Age: Britain between the Wars* (London, 2009), 254

34 Don Lattin, *Distilled Spirits* (Berkeley, CA; Los Angeles, 2012), 146–7

35 Bedford, *Aldous Huxley*, vol. 1, 341

36 Donald W. Whisenhunt, *Utopian Movements and Ideas of the Great Depression: Dreamers, Believers, and Madmen* (Lanham, MD, 2013); Joshua Lockyer, "We Try to Create the World That We Want': Intentional Communities Forging Liveable Lives in St Louis', working paper 2011, 3

37 C. J. Maloney, *Back to the Land: Arthurdale, FDR's New Deal, and the Costs of Economic Planning* (Hoboken, NJ, 2011). The dinner is discussed by Joseph P. Lash in a letter to the Elmhirsts, 27 September 1968, LKE/USA/4/A, and is recounted in his book, *Eleanor and Franklin* (London, 1972), 396.

38 D. H. Lawrence had long talked about building a socialist utopia, which he called Rananim, in America. He had even invited Aldous Huxley to join it. But when Lawrence arrived in Taos he merely settled with his wife on a ranch bought for him by Mabel Dodge Luhan.

39 Flannery Burke, *From Greenwich Village to Taos: Primitivism and Place at Mabel Dodge Luhan's* (Lawrence, KS, 2008)

40 Gerald Heard to H. R. L. Sheppard, 26 October 1937, Lambeth Palace, Sheppard Papers MS 3745.162, quoted in Eros, 'Heard', 11

41 Peter Parker, *Isherwood: A Life* (London, 2004), 433

42 Christopher Isherwood, *Diaries*, vol. 1: 1939–1960, ed. Katherine Bucknell (London, 1996), 24–5

43 Swami Prabhavananda was a member of the Vedanta Society, a missionary arm of the Hindu revival movement with which the Tagore family was involved in late-nineteenth-century Bengal. The organization promoted tolerance of all religions, social reform, recognition of a higher reality, and inner peace – inclusive themes that many Americans found attractive in the 1930s.

44 Gerald Heard to Margaret Isherwood, 23 November 1932, DWE/6/F1

45 Gerald Heard, *Pain, Sex and Time: A New Hypothesis of Evolution* (London, 1939), 2; Gerald Heard, 'Men and Books', review of *Letters of George III* by B. Dobrée and *Government in Business* by Stuart Chase, *Time and Tide*, 9 November 1935, 1619–20

46 For the place of eugenics in progressive thinking, see Chris Renwick,

British Sociology's Lost Biological Roots: A History of Futures Past (Basingstoke, 2012), especially chapter 2; and Michael Freeden, 'Eugenics and Progressive Thought: A Study in Ideological Affinity', *Historical Journal* 22 (1979), 645–71

47 *Trabuco Prospectus*, September 1942, LKE/G/17/E

48 Llano del Rio (1914–18) aimed to free people from the evils of drudgery and capitalist exploitation. At its height it housed 900 people, but its power dynamics never stabilized and, after a series of arguments, the colonists dispersed. Huxley wrote that, 'Except in a purely negative way, the history of Llano is sadly uninstructive.' Aldous Huxley, 'Ozymandias, the Desert Utopia that Failed', in *Tomorrow and Tomorrow and Tomorrow and Other Essays* (New York, 1956), 7–8

49 Quoted in Murray, *Aldous Huxley: An English Intellectual* (London, 2003), 316

50 Felix Greene was the cousin of Heard's friend Christopher Isherwood and also of the novelist Graham Greene. Jeremy Lewis gives a vivid portrait of this family in *Shades of Greene: One Generation of the English Family* (London, 2011).

51 Ibid., 256

52 Lattin, *Distilled Spirits*, 141

53 Ibid., 142

54 Gerald Heard quoted in Christopher Isherwood (ed.), *Vedanta for the Western World* (London, 1948), 58; similarly in Franklin Zahn, 'Temporary Monk', 1984, https://www.geraldheard.com/writings-and-recollections/2017/8/2/temporary-monk [accessed 20 August 2020]

55 Gerald Heard, 'The Way of Life at Trabuco', T/DHS/B/15/D

56 Isherwood, *Diaries*, vol. 1, 21–2

57 Isherwood quoted in Alison Falby, *Between the Pigeonholes: Gerald Heard, 1889–1971* (Newcastle, 2008), 107

58 Swami Yogeshananda, 'Trabuco College Tryout', [n.d.], https://www.geraldheard.com/writings-and-recollections/2017/8/2/trabuco-college-tryout [accessed 20 August 2020]

59 Falby, *Between the Pigeonholes*, 107, 113

60 Anne Freemantle, 'Heard Melodies', *The Commonweal* 43 (25 January 1946), 384–5

61 Maria Huxley to Grace Burke Hubble, 9 January 1944, mssHUB 1083, Huntington Digital Library

62 Alan Watts, *In My Own Way* (New York, 1973), 208; David Robb, 'Brahmins from Abroad: English Expatriates and Spiritual Consciousness in Modern America', *American Studies* 26 (1985), 45–60, fn. 22

63 Lattin, *Distilled Spirits*, 169

64 Heard dedicated an entire book, *Pain, Sex and Time: A New Hypothesis of Evolution* (1939), to explaining how, by controlling their lustful energies, men could reconnect with their capacity to evolve further psycho-

logically (he didn't mention whether this was possible for women). Through celibacy, he wrote, egotism would be replaced by willing co-operation and an understanding of the 'universal reality'.

65 Marvin Barrett, quoted in Falby, *Between the Pigeonholes*, 114

66 Miriam King, 'Life at Trabuco', [n.d.], https://www.geraldheard.com/writings-and-recollections/2017/8/2/life-at-trabuco [accessed 20 August 2020]

67 Maria Huxley to Grace Burke Hubble, 9 August 1943, mssHUB 692, Huntington Digital Library

68 Aldous Huxley, *The Perennial Philosophy* (New York, 1945)

69 Lewis, *Shades of Greene*, 259

70 David King Dunaway, *Huxley in Hollywood* (Bloomsbury, 1990 [1989]), 114

71 Leonard Elmhirst to Margaret Isherwood, October 1948, LKE/G/17/E

72 Laurence R. Veysey, *The Communal Experience: Anarchist and Mystical Communities in Twentieth-Century America* (Chicago and London, 1973), 273

73 Maria Huxley to Matthew Huxley, 1947. Quoted in Sybille Bedford, *Aldous Huxley: A Biography*, vol. 2 (London, 1974), 81

74 Lewis, *Shades of Greene*, 262

75 Alan Watts, *In My Own Way: An Autobiography 1915–1965* (New York, 1973), 208

76 Aldous Huxley, *The Doors of Perception* (San Francisco, CA, 1954), 26

77 Ibid., 17

78 Ben Sessa, *The Psychedelic Renaissance: Reassessing the Role of Psychedelic Drugs in 21st Century Psychiatry and Society* (London, 2017)

79 Aldous Huxley, *Island* (London, 2005 [1962])

80 Walter Truett Anderson, *The Upstart Spring: Esalen and the American Awakening* (Reading, MA, 1983), 12–13; Michael Murphy, 'Totally on Fire', [n.d.], https://www.geraldheard.com/writings-and-recollections/2017/8/2/totally-on-fire [accessed 19 August 2020]

81 Lattin, *Distilled Spirits*, 2; Jeffrey J. Kripal, *Esalen: America and the Religion of No Religion* (Chicago, 2007)

82 Yogeshanada, 'Trabuco College Tryout'

83 Ibid.

84 Miriam King, 'Life at Trabuco', [n.d.], https://www.geraldheard.com/writings-and-recollections/2017/8/2/life-at-trabuco [accessed 20 August 2020]

CONCLUSION: Radically Different Ways of Being

1 Landon Jones, *Great Expectations: America and the Baby Boom Generation* (New York, 1980)

2 See, for example, Benjamin Zablocki, *Alienation and Charisma* (New York,

1980); Philip Wallmeier, 'Exit as Critique. Communes and Intentional Communities in the 1960s and Today', *Historical Social Research* 42 (2017), 147–71

3   Carol Hanisch, 'The Personal Is Political' (first published in 1970), reprinted in *Radical Feminism: A Documentary Reader*, Barbara A. Crow (ed.) (New York, 2000), 113–7

4   Wallmeier, 'Exit as Critique', 154

5   https://www.auroville.org/ [accessed 22 August 2020]

6   See, for example, Andrew Marantz, 'Silicon Valley's Crisis of Conscience: Where Big Tech Goes to Ask Deep Questions', *New Yorker*, 19 August 2019

7   http://www.matavenero.org/ [accessed 19 August 2020]

8   http://www.suderbyn.se/ [accessed 19 August 2020]

9   Ernest Callenbach, "Ecotopia' in Japan?', *Communities Magazine* 131 (2006), 42–9; https://www.yamagishi.or.jp/?page_id=3565 [accessed 25 August 2020]

10 Krishnan Kumar, 'The Ends of Utopia', *New Literary History* 41 (2010), 549–69, at 564

11 Yaacov Oved, *Globalization of Communes, 1950–2010* (New Brunswick, NJ, 2013), 5–7

INDEX

Page numbers in **bold** refer to illustrations.